CRADLE CRUISE

*To my grandson, Eddie Asala,
who once upon a time asked me,
"What did you do in the Navy, Papa?"*

CRADLE CRUISE

A Navy Bluejacket Remembers
Life Aboard the USS *Trever*
During World War II

Lon Perry Dawson
SF 2/C USN

Wind Rose Books
Chicago, Illinois

CRADLE CRUISE
© 2009 Compass Rose Technologies. All rights reserved.

ISBN 10: 1-880954-07-9 / ISBN 13: 978-1-880954-07-2

Edited by Joanne Asala. Associate Editors: Robert Calhoun, Kim Gaetz, Andrea Hines, Lisa Jo Lupo, Andrea Preziotti, and Sherri Ryan.

Author's Note: The term "cradle cruise" was US Navy slang designating the enlistment of a recruit who was less than eighteen years of age. It extended to his 21st birthday, rather than the specified four- to six-year hitch. My cradle cruise was the most memorable, happiest, and certainly the most formative period of my life. This book is an account of how I came to join the United States Navy and my personal recollections of my experiences and observations as a bluejacket. Admittedly, it is fictionalized to some extent for the sake of storytelling, and for reasons of confidentiality. Comments of individuals have been paraphrased, and some people are composites of the many men and women I came to know. There will, I suppose, be those who will read this book and think to recognize themselves. Others may not. It is their choice some fifty years after it all took place. —LPD

Front cover image: *Fight! Let's Go! Join the Navy* by McClelland Barclay for the US Navy; modified. Image courtesy of the United States Library of Congress Prints and Photographs Division, LC-USZC4-5868. Back cover: Photos of Lon Dawson courtesy of Donna Asala and used with permission. Photo of the USS *Trever* is an official US Navy photograph, from the collections of the Naval History and Heritage Command.

Editor's Note: While the events of this book are true, all names—including those of commanding officers—have been changed by the author. A limited edition of 100 copies of *Cradle Cruise*, © 1996 by Lon Dawson, was originally published by Kalevala Books and distributed by the author.

Published by Wind Rose Books
an imprint of Compass Rose Technologies, Inc.
PO Box 409095, Chicago, IL 60640
www.compassrose.com

About the Author

Lon Dawson joined the US Navy in 1941, shortly after finishing high school. He was stationed in San Diego, California, awaiting further transfer, on the day Pearl Harbor was attacked by the Japanese, and served most of World War II aboard the USS *Trever*, an ancient four stack destroyer of World War I vintage, which was awarded five battle stars and a unit commendation.

After the war, Lon returned to Chicago, where he worked as a freelance designer and display manager for Sears. Upon retirement, he moved to Christopher, in Southern Illinois, where he began a second career as a columnist. His credits include a community column entitled "Speak Out!" and a theatrical column, "Playhouse Patter," which were syndicated in several Southern Illinois newspapers.

When his wife Ellie's breast cancer returned, they moved to the Illinois Veterans' Home in Quincy, Illinois. Lon was president of the Residents' Action Group at IVH and a regular contributor to the home magazine, *The Bugle*, as a staff writer and member of the editorial board. He is the author of *A Promise Kept, the Story of the Illinois Veterans' Home*; *Also Known As Albert D. J. Cashier: The Jennie Hodgers Story*; and editor of *Culinary Campaign: A History of Military Cuisine*. He died in 2004, at the age of 80.

Foreword

When I was growing up, my father never talked much about World War II. I knew he had been in the Navy, having joined and completed basic training before the Japanese assault on Pearl Harbor, and that he had arrived in Pearl a few weeks after the attack. Outside of a few stories of his time on the USS *Trever*, he kept his experiences to himself. That is, until one day, when my then-young son, Edwin, asked, "What did you do in the war, Papa?" Thanks to his grandson's innocent question, my father began to remember and share his stories. Some of them were funny, and some were not. Many of them he eventually wrote down and gathered together for this volume.

My father is gone now, but I know the stories found in *Cradle Cruise* will help keep him alive in the hearts of his family and friends, and will help future generations understand what it was to be a common sailor in wartime.

Donna Asala
Chicago, 2009

Prologue

Around three in the morning, the general quarters alarm sounded. With my lifejacket and steel pot in hand, I rushed to my station with the after ammo party, taking my place by the hoist. In a few moments the word was passed: "All battle stations manned and ready." But were we really? Most of our crew had some prior combat experience, but this was different. This was the Big One, and everybody knew it. As the invasion fleet moved ever closer to the islands, our eyes became accustomed to the darkness, and I was surprised at how much could be seen despite there being no moon. The silhouette of the enemy stronghold reared up against the horizon, and we could see the ships of our task force gliding into position. The sea was calm, and from time to time there was a smell of rotting jungle on the early morning breeze. Exhaling with disgust, I wondered why anyone would want such a place badly enough to fight for it, and maybe die.

It has been said that to the individual fighting man, the battle is limited to his own experience. What he sees; what he hears. What he may or may not do. Standing there with one hand resting on the chain hoist, I realized that if our main battery was to continue firing when needed, the ammo party would be hard pressed.

There would be no time for sightseeing. This was no movie. I would have to wait until it was all over to compare notes with my shipmates and find out what actually took place. Strangely enough, it never occurred to me I might die before that time came.

The silence was almost oppressive, broken only by the swish of the *Trever*'s hull cutting through the water and the scuffling sound of shoes on the steel deck as gun crew and ammo party shuffled nervously at their battle stations. Waiting...waiting...would it never begin?

Then, suddenly, the world seemed to split asunder as the cruisers opened fire. So bright was the flash of their heavy guns we were able to see individual ships clearly. Between salvos, it was possible to watch the glowing shells pass through the air, only to flash again as they exploded on target. The stench of burning powder floated across the waters and I heard someone mumble, "I never thought war would stink so much."

How long the bombardment continued, I don't know, but it seemed to go on forever, until the first streaks of dawn began to lighten the horizon. Surely the island would sink from the sheer weight of the shells being dropped on it. Yet there was no response from the Japanese ashore. What could be happening? As the sky lightened, the action became more visible. We watched as the fifteen-gun cruiser USS *San Juan*, with her main battery firing continuously, backed down more than once to get out of her own smoke and give her gun crews a clear view of the beach.

The firing ended as abruptly as it had begun. In the deathly silence that ensued we could hear the word being passed on our troop carriers: "Now land the landing parties...

Now land the landing parties." As the Higgins boats headed for the beach carrying our combat-laden marines, it came to me that a lot of good men were going to die that morning.

Contents

High School and the Family 12
Uncle Sam Wanted Me 16
From Khaki to Navy Blue 19
First Physical 22
I Do Solemnly Swear 25
Boot Camp: Day One 29
Stencil It—It's Yours 35
Tear Gas and Lifejackets 41
Maggie's Drawers and Mess Duty 45
Paradise, Payday, and Away We Go! 49
Rooster, Tater Pie, and Graduation 53
School Days, School Days 60
Boots, Gun Grease, and I Turn Eighteen 66
For Further Transfer 70
San Diego, Pearl Harbor—and War! 76
Pearl Harbor and a Merry Christmas 82
Whitney to *Rigel* to *Trever* 85
Permanent Duty 89
From a Greasy Hole in the Afterdeck 94
Cold Iron and a Steaming Watch 99
Battle Stations, Fire Room Frustrations 104
Honolulu Liberty—Tourist Style 110
Honolulu Liberty with the Old Salts 114
And We Watched Her Die 118
Old Salts and the New Breed of Sailor 124
Soupy, Soupy, Soupy 129
A Sailor Goes Home 134
Back to Pearl 138
South of the Equator 143
Crossing the Line 149
Look out Tojo, Here We Come! 156

Invasion of the Solomons	161
Counterattack!	166
So Wave to the Pretty Ladies	170
Fishing from the *Trever*	176
Back to the Solomons	182
Flight Through Nggela Channel	188
And Commit Their Bodies to the Deep	195
Pago Pago is Real	199
Navy Strawberries for Thanksgiving	205
A Cat Called Gladys	208
Woolloomooloo and the *Trever* Too	212
And a Good Time Was Had By All	220
New Zealand Stopover	227
Mess Cooking and Worse	231
Shipfitters' Gang	236
Two Stars and a Crow	241
Fourteen Days' Leave	246
US Navy Fire Fighting School	250
National Guard Commandos	256
1943 — A Lull in the War	261
And You're a Gun Captain?	265
Dirty Fingernails and Apple Pie	271
Asiatic Earrings	275
Misfortunes of War?	282
Back to Normalcy	287
Typhoon Cobra	291
Pearl Harbor and Home	300
A Sailor Ties the Knot	305
That Chickenshit TADCEN	310
San Diego Naval Repair Base	317
The War is Over	323
USS *Indian Island*	327
Time to Swallow the Anchor	333
Glossary	338

High School and the Family

My US Navy "cradle cruise" was launched at age thirteen, when I started my freshman year of high school (rather than with my enlistment four years later). I began studying subjects that in no way prepared me to earn a living. I suppose I should have been more selective in choosing my program, but kids in those days—at age thirteen—were not very sophisticated, nor were they inclined to think for themselves. Instead, you were influenced by family and friends who thought they knew what was best for the younger generation. With the country just emerging from the Depression, college was still out of the question for me. It was a matter of choosing subjects that might help me get a job later. Not just anything, but a Man's Job. You could hear the words being capitalized as they were spoken. Which was often. To this day, I'm not quite sure what was meant by the term, coming as it did from people who drove a truck, worked in a factory, pumped gas, or filled their time at a politically acquired job of some sort—the kind of work that put beans on the table, but wasn't very exciting. There had to be something better.

Always having a fair hand with a pencil or paintbrush, I had an idea of taking art as a major subject in school, along with anything else that might be of value in that field.

Mention of this at home, however, was almost immediately ridiculed with the admonition, "For chrissake, try and study something that will help you get a Man's Job!" Consequently, my first two years in high school were spent in business training, bookkeeping, typing, and something called "commercial law." None of these seemed very manly to me, but they were all family approved.

I dropped commercial law after a few weeks when the teacher was honest enough to tell me that I would never understand it. He was probably right. In fact, I never really understood business training or bookkeeping, either, and barely squeaked by with passing grades. (It was probably because of my resentment at having to take them in the first place.) Typing was the one course that was of any real value to me, although if my old typing teacher, Mr. Lewison, were to watch me now, he would probably cringe, just as he often did back then.

In my junior year I began to realize some changes had to be made, even at the risk of the family's displeasure. So throwing caution to the winds, I began to go for subjects like chemistry, zoology, algebra, and a newly developed course known as "careers." Supposedly, it was intended to help a student plan for his future. None of these classes were destined to do me any good, but were taken because they looked like fun, were reputed to be easy, or because they were being taken by a pretty girl I wanted to know better. I was at that age where the differences between girls and boys was becoming *very* obvious.

There was one course in school I did enjoy and, as later events would show, served to my advantage. That was ROTC—Reserve Officers' Training Corp. For the uninformed,

Cradle Cruise

ROTC was a kind of low-pressure military or cadet course that might be substituted for gym. That in itself appealed to me. After undergoing two or three periods of what was called "athletics," it was obviously not for me. Running the full length of the gym, patting a green line three times, and then running back to holler "okay!" didn't make much sense. ROTC offered an interesting alternative.

"RO," as we called it, consisted of close order drill; discussions on military customs, courtesies, and traditions; and military history. I ate it up. Besides, they issued a uniform that we were required to wear to school twice a week. After a while, I began to volunteer for such things as flag detail, color guard, charge of quarters—almost anything that required my being in uniform. That way I was able to wear some decent clothes for three or four days a week, something other than hand-me-downs. My grandma, who had raised me from age one, was pretty proud when I started off to school in the morning with brass buttons sparkling and my cap cocked over one eye. She never did say anything, but it showed in her face and that meant a lot to me. Later, when I became a cadet officer and was permitted to wear a sword, she wasted no time telling the neighbors about it. More importantly, she bragged to the family. By graduation, I had been promoted to cadet commander of the school ROTC battalion. There was no living with the old girl after that. I was her boy!

I was able to get out of high school with a couple extra credits, but still not much of an education. A G+ average was just not very impressive to a prospective employer. So there I was, in January of 1941, out of work, with no skills or abilities to offer, and with no idea at all of what I was going to do. Daily I was hearing, "Damn it, if you had only listened to us, you would be able to go out and get yourself a real Man's Job!" God, how I hated that expression. But it was beginning to look as though they might be right, and that bugged me. It *really* bugged me. Like thousands of other recent graduates, I was facing a world feeling scared, confused, and almost useless. But the family decided to rescue me from my fate; in a way, I kind of expected it.

My Uncle Ernie owned a gasoline service station that he ran with the help of his son, Charlie. I had already been working there on and off during the past year, making myself generally useful. It brought in a few bucks, which helped with school expenses in my senior year. So after graduation, with no job prospects in sight, it was decided that I would go work for Uncle Ernie. He and my cousin Charlie would teach me the business and there would be something for me to look forward to. In just a few weeks, I became very proficient at pumping gas, checking oil and water, mopping floors, and cleaning restrooms. I was at long last learning what was meant by a Man's Job! I didn't like it.

Grandma and I sat down and talked about the problem. She felt I ought to appreciate what was being done for me, but at the same time it would be a good idea to look around for something else. According to her, listening to the family was one thing, but working for and with them was a different kettle of fish. We agreed I would look for another job, but without telling anyone. If and when something turned up, we would face the wrath of the family together. It became very apparent that in spite of her own limited education, Grandma was smarter than all of them put together. But then, grandmas are like that.

Uncle Sam Wanted Me

With my grandma's advice in mind, I headed out into the job market at my first opportunity, only to find there was simply nothing available for a seventeen-year-old kid with no experience or skills. My recently acquired expertise at mopping floors and cleaning restrooms had no dollar value. I wasn't sure what I should do.

Then, while bouncing along on the "L" train on my way downtown, the answer to my predicament materialized. I had been sitting there, gazing off into space, when my eyes focused on a poster at the other end of the car. It was a picture of a guy in a red, white, and blue suit and a top hat. He had white chin whiskers and he was pointing right at me. He had to be. There was nobody else there. More importantly, he was saying "I WANT YOU!" I had to look again and ask, "Me?" I swear he nodded his head and answered, "Yep, you." It was a recruiting poster for the United States Army. Sitting there, staring at that poster, a plan began to form in my mind. Four years of ROTC and now join the Army? Why not? According to the poster, the Army would give me a chance to travel, make a lot of new friends, and learn a good trade—something that might even get me a Man's Job! It began to make a lot of sense. The starting pay sure wasn't much, but when you had nothing, it did look pretty good. I could even send Grandma a few bucks. So that was it. I'd join the Army. Sitting back, I relaxed. My problems were solved. Going the rest of the way downtown, I jumped off the train and went looking for a recruiting office. I found one and walked in, full of confidence, feeling that for once in my life my decision would be my own.

The sergeant in charge seemed to be very glad to see me, probably because he had not made his quota for the month. He stood there, resplendent in a uniform that looked so good it had to be tailor made. With silken chevrons, a chest full of ribbons, sleeves laden with hash marks, and even a wound stripe, he was beautiful. I could imagine myself in his place some years away.

In no time at all he had pitched a career in the US Army. All about the training, the travel, medical care, opportunities to learn a trade, chance for rapid promotion, security during the bad times of the post-Depression, and a lot more. I was suitably impressed. When he found out that I was only seventeen, he slowed down just a smidgen. Just long enough to tell me that I would need my parents' consent. When he found out that my parents were divorced, he slowed down even more. I'd need consent from *both* of them. But because of my obvious enthusiasm about enlisting, he assured me things could be worked out. So with a shake of his hand and a pat on the shoulder, he escorted me to the door. Floating out, I headed for home with a handful of literature all about the Army and what it could do for me.

On the ride back, there was plenty of time to think about it pretty carefully. It was a good idea, at least in my mind. Even the starting pay of $21 a month didn't seem too bad. I figured, "What the hell, the Army will give me everything

I need. That $21 will be clear. More money than I've ever had in my life." By the time I got home and was ready to tell Grandma all about it, the future looked very bright indeed!

We talked about it at some length that evening. There didn't appear to be any likelihood of a war in the foreseeable future, and Grandma gave me her blessings. Even though her approval was not legally required, because she was not my guardian, her okay had been my first concern. I still needed the consent of both my parents, but good old Grandma assured me that was her job. That, and dealing with any comment from the family. We decided that in a day or two I would make another trip downtown to see the recruiting sergeant, fill out all the necessary papers, and get the consent forms. This boy was going to be a soldier.

Something came to my mind then. In our high school yearbook the committee had written "Lon Dawson will a general be, with medals on his chest." Well, not a general, maybe, but otherwise they might not be wrong. That night my dreams were of the Army of the U. S. of A. Everything was going to be great.

From Khaki to Navy Blue

Having decided the Army would be my new way of life, I was soon back on the Fullerton Avenue "L" platform, waiting for a train to take me down to the recruiting office for another visit with the sergeant. However, it was on that same platform Fate intervened again, this time in the person of Kenny Sidletch.

Kenny, while not a real close buddy, was a neighbor kid I had gotten to know fairly well over the years. We had a lot in common: our age, the fact that our parents had split up when we were quite young, and the fact that we had both been raised by our grandmothers. Also, we each had the feeling that we were on a merry-go-round taking us no place. I hadn't seen him for a month or so because, as it turned out, he was preoccupied, much as I was. When he bounded up the stairs from the ticket seller's cage, he spotted me and the conversation went something like this:

"Hey, Lonnie, where ya goin'?"

"Hiya, Ken. I'm goin' downtown to join the Army."

"Hell, why the Army? Do like me. I'm joinin' the Navy!"

Realizing that we were both facing up to our problems in much the same way, we started talking about it as we waited for our train. As we talked, the train pulled into the station... and pulled out. We still talked. Kenny was convinced the Navy was the better way to go. He sounded so enthusiastic that I began to wonder if it wasn't worth looking into. At least I could talk to the man. Nothing had been signed with the Army yet. Besides, as Kenny said, we could join together.

It sounded kind of neat, so I agreed to go with him and talk to the recruiter. Then I could decide for myself which was the better deal, Army or Navy. After all, whichever way I went, it was going to be for some years.

The next train was ours, and we jumped on, heading downtown. The US Navy Recruiting Office was somewhat bigger than that of the Army. It seemed much brighter and more cheerful. The guy in charge, an officer of some kind, took us right into an inner office to talk.

He was dressed pretty sharp. Well-fitting blue uniform, white shirt, and a tie. There were fancy gold stripes and badges and colorful ribbons all over his jacket. And he really seemed to know his stuff. I found out later that he was a chief quartermaster with over twenty years of service. The chief gave us a rundown on what the Navy had to offer. As he was telling us all about it, my eyes kept roving around the room. There were big pictures of fighting ships and of sailors in dress uniforms in exotic places around the world. There was no doubt about it; the uniforms did look a lot better than the drab khaki the US Army would give me. Those tight-fitting bell bottom pants and that salty white hat cocked over one eye were as impressive as hell. I could see myself as a sailor with a girl in every port, just like in the movies.

And, from a practical viewpoint, the Navy had more schools to choose from. Trade schools—that's what I needed. Why, they even had a school for artists! It was a lucky day when Kenny Sidletch came running up the stairs to the train platform.

We were there about an hour and a half before we left with hands full of literature, photos, and even the consent forms for our parents' signatures. On the way home we talked about it some more. By the time I was able to sit down and tell my grandma all about it, my mind was made up. It would be the US Navy for me.

Of course, it wasn't easy to convince her that I had changed my mind and why. "I don't understand. Why the Navy? Damn it, Lonnie, *you can't even swim!*" She was right there, but the Navy would teach me. And besides, who ever fell off a battleship? Eventually, she came around to my way of thinking. Mainly, I suppose, because of the bigger list of schools and the fact that there was a guaranteed thirty days of vacation each year. Finally she said, "If that's what you want, my boy, go ahead."

When Kenny and I got back to see the chief, he gave us a hearty welcome and quickly dealt with the myriad of papers to effect our enlistment. I guess he had a recruitment quota, just like the sergeant. He probably wanted to get us in before we changed our minds. Afterwards, he took time to shoot the breeze with us about the Navy in general. "Shooting the breeze"—that's Navy jargon for idle conversation. When we left he told us that in a couple of days we would receive a letter telling us where and when to report for our first physical examination. Hot damn! I didn't know about Kenny, but I could hardly wait. The next day, when I went to work at my uncle's station, I didn't mind cleaning the restrooms. All that was on my mind was being a sailor on one of those big, beautiful, sparkly clean United States Navy fighting ships. It never occurred to me at the time who kept them looking that way.

First Physical

In a couple of days we did receive our notice to report to the naval medical center downtown—at 0700 hours. More Navy jargon for us—it meant 7AM! We were on the "L" once more, only this time it was different. It was the big day when we found out if we were going to be in the service or not.

When we arrived, there were about thirteen other guys waiting. In no time at all our papers had been collected and we were standing stark naked in a goose-pimpled line to brave the cold hands of the medical officer. It wasn't much as exams go. I don't think they examined eyes as much as counted them. If you had two, you passed. There was the usual "bend over and spread your cheeks," and the icy clutch of your vitals as you were told to "turn your head and cough." Looking back at it all, I know it wasn't much to contend with, but to a seventeen-year-old kid who had never been through anything like it...well!

What scared and confused most of us, I guess, was the first time we had a medic tell us to "skin it back and milk it down" as he pointed a lighted flashlight to what writers so often refer to as our manhood. You would be surprised how many of us just stood there and wondered what in hell he was talking about.

The exam was brief and very basic, yet it was thorough

enough to reject an applicant. It was still peacetime, and the Navy could afford to be choosy. Of the fifteen guys who walked into the medical center that morning, thirteen were turned away. Kenny was one of them. The poor guy had a heart murmur he didn't even know about. It was sad seeing him turn and slump away like he did. He didn't even say good-bye.

I thought for a moment of how ironic it was. He had talked me into going to the Navy recruiter in the first place. I suppose if I had been a real buddy the thing to do would have been to walk out with him. But knowing what that would lead to at home, and having made a commitment to myself, it just couldn't be. I stuck it out.

When the physical was completed, only two of us had passed—me and a guy with only one testicle. No kidding, he only had one such vital gland. I can still remember the look on his face when the doctor informed him of the condition. He stood there, holding himself with one hand, looking all around the room as though it had just happened and he might see it rolling around somewhere. It probably didn't help when the doctor said, "Don't worry, son, where we're going to send you, one nut will do you just fine."

In my case, although I passed the exam, there was a problem. In checking my teeth the doctor found considerable work was needed, and it would have to be completed at my expense before they could accept me. But there would be time to take care of it. With that we were sent home to wait for another notice to appear for a more extensive physical, and then be sworn in. The medical officer said it would be around the 18th of April, and we had better be prepared to stay. That was the good news, because it gave me time to get my teeth up to acceptable standards.

Grandma was not at all surprised when I told her about my teeth. Few people at the time went to their dentist twice a year. You waited until you had trouble and the money to take care of it. A couple of days later, it was off to the dentist for me, although where the money was to come from I had no idea. But leave it to Grandma. I knew she didn't have any, and I sure didn't. Asking the family was out of the question. Some arrangements had been made, however, because when the dentist went to work on me he didn't seem concerned about being paid. I found out later that my parents had split the expense. More of that Grandma magic! The dentist did a good job; he even put in some kind of porcelain filling instead of the usual silver stuff we were used to. He told me that if I took care of my teeth, the porcelain would last forever, and the Navy would be happy to see such good work. I hoped he was right; I had never heard of porcelain fillings. Grandma said if the Navy did not approve of the work, she would go down and talk to them. That scared me, because I doubted even the US Navy was ready to face an infuriated grandmother.

It wasn't long before my notice to report arrived. When it came, Grandma and I both knew that was it. When I left that time, there would be no turning back. Still, there were no tears; not then, anyway. On the morning of the 18th I said my last good-bye and headed off to my big adventure. As it turned out, it was a much bigger adventure than planned. The callow seventeen-year-old kid was about to disappear and be replaced by someone else. Just who remained to be seen. But one thing was for sure: On the 18th of April, 1941, I did grow up, taking that first step to becoming a man. There was no other choice.

I Do Solemnly Swear

Riding the "L" downtown that last time was a lot different from all the trips I had made before. As the train rattled along, so many things came to my mind: How I had almost joined the Army, the way Ken Sidletch had slipped out of the examining room without so much as a "so long," and how I hadn't seen him since. I wondered what he was doing. I thought of how the family hadn't seemed very concerned that I was leaving. And I thought of my good-bye to Grandma. There wasn't a great deal of emotional carrying-on between us. We had never been very demonstrative. Instead, she gave me the usual lecture to "be a good boy, and don't get into any trouble." That sort of thing. It was as I stepped out the door that her feelings really showed. She threw her arms around me, kissed me on the cheek, and whispered, "You go now, my boy, and show 'em all. Make me proud. Make me proud." I swore to myself then that if I did nothing else all through my time in the Navy, I would do that one thing. I would make my grandma proud.

Arriving at the medical center, I found about fifty guys milling around, all waiting for something to happen. Most were around seventeen or eighteen years old, although a few were in their early twenties. Also present were a few fathers who apparently had come down with their sons to say their last good-byes. It wasn't long before a chief pharmacist mate (medic) came into the room to collect our report notices and to inform the parents that they might say good-bye then, or wait until we had completed our physical and witness the swearing-in ceremony. They opted to wait. We were herded into another room to begin processing.

Before we began our second examination, we were all sent down the hall to the shower rooms. None of the medical people wanted to touch some smelly recruit. From what I saw and smelled in that shower room, it was understandable. Finally, we were all lined up buck naked to face a battery of doctors and pharmacist mates. The physical check the second time around was a lot more detailed than the one we had received earlier.

Our eye exam was complete with all the fancy charts, tuning forks were used to determine the level of our hearing ability, and there was a close check of our teeth—where I was happy to find out my recent dental work was acceptable. We jumped up and down to test the soundness of our heart and lungs, and there was the time-honored "short-arm" inspection administered by a third-class pharmacist mate who was very laughingly referred to by the rest of the team as the "resident pecker checker." Apparently, the unenviable task was usually assigned to the lowest-ranking medic present. Altogether, it was a pretty damned thorough examination; thorough enough, in fact, to wash out another five or six guys.

When it was all over, we were hurriedly taken back to the outer room to wait for someone to take us to lunch. The fathers were still patiently hanging in there. In a little while a couple of petty officers came along to take us to a local restaurant. Fathers were permitted to accompany the group, giving them a last opportunity to spend time with their bewildered offspring. After noon "chow" it was back up to the medical center, where we would wait for our swearing-in.

It wasn't long, however, before the chief was there to escort us to yet another room. The Navy seemed to have a different room for every activity. This room was impressive: carpet on the floor, flags, and pictures of warships all over the place, and a platform up front with a lectern bearing a great big seal of the US Navy.

As we stood there, an officer came striding into the room, looking sharp as can be in a tailored uniform encrusted with gold and covered with ribbons and badges. He introduced himself as Commander E. M. Senn. The Commander explained to us the seriousness of the oath we were about to take. He also told us that we would be sworn in as apprentice seamen at a salary of $21 a month. After four months we would automatically be promoted to seaman second class at $36 a month. Advancement after that would depend upon our studying for and passing rate examinations, as well as proficiency shown at any service school we might attend. We would also be assigned a service number that we would do well to remember, inasmuch as everything we did or received in the Navy would be tied to it. That was over fifty years ago and I still remember mine: 300 43 98.

Finally, the moment of truth had arrived, the moment when we would commit ourselves to something that was going to change our lives forever. Standing before the commander, our eyes fixed on the colors up front, we raised our right hands and repeated the Oath of Allegiance to the United States of America:

Cradle Cruise

> *I, Lon Perry Dawson, do solemnly swear that I will bear true faith and allegiance to the United States of America, and that I will serve them honestly and faithfully against all their enemies whomsoever, and that I will obey the orders of the President of the United States and the orders of the officers appointed over me, according to the rules and articles for the government of the Navy.*

The oath completed, hands dropped slowly around the room and the silence was almost scary. All that could be heard was the breathing of some fifty new recruits as we realized the significance of the words we had just spoken. I don't care what anyone may say about a time like that. To me it was awe inspiring, almost spiritual. I looked back to where the fathers were standing, and saw more than one wet cheek.

Commander Senn congratulated us and welcomed us into the greatest navy in the world. Wishing us Godspeed and good sailing, he hurried out of the room. I suspect what he really meant was that although our souls might still belong to the Lord above, our collective and individual asses now belonged to Uncle Sam and the chief of naval operations. And it was all, to put it into proper naval terminology, "Subscribed and sworn to on the 18th day of April AD 1941 and contract perfected." All we had to do then was sign a copy of the oath, which I suppose made it legally binding. Every recruit received a copy for his own use as he saw fit.

After that, it was time for the fathers to wipe their eyes, say good-bye, and leave. The new draft of recruits sat down to wait once more—this time for transportation to boot camp.

Boot Camp: Day One

Basic recruit training was to take place at the Great Lakes Naval Training Station, located at Great Lakes, Illinois. About 35 miles north of Chicago, it was a fairly large, rambling installation on the shores of Lake Michigan. It would be the real beginning of our Navy experience, where raw civilians would be turned into something that at least resembled sailors before being sent on to service school, or out to the fleet. There was a certain bit of magic about it. Just passing through the gates, we were transformed from what were politely referred to as recruits to something called "boots." Or, to be more accurate, using the description frequently voiced by our training chief: "A bunch of left-footed, raggedy-ass, hopeless—*my own personal curse*—BOOTS!" The last part was always delivered in a near shout.

The bus trip out to Great Lakes took something over an hour, the driver being in no great hurry and in deep conversation with the first-class pharmacist mate in charge. All the guys in back seemed unusually quiet, preoccupied, I suppose, with their own thoughts of what lay ahead. In time, we did pull up to the main gate of the base. I remember how impressive it looked. It had big red-brick columns and a gatehouse, wrought-iron gates, well-kept lawns and shrubbery, and guards in sparkling white uniforms, guard belts, and leggings. After the guards checked the first class's paperwork, we proceeded onto the base.

Just inside, we passed a low structure that we were told was the hostess house. There we might entertain visitors, go to the soda fountain (known in the Navy as a gedunk), and buy souvenirs and personal needs at the ship's store. Although we didn't know it at the time, that was a luxury still some weeks away. As our bus rattled and rolled down the street, we passed several big, red-brick barracks, and more well-kept grounds, along with a humongous field with grass so neatly cropped it looked like velvet. I figured this was going to be great. No matter what we were told, boot camp was going to be a snap. But when the bus continued to rumble down the street, things began to look different—a lot different.

The paved street turned into a gravel road. The well-groomed lawns and all that beautiful landscaping, along with the acres of velvety fields, disappeared as we passed through rising clouds of dust. After a bit, we pulled up in front of a big, two-story wooden barracks. Peeling paint, a dented garbage can standing by the doors, the nearby parade ground dominated by dust devils, and a general feeling of neglect took away any enthusiasm we had felt. When the bus stopped bouncing after coming to an abrupt halt, we heard, "Okay, all you civilian suckers, get out and form two lines." We did, and numbly stood there. The first class in charge of our draft handed a folder full of paperwork to one of our guys as he swung back aboard the bus. "Just give that stuff to the chief when he comes out. I gotta go—liberty tonight!" With that, the bus pulled away, rattling, banging, with lots of smoke, leaving us standing there wondering what the hell kind of navy we had joined. We didn't have to wonder for very long.

In a couple of minutes some older guy came out of the building wearing a rumpled blue chief's uniform. He was followed by a funny-looking little brown-and-white dog that scooted along on three legs. So help me, three legs! That's all he had. The two of them moved down the steps and over to where we were gathered in our two sloppy lines. They stopped, and the chief leaned back on his heels with that three-legged dog sitting next to him. Both of them were looking at us as though we were a collection of something unclean. Then the chief began to yell.

"Now hear this! I'm Chief Bos'n Mate Buck Walters. You can call me Chief Walters, you can call me Mr. Walters, but you damn well better call me 'Sir' while you think of me as God. I'm gonna be your company training officer for the next eight weeks. This little swabbie next to me is my dog. His name is Salty, because he has probably peed more salt water than most of you people will ever sail over. Treat him with respect and maybe he won't bite nobody."

He stopped at that point to take a breath, and then started in again. "Okay, now open your ears and listen up. I don't tell you people nothing twice." Then he began to pace back and forth in front of our double line, with Salty tagging along behind. The chief gave us a brief run-down on what to expect. It did not sound encouraging.

We would spend our first three weeks in detention (quarantine), just in case we had something that no one else wanted. During that time we would receive yet another physical, a vaccination check, and all our shots, including "one in the left nut with a square needle to curb your carnal desires over the next eight weeks; maybe longer." We would learn how to march, how to wash our own clothes in a bucket, and anything else the Navy thought we ought to know. We were to "Sir" everyone except another boot, and salute everything and everyone that moved, including Salty. If we survived the next three weeks we would be allowed to pass over to Paradise for the balance of boot training. What and where Paradise was he didn't say. It sounded ominous, and nobody wanted to ask.

Having given us what was apparently the standard Navy welcome, Walters and his dog took us inside, where we were treated to a tour of our new home. It was, I suppose, like most military barracks, and surprisingly clean inside compared to what we saw from outside. It had two stories, with the second floor being known as the "upper deck." It was there that we found the ladders (stairs), hatches (doorways) to the washrooms, and gear lockers (broom closets). We were learning an entirely new vocabulary. On the main deck (first floor) was the chiefs' quarters. He was not to be disturbed—under the penalty of death—except for dire emergencies. What was most unsettling were the dormitories.

Each was divided into two areas called "crew spaces" where we would sleep. Between them was an area with several big picnic-style tables for studying, writing letters, or whatever we chose to do if and when we had any free time. The crew spaces were something else, consisting of nothing but big frameworks of six-inch pipe called "jackstays" from which were suspended row after row of hammocks. That's right, hammocks!

We were ordered to stand by a hammock, which would then become our "sack" from that moment forward. Everybody rushed over, newly made friends together, to pick what they thought were choice spots. A few of us didn't move quickly enough and were told we would be assigned sacks on the upper deck.

The canvas hammocks were all brand new, and stretched so tight that if you hit one with your fist it reverberated with a deep "thrumm." Walters showed us how to let up on the clews (ropes) at each end to give just enough slack so we might get into it and sleep without falling out. In each hammock we found a mattress, pillow, covers for each, and two new woolen US Navy blankets. In a very, very quick demonstration, the chief opened one of the sacks and showed us how easy it was to get into. He also showed us how dangerous it was to thrash and turn in our sleep by quickly turning over and falling out. He covered his obvious goof by saying, "That's what happens if you people don't pay attention." He also warned us not to tuck in our blankets because if we did fall out, they would bind our legs, making us fall out on our head. That he did not demonstrate.

After hammock familiarization, he took us into the washrooms, where we were shown the showers and basins. There was a supply of soap and towels, which were for our use that night. We would be issued our own clothing and other gear the following day. After that, with a promise to come back later and march us to evening chow, he left us on our own to think about what we had gotten into. We were not sailors, but were most definitely in the Navy. I went upstairs—*whoops! I mean the upper deck*—where those who had not yet been assigned hammocks were to be quartered. I decided to pick a hammock next to the jackstay, figuring it was something to hang onto until I mastered the technique of sleeping in a canvas bag. A few of the guys laughed at my precautions, but the next morning there were several who wanted to change their sacks. The chief nixed the idea in a hurry because he had more boots coming in and nobody wanted a warm bag, what he was constantly referring to as a fartsack. Why he called them that became very apparent after a few days.

In case you're wondering why the Navy still used hammocks in the enlightened forties, it was not just tradition. On board ship they were more comfortable and safer to sleep in because of the pitch and roll of the ship. Anyone in a bunk might easily be tossed out onto the steel deck in rough weather. So they just got you accustomed to hammocks in boot camp, and you carried it with you wherever you might go. That was US Navy efficiency for you.

Stencil It—It's Yours

Around 5:00 PM or so, Walters emerged from his cave to take us all to chow. We marched over to the mess hall and got into line. It was pretty much as you would expect—a great big room filled with tables with built-in benches. We were handed metal trays and the food was passed out along a serving line of steam tables manned by sailors in clean white uniforms and aprons. The food was good, although I can't remember what we were served. What was hard to understand, and will never be forgotten by anyone who went through boot camp at the Lakes, was the coffee. Served in big aluminum pitchers set out on the tables, it was lukewarm, not very strong, and with milk and sugar already added. You drank it that way or did without. It also had a strange flavor that no one could identify. We found out later it was something called "saltpeter," a chemical additive which supposedly reduced our biological urges, much as the shot with the square needle was intended to do. After drinking that stuff three times a day for a few weeks, we would go on our first liberty without getting into any trouble at all. Or, as the chief put it, we would be going into town representing the United States Navy, and while we would be honest and true, we definitely would not be upright! The scuttlebutt (rumor) going through the company said that we would not even be issued the prophylactic kit usually passed out to sailors as they went through the gate for a few hours of freedom. Chief Walters, chuckling as he did so, said that after a few days the coffee would also begin to reduce what might otherwise be a rash of "midnight manipulations."

The first day ended rather quickly. We were all pretty exhausted, and by 9:30 that night most of the guys were already in their hammocks. I remember carefully swinging up into mine, hanging onto the jackstay as I did. It wasn't so easy going to sleep with one arm wrapped around that pipe, but eventually I did drop off. My rest was fitful, however, because like all the others, I was so keyed up. Besides, during the night there were periodic thumps as some guy fell out of his sack, followed by a very disgusted, "Son of a bitch!" But altogether, it had not been all that bad, and I guess we were all looking forward to the future. I didn't know it then, but for me that was going to be four years, five months, and thirteen more days—with a war thrown in.

CRASH! BANG! BOOM! "Wakey, wakey, rise and shine!" It seemed we had just dropped off to sleep when Chief Bos'n Walters was running through the barracks, banging on an empty bucket with a stick and screaming something about "wakey, wakey!" It was the ungodly hour of 5:30 AM, and the chief was making reveille, the kind of morning call we would learn to expect as normal. That crazy call of his we were later told was a tradition going all the way back to the early British Navy. In full it went like this:

> *"Wakey, wakey, rise and shine,*
> *You've had yours and I've had mine.*
> *The cook's in the galley, the fire's below,*

Lon Dawson

Show a leg, show a leg, let's go, let's go!"

The "show a leg" part was really necessary in the Brit's navy because in days long past sailors were sometimes permitted to take their wives (or doxies) along with them when they went to sea. Of course, having probably worked hard all night and being civilians who were not required to get up to stand watches, they could sleep late. By dropping one leg out of the hammock, they could show the master-at-arms that they were women and would not be spilled out of their sack.

Walters seemed to be real big on tradition, or else he just got his jollies with those kinds of tricks. Scuttlebutt had it that he was nearing retirement and was mad at the world. We all crawled or fell out of our hammocks and made ready to face the day. Breakfast was our introduction to an old Navy standby, S.O.S. It was some kind of ground meat and gravy poured over dry toast. We learned to like it after a few weeks, despite its unappetizing name. S.O.S. is an abbreviation for "shit on a shingle." Everybody dug in with gusto to fortify themselves for whatever was to come. And after chow we filed outside to march over to the storekeeper's shack (supply warehouse) for our clothing and gear issue. It was to be the last time we would wear civvies while in the Navy.

The storekeeper's shack was just a big warehouse with long counters running down both sides, behind which there were a lot of sailors and piles of clothing and other assorted Navy gear to be issued. The first thing we were given was a mattress cover. Moving down the line, we held it open like kids playing trick or treat on Halloween, while the guys behind the counter threw everything into it. Sometimes they even asked our size. That mattress cover got heavier and heavier, until by the time we reached the end of the last counter, it was dragging on deck. They gave blue uniforms and white ones. White hats and blue ones. Skivvies (underwear), shoes, and socks. Just about everything you could think of, plus a seabag (canvas bag) to carry it in. There was also an issue of toothbrush and paste, soap and a razor, shoe polish, and a lot of other personal stuff I don't even remember. I do remember that we had to pay for the personal items later on. All those little things went into a cute little canvas sack called a ditty bag. Both bags were later to be hung from the jackstay by our hammock.

Once we had everything coming to us, it was a struggle to carry it all to a nearby drill hall, to line up at long tables to stencil our name on everything. We had to strip to the buff and pack our civvies into a box for shipment home. There we stood, over a hundred of us, stark naked with a lot of stuff to be marked, but waiting for instructions. *You did nothing in the Navy without instructions!* Finally, we were shown how, and ordered to stencil a pair of skivvie shorts first and put them on so as not to offend the sensitivities of anyone walking into the building. We wondered just who the hell they were expecting.

In a hurry to do it right, I used too much ink and it soaked right through the fabric. Still wet when I pulled them on, the ink was transferred to my belly. I didn't notice it at the time, but when I took my shower that night, there it was. Right on my little Navy belly was my name, clear as it could be. Being waterproof ink, of course, it wouldn't wash off. When the chief spotted it, he wasn't too helpful. "Don't worry about it, sailor. It's your belly and you were told to stencil everything. Just be careful when you go into town—no sense in letting those little girls know your real name!"

Thanks, Chief. Thanks a lot!

When we finished the stenciling operation, it was back to the barracks, where we were shown how to fit all our belongings into that seabag. There was a real trick to it. The trick was to roll everything into tight little packages and to pack it away according to a set pattern. When you took anything out to wear it was supposed to be wrinkle free. Walters made the comment, "Each piece has to be rolled so tight it won't bend. Even those little girls in Waukegan don't like anything that bends in the middle." Waukegan was the name of a nearby town popular with the local sailors.

After getting everything properly made up, we learned how to lay it all out for inspection. You spread a clean mattress cover on the deck and then arranged everything on it according to a set pattern. Then you stood by as the inspecting officer came to check it out. Ours was a reserve lieutenant who had been recalled to active service, and didn't like it a bit. It seemed he took out his anger on all the boots. Woe be it to the guy who didn't pass inspection. It was not uncommon to have your entire issue thrown out the window. This meant that everything had to be picked up, washed, re-rolled, and repacked. Nobody ever failed inspection twice.

Next on the schedule was how to wash clothes. Walters came into the quarters with a couple of buckets, soap, a small brush called a "kiyi," and a pair of somebody's skivvies. He sat down on one bucket, the other being filled with water, and showed us how it was done. The kiyi was for white hats and, occasionally, to remove what were called "hash marks" from our shorts—the unsightly brown stains that were the result of a buddy grabbing your pants and shorts from behind, yanking them up between your cheeks, and gleefully screaming, "Hash marks!"

When the day was over we were again so fagged out that our sacks looked very good. Maybe fewer guys would fall out that night. For me, it was one more night of hanging onto the jackstay for safety. Before lights out the chief came in once more to yell, "Listen up. Sweepers, man your brooms. I want a clean sweep down fore and aft!" I wondered why he didn't just tell us to sweep the decks and let it go at that. But then, that wouldn't be Navy, and Chief Bos'n Mate Buck Walters, if nothing else, was Navy all the way.

Tear Gas and Lifejackets

It took us a few days to get squared away. Our talk began to get salty, and we were looking forward to completing our three-week detention and heading over to Paradise. We knew by then it was the training facility on the other side of the base. We would be living in the red-brick barracks we had passed on our arrival, have access to the hostess house, and, best of all, an opportunity for our first liberty. There wasn't much time to dwell on such things, however, because our company was keeping pretty busy.

There was another physical exam, those guys who had never been vaccinated were taken aside for their needlework, and we were all set up for shots that were intended to protect us against everything from the clap to collywobbles, whatever that was. The one shot that did not become a reality was the often-threatened one with the square needle. When we discovered it was nothing but a sick medical joke, we all heaved a sigh of relief.

One of the more interesting classes we attended was one for gas mask instruction. We marched out to the lake front where a small brick building about twenty feet square served as a gas chamber. There was a door in front, one in back, and a big sign reading DANGER—TEAR GAS! We were to be exposed to the real thing. After careful instruction on

41

how to properly use the equipment, the company was broken down into groups of about fifteen men each. There were a number of Navy medics present, experienced in dealing with exposure to tear gas, and gunner's mates to handle the chemical itself.

Each group was directed to enter the building, whereupon it was sealed and the gas pumped in. After a few minutes in the gas-filled chamber, we were ordered to remove the mask and get out quickly. The idea was to get accustomed to the mask and yet experience the effects of the gas. Outside there was a lot of hacking and crying, with more than one boot losing his breakfast; but we all survived. After a break to wash up at a convenient water outlet, we were lined up for phase two. The second time around would prove to be a bit more difficult.

The program called for us to carry our gas mask in hand, take a couple of deep breaths, and go into the chamber, unprotected. Once inside with the door closed, we would put on the mask, clear it of gas as instructed, wait a couple more minutes, and then leave. Several of the guys screwed up as might be expected and went panicky inside. If they had listened to what they had been told there would have been no trouble. The trick was to get into the chamber holding a deep breath, put on the mask, pop open a little valve in the side, and then use the pent up breath to blow out the gas. Sure, there was some residue left inside, but not enough to really do any damage.

All in all, we got through it with no fatalities, but on the way back to the barracks even the tough old chief had tears in his eyes. Once safely back home, we spent the rest of the day washing the traces of gas from our uniforms and taking long showers. Those needing it received medical attention from a pharmacist mate who was waiting for us. That was over fifty years ago, but thinking about it now I can still feel the burning sensation of that gas. It was one of the more memorable aspects of boot camp. It's interesting to note, however, that of all the things we learned, the use of a gas mask was one thing we never had to fall back on. Even during the war.

Another important detail of those days was an opportunity to buy life insurance. National Service Life Insurance, it was called, a government policy available to us in amounts of $5,000 and $10,000. Most of us opted for the $5,000 coverage because with no war on, nobody was expected to die. Besides, that $3.65 monthly premium took a big bite out of our salary of $21.

A great deal of time was spent listening to lectures on Navy customs and courtesies, health and personal hygiene, and naval history. There were classes in knot tying, and even a visit to the base swimming pool where we all had to qualify as swimmers if we wanted to graduate with our company. Those who could not would be held back to go through boot camp with another company, and the time lost would be added to their enlistment. Nobody wanted to fail, of course, but there was no need to worry. The petty officers in charge of the pool wanted us all to qualify as much as we did, so they resorted to an old Navy practice to guarantee our success—they cheated! Those who could swim leaped into the pool, struck out for the other end, and climbed out. Those like me, with the aquatic ability of a rock, were strapped into a kapok lifejacket and unceremoniously thrown into the pool. If we could swim, fine, if not we floated and were dragged to the far end with a boat hook. Presto—we were swimmers!

I couldn't stand the idea of being towed and searched for a solution. I found it. Noticing that all the lift of the jacket was in the front, when I was thrown in I let it flip me over on my back and then backstroked to the deep end. My grandma didn't raise no dummy. As they pulled me from the water, one of the petty officers asked if I'd had any previous experience with the jacket. I just smiled in what I hoped was a conspiratorial manner and said nothing. Whatever they thought, Apprentice Seaman Lon P. Dawson was logged into the records as a swimmer.

When we were not in class, attending lectures, taking physicals, or standing inspections, we were out on the drill field, raising dust as we shuffled around in close order drill. By that time, our mob had been organized and designated as Recruit Training Company 69. With two platoons, we had our own people appointed as company, platoon, and squad leaders. A guy with previous National Guard experience was our company commander. Another boot and I, because of our high school ROTC experience, ended up as platoon leaders. I drew second platoon. One great big guy was appointed barracks master-at-arms to maintain order when the chief was not around and to supervise general clean-up.

Being a platoon leader had its good points. I was not required to carry a rifle during drill period, and there were no more bag inspections. Best of all, no night guard duty. We were sarcastically referred to by the rest of the company as "square knot admirals." I didn't mind. This admiral got a full night's sleep and didn't stand inspections, so go ahead and laugh!

Maggie's Drawers and Mess Duty

There was one aspect of the drill routine that nobody liked—canvas leggings. Stiff and uncomfortable, the damned things laced tight from the instep to just below the knee. The worst part was that our pants legs had to be folded and tucked into them, so that from waist to ankle we presented a nice, smooth, tapered line. This was a trick not easily acquired. The first time we fell into drill wearing leggings we looked like a bunch of baggy-pants paratroopers. You should have heard Walters yell.

"What's the matter with you people? Look at those pants! They look like Maggie's Drawers. I never saw so many baggy-kneed britches outside of a Chinese whorehouse!" He jumped up and down, threw his cap on the ground, and proceeded to kick it around. Then he broke into the chorus of an old Navy drinking song:

> "They were ruffled at the top,
> and for a dollar they would drop,
> Those baggy old red flannel drawers
> that Maggie wore.
> They were baggy at the knees,
> and the crotch was..."

Although the chief sang the entire verse for us, I can't go on. My sense of propriety forbids it, even though this is a story about the US Navy.

We all filed back into the barracks, where we spent the better part of the day learning to wear leggings correctly. Eventually, most of us were trim as we could be. The couple guys who never could master it were relegated to the inner ranks of the company where they wouldn't be too visible.

It was almost three weeks into boot camp when we lost our by-then-well-liked Chief Bos'n Mate Walters. One morning we were called by a different kind of whistle and somebody calling out, "Okay, recruits, up and at 'em. Reveille!" It was almost polite. We knew something was definitely wrong. When we fell out for morning chow, we were told that Walters had been unexpectedly transferred. In his place we had this new guy.

"My name is Daniels, Chief Bos'n Mate, United States Navy. I'll be your training officer for the balance of your recruit training." That was it. Came right to the point. No frills. With that he marched us off to breakfast. He was a nice enough guy, and we probably learned a lot more real Navy stuff from him than we would have from Walters, but he wasn't half as much fun. With our new boss there were no more snide remarks about personal habits, no demonstrations of how to fall out of a hammock, no advice on dealing with the little girls in Waukegan, and no more dirty songs. Daniels was all business.

It was just a few days later that he lined us up to inform us our time in detention was at an end. No more quarantine, no more bag inspections, and best of all we could look forward to our first liberty. Everybody cheered the last. But then he dropped a bomb. Before moving to Paradise, we would put in a week of mess duty.

"Mess duty? What is that?" a little voice in the back of my mind asked. Then I remembered those guys in white uniforms who were dishing out the S.O.S. and it hit me—*we* were scheduled to spend a week in the mess hall. The chief said we would begin that Saturday at 0500 hours, meaning reveille would be at least an hour earlier. We would have Friday to get everything cleaned up and squared away so that there would be nothing else for us to do that week. Ousted out of our sacks at 4:00 AM, we would be working until about 7:30 in the evening. Having given us all that good news, the chief left us to contemplate our misfortune and prepare for the long week ahead.

Saturday morning came all too soon, and we were off and running before the sun was up. Heading over to the mess hall, I wondered how duty stations would be assigned. As a platoon leader, I expected some cushy job like master-at-arms or maybe supervisor of the serving line. But when Daniels handed our company roster to the chief cook, my hopes died. "Cooky" was only interested in warm bodies to fill work slots. I watched as jobs like butter boy (who used a machine to cut pounds of butter into cute little pats), bread boy (who sliced up innumerable loaves of bread), and coffee master (who did nothing but keep those pitchers filled with the sickening saltpetered coffee) go to rear rank sailors as he passed over the square knot admirals.

When he came to the really good jobs, I heard my name called. "Dawson, sink number two!" What a come down. I was going to be a pot walloper! For a solid week it would be my fate to scrub pots and parts, buckets, and anything else the cooks might throw on that pile behind me. Oh sure, I would be wearing a white uniform, but also a heavy rubber apron and boots to my knees. We found out later that all the square knots were given sloppy jobs to keep their heads from swelling because of their otherwise exalted rank. The really bad thing about working on a sink—or worse, the garbage dock where our company commander was assigned—was the fact that we would have to wash out a suit of whites every night. Guys like the bread-and-butter boys could go for two, three days on a uniform.

One good thing that did happen at the time was those of us who had been appointed to leadership positions had it entered in our service records. According to mine, I had been temporarily promoted to apprentice petty officer first class—platoon leader. It didn't mean a great deal other than to add to my overall conduct ratings for service in general. But then, that wouldn't hurt.

Despite the lack of sleep, extra uniforms to wash, and the dirty jobs some of us drew, the week passed quickly enough. Mostly it was because we knew that when it was behind us better things were coming. On the last day, when we returned to our dormitories, Daniels made the rounds and let us know we could scrub up for the last time, pack our gear, and stand by to move out. On Saturday morning we were going to Paradise! And on Sunday we would be turned loose for our first Navy liberty. One guy, "Timber" Baldasario, who had come from some place up in the North Woods and wasn't really accustomed to civilization, let out a whoop and a holler. "Okay, look out all you civilian people; lock up yer chickens and dotters. Timber is comin' to town!" For just a moment, I thought Buck Walters was back.

Paradise, Payday, and Away We Go!

That Saturday morning there was no need for the chief to hold reveille. We were up before the first blast of his whistle, rushing to "lash up and stow" and move off to our new home. That meant to roll our mattress and pillow inside our hammock and tie it nice and tight into a sausage-like roll, which was then wrapped lengthwise around our seabag. It made for a neat, easily handled package for storing or transfer. In our case, it was dropped out by the street in front of the barracks, loaded on a truck, and shipped across the base. In no time at all the company was ready for chow. When we got back, our dunnage had already been picked up. All we had to do was make a final sweep down and fall into ranks for the march to the long-awaited Paradise. And off we went with our ditty bags slung over our shoulders.

It was a long walk, but nobody complained. When we arrived at the red-brick barracks, we filed inside to be assigned our hammock numbers. Once again I drew space on the upper deck. The building was laid out much the same as the old one we had occupied, with dormitories and a well deck between. Washrooms, showers, and heads, however, were all in the sub deck. Lord help anyone who referred to it as a basement! We had been told that we no longer would be sleeping in hammocks four feet off deck. That was encouraging; at least, until we walked into the crew spaces. We found that the jackstays came from the overhead, and were eight feet up! A catwalk about four-feet high ran the full length of the room to give access to our sacks after they were slung. Anybody who fell out of his fartsack from that height was going to kill himself.

Most of the company, while not exactly thrilled about sleeping eight feet up in the air, did get their rigs up to the chief's satisfaction. The square knot petty officers, in recognition of our exalted rank, were provided with folding wood and canvas cots, which we set up each night and stowed away each morning. So for the time being, at least, this boy did not have to sleep in a bag. Instead, our hammocks were to cover our bedroll when it was stowed. In return for our luxurious sleeping accommodations, we had to stand night watches as junior officers of the deck. That didn't amount to much. We just had to stay awake in the barracks' office and man the telephones in the event of any incoming calls and call Chief Daniels in an emergency. It was usually pretty quiet, giving us extra time to study. Watches were on a four-hour rotation—from eight in the evening until twelve, from midnight to four in the morning (known as the midwatch), and from four in the morning to reveille, when the junior officer would help the chief make the morning wake up. With the number of square knots in our company, I pulled a watch about once every three days and it rotated so I would have a different one each time. All that would begin when we returned from our first liberty. As luck would have it, it fell on me to start the program with a midwatch coming in that Saturday night.

Our new barracks had a telephone on the well deck so those who could afford it could call home, a girlfriend, or whomever. Another feature that called for a lot of comment was the shower facilities. They consisted of no more than a bunch of showerheads jutting from a maze of pipes in the overhead of the basement. (There, I said it: basement!) The concrete deck beneath was slanted to a drain in the center. That was it. Come shower time we had about twenty-five boots scrubbing, rinsing, and catcalling to one another about their sexual equipment.

Singled out in particular for that kind of attention was one of the older guys who had come from a southern state. His name was Dangle, and, according to him, he got into the Navy one step ahead of the sheriff, who was after him following charges of misconduct. It had something to do with his physical endowment and sexual prowess. It was not for nothing that we called that ridge runner "Dingle Dangle."

The Navy also held a special payday for us that afternoon. Usually it fell on the 15th or 30th of the month, but because we had been in detention, and had a liberty coming up, the brass relented. We received money for about a half month. After deductions it left us with about $6. Nobody was going to get far, or in much trouble, with that. Still, $6 was a lot of money to guys who never had very much, so we were ready to take it and go.

It took the rest of the day and evening to get organized. Most of the guys then went to sleep in those high-flying hammocks and, for the privileged few, there were the cots. Fortunately, no one fell out that night, probably because we were all awake and thinking of the next day's freedom.

In the morning, all hands were up before reveille again. Sacks were lashed where they hung, and we were off to chow with everybody in our dress blues. Right after breakfast there were church services for those so inclined, and then liberty call! Once we were released, there was a mad dash for the main gate. For those too far from home, it was Waukegan, about five miles away. Guys with a few bucks to play with headed for Chicago. Me, I went home. Liberty was up at midnight, but for me, having the midwatch, it was even shorter. Still, it did give me time to see my grandma and tell her of the happenings of the previous weeks. Then, by the time I said hello to the family and a few friends in the neighborhood, it was time to return to the base. But not before letting folks know that graduation was in just a few weeks and I would be back.

Arriving at the barracks, I changed uniforms and took over the junior watch. Considering that the midwatch would be the time when all my shipmates would be coming in from liberty, it was a quiet four hours. I guess nobody had enough money to get into any real trouble, and with the heavy dosage of saltpeter we had absorbed over the previous four weeks, everybody behaved themselves. What other choices were there? A few hardy individuals like Dingle Dangle, who had steadfastly refused to drink the coffee in preparation for his first night in town, may have scored with the local belles, but there were no negative reports. To quote an old sage, "All's well that ends well."

Rooster, Tater Pie, and Graduation

With that first liberty behind us, Company 69 settled down to the remainder of our training period. There were lectures and more classes in knot tying, seamanship, history, and naval tradition. We also took a series of tests to determine what service school, if any, we might be assigned. Those recruits that showed no specific aptitude would be shipped out to the fleet for duty. Others, depending upon their test scores, would have their choice of a number of schools then available. I was classified for what was called "Group II Artificer Skills." These included specialties like carpenter, mold maker, machinist, boilermaker, shipfitter, and metalsmith.

I chose metalsmith school. It would consist of a month of basic training instruction right there at Great Lakes, and three months of specialized training at the new US Navy Service School set up by the Ford Motor Company in conjunction with the Navy. Our training would take place right in the auto manufacturing plant, where we would be working alongside union tradesmen who, to a very large degree, would be our instructors. It was definitely something to look forward to.

Aside from our testing, classes, and other basic routines,

Cradle Cruise

there was still more close order drill—but with a difference. After the regular Saturday morning inspection and parade afterwards, each company was judged for excellence. The best would be designated rooster company for the week. That meant we would carry the rooster-emblazoned guidon, or flag, for our drill periods and parades. More importantly, it included a liberty the following day. The 69th only captured the rooster once, but when we did it was with the highest overall score ever compiled in the history of the rooster program.

That Sunday it was home again to tell Grandma all about it. She lost no time in telling anyone who would listen that her boy and "his" company had won the rooster. I don't think she really understood how it worked, but that made no difference. As far as she was concerned, my company was better than all the rest.

During those final weeks we also had a day out in the boats. Split up into crews of sixteen or eighteen men each, we were plunked into big thirty-foot oar-powered lifeboats and out on the lake we went to learn how to pull an oar and steer.

As platoon leader, it fell on me to be boat cox'n in charge, and to do the steering. There was a turn at the oars, of course, but mostly it was up to me to handle the tiller. Quite frankly, it scared me to death. Not only were the boats hard to handle, but the other guys were not too keen on taking orders from some square knot admiral who was really no better trained, no wiser, and no better a seaman than any of them—especially when our chief was in another boat.

Hancock, first platoon leader and cox'n of his own boat, was obviously too big for his Navy britches. As soon as we were on the water he began screaming orders at his oar men. They promptly threw him overboard. With my own rock-like swimming style, I was not about to antagonize my own crew. So the day passed without anyone other than the wiseass Hancock going into the drink, and no boats were lost. Just how much we learned is debatable, but the training schedule said we would spend a day in the boats, and spend it in the boats we did. I think the chief was as happy as we were when it was over.

One really nice thing about Paradise was the hostess house. Whenever we could find the time, we would head over there for an hour or so. It was a low, rambling building about a block or so from our barracks. A big visiting room was available where recruits would entertain friends or family who might come to the base. There was also a ship's store, the Navy equivalent of the well-known Army PX. It was a kind of general store where we could buy personal necessities as well as souvenirs. One entire side of the house was given over to the gedunk, a Navy type soda fountain and coffee shop that offered soda pop, ice cream, candy, cake, pie, and coffee without the familiar taste of saltpeter. It was at the gedunk that one of our boys became aware of all the goodies that the Navy made available—things he never saw back home.

He was an escapee from the hills of Arkansas when he enlisted, and was immediately tagged with the name of Arky. (What else?) His real name was something like Marion Billy Bob, which nobody could say without laughing. And you just did *not* laugh at Arky; but a nicer guy you'd never meet. Always happy, never complaining no matter what we were asked to do. He was instantly amazed at the things he ran into in his new life. He had two pairs of shoes of his very own, "all them new clothes," and a chance to go into the big city "all by my own self!"

He was flabbergasted to see mustard and ketchup on the mess tables every day, and to receive ice cream every Sunday. For Arky, life was sweet. I often wished I could have read some of those letters he was writing home. They had to be collectors' items.

One Saturday afternoon, we were hanging around the barracks writing letters of our own, washing clothes, or studying, when our mountain boy came rushing into the dorm more excited than we had ever seen him. "Hey fellers, guess what! We'uns is havin' pie fer supper!" Now that, we thought, was indeed cause for rejoicing. "What kind of pie, Ark?" we asked. He stopped dead in his tracks, looking at us as though we had lost our collective minds, and blurted, "Why, tater pie of course. How many kinds of pie you think they is?" It turned out that the poor guy had never tasted anything other than sweet potato pie, and back home that was a holiday delicacy.

When we told him there were lots of different kinds, he backed off. "Aw, come on, fellers, you're funnin' me." There was nothing to do but take him down to the hostess house. He had not been there yet because he was sending money home, not keeping anything for himself. About five of us took him in tow, and down to the gedunk we went. He couldn't believe what he saw. "Them's all pie?" We bought him a piece of pie—apple, I think. He was a joy to watch. By the time we were finished he had inhaled five slices, including one piled high with whipped cream that I don't think he believed existed, even as he ate it. Finally he leaned back and said, "Golly, thanks, fellers, but you can't do it no more. I 'llow as how you ought to be spendin' your money on your own selves. 'Sides, iffen I eat any more, I won't be able to eat supper. And we'uns is havin' pie!"

Days came and went, and slowly we became sailors, although admittedly the dry land variety. And on June 19 the battalion fell out on the drill field before a crowd of family, friends, and well wishers—as well as the commander and his staff—for our final dress parade. We were resplendent in dress blues, with our shoes shining, as Arky put it, "Bright as a new dime in a billy goat's behind!"

There was a Navy band on hand, and as it struck up the familiar *Anchors Aweigh*, we stepped off to pass in review. I can still remember strutting along at the head of the second platoon. Head high, but with a slight catch in my voice as, passing the review stand, I called out the command: "Eyes... Right!" And moments later feeling that snap of heads when giving the command: "Steady...Front!" We continued down the field to the far end where the battalion was halted and dismissed. It was all over. We had graduated. Walking back to the barracks, I felt a strange emptiness inside, realizing that I would probably never see most of these guys again. Although they were strangers just a few weeks earlier, they now seemed closer to me than family.

A lot of sailors (boots no longer!) raced to the spectator section to greet family and friends. The rest of us headed back to the dorm to pick up our ditty bags and leave papers. It didn't take long for a fast "see you later, guys" and a beeline for the gate.

My leave was spent much as was my first liberty—visiting a few friends in the neighborhood, talking to the family a bit, and telling sea stories to my grandma. She seemed pretty happy for me, and I think she was also kind of proud.

Cradle Cruise

She insisted I take a day or two to visit with my mother and father, and, to tell the truth, I felt better when I did. Leave it to Grandma, she always seemed to know what was best for me.

Foremost on my mind, however, was getting back to the base. There was a long hitch ahead of me with places to go, things to see, and—although nobody knew it at the time—a war to fight. I wanted to get on with it. Having grown into my Navy blues more and more every day, I was beginning to have some very definite feelings where Uncle Sam was concerned. It was kind of a love/hate relationship. I certainly felt qualified to brag about it, while at the same time entitled to a complaint now and then. There is an anonymous poem entitled *A Sailor's Prayer* that, if carefully read, explains my feelings at the time.

> *Now I lay me down to sleep,*
> *And pray the Lord my soul to keep.*
> *Grant no other sailor take*
> *My shoes and socks before I wake.*
> *Lord, please guard me in my slumber,*
> *And keep my hammock on its number.*
> *May no clews or lashings break*
> *And let me down before I wake.*
> *Lord, keep me safely in thy sight,*
> *And grant no fire drill tonight.*
> *And in the morning let me wake*
> *Breathing scents of sirloin steak.*
> *God, protect me in my dreams,*
> *And make this better than it seems.*
> *Grant that time may swiftly fly*
> *When myself shall rest on high,*

Lon Dawson

In a snowy featherbed
Where I long to rest my head,
Far away from all these scenes,
And the smell of half-cooked beans.
Take me back onto the land
Where they don't scrub down with sand,
Where no demon typhoon blows,
And where the women wash the clothes.
God, thou knowest all my woes,
So feed me in my dying throes,
Take me back, I'll promise then
Never to leave home again.

It has been reported that four years later that same sailor wrote *Our Father, Who Art in Washington:*

Please dear Father, let me stay,
Do not drive me now away.
Wipe away my scalding tears,
And let me stay for thirty years.
Please forgive me all my past,
And things that happened at the mast.
Do not my request refuse,
And let me stay another cruise.

School Days, School Days

With boot leave over, I returned to Great Lakes, and back to the same barracks I had left. But everything had changed; Company 69 was no more. Most of the battalion had been moved out to sea or to other quarters to await transfer to school, and the dormitories were filling up with new faces. Guys were coming in from other training battalions or even from ships at sea. The only sailors I knew were those from my company who had been assigned to Group II Schools as I had.

The barracks became the responsibility of a couple of first class petty officers who had shore duty at the Lakes, and a few section leaders chosen from the older fleet sailors. Some of us would be picked for night security fire watches; we would still have Saturday morning barracks inspection by some station chief, but that was about it. No more personal inspections, no drill or marching to chow. So long as we kept our quarters clean and caused no trouble, we were free to concentrate on school.

School, which began almost immediately, occupied four and a half days a week. Friday afternoon was given over to a field day (clean up) in the building. There would be liberty on the weekends for those who chose to take advantage of it, but few did. Many preferred to crack the books instead, because if we failed to maintain a specified average we would be dropped from school and transferred to other assignments.

Classes were much like those so many of us had just left in high school a few weeks earlier. A lot of time was devoted to the old "readin', 'ritin', and 'rithmetic." A little simple math, some geometry, and mechanical drawing, as well as a familiarization course with basic hand tools—a well-rounded program designed to prepare us for what was to come in Michigan. Nobody had any real trouble making it, except a few of the country boys, and the rest of us tutored them so our class would stay together. Anyway, the first month was behind us before we knew, and we were packing for the trip to Dearborn.

On July 29, our group of about 200 was jammed into buses, our seabags tossed into a truck, and we were off to the railroad station. Then it was on to Detroit. Once there, we scrambled out of the carriages and lined up on the railroad station platform. There were several of the usual shake, rattle, and roll Navy vehicles to take us to the base, but first a harried lieutenant came racing up to leap on the hood of one vehicle and in a very loud voice yell, "Now hear this! I want to welcome all you people to the United States Navy Henry Ford Service School. Before we go anywhere, I want to tell you two things. First, the legal age of consent in the state of Michigan is sixteen. Second, if you just have to be sociable with the little girls in town you damn well better put a boot on it!" With that he jumped down, climbed into his Navy sedan, and roared off. A gnarly old chief who looked as though he hated the world appeared out of nowhere and snarled, "Okay, everybody into the buses." That was our official welcome to our new duty assignment.

You can imagine the conversations on that ride to the base. Everybody was curious about the reference to the legal age of consent. A few of the younger guys were asking, "What did he mean, 'put a boot on it'?" It looked as though we would have an interesting three months.

As our little convoy rolled up to the school grounds, what met our eyes was a far cry from what we expected. We had been told it was a new installation, but that was an understatement. Located on the banks of the Lower Rouge River, it was almost all wood frame construction, surrounded by a chain link fence. The gates were wide open and the guards were seamen in whites with guard belts. There were no petty officers in evidence anywhere. It seemed like a pretty slack operation. Not Navy at all. Further inside were several two-story barracks, much like those we had lived in during our detention period. When we off loaded and went inside to our assigned dormitories, we discovered one big difference—the absence of jackstays. We would be sleeping in double-decker bunks. That, at least, was good news. We settled in pretty quickly, prowling all over the building to familiarize ourselves with the facilities, and to see where our friends might be located. After that, it was chow time, and we found it was a base that fed good; another mark in its favor.

Later that evening, we were taken on a walking tour of the grounds by a first class petty officer who used a bullhorn to describe what we were seeing. Besides the barracks, there was an administration building for staff offices, and the base police department. Base police consisted of a Regular Navy chief, several petty officers, and a few seamen, all of whom had shore duty there. Further down the street we found the sick bay, and a big empty recreation hall, empty except for a gedunk in one corner and a lot of picnic tables. Recreational equipment had yet to be delivered. There was a fire station, a mess hall, and another big gate at the far end of the street. Like the main entrance, it was guarded by several sloppy-looking seamen in dingy whites.

The fact that Henry Ford had built, and probably paid for, the installation was quite obvious. His name was on just about everything—every tray, every knife, fork, and spoon. Even the pots and pans in the galley carried the Ford logo. The fire engine, base police vehicle, utility trucks, buses, and even the commandant's car were all Fords.

The tour over, we were again taken to the mess hall for an indoctrination speech. The earlier reference to the state age of consent and the "boot" very quickly became clear. Apparently, when the Navy first moved to Dearborn, the officers and enlisted men alike were a randy bunch and wasted no time in establishing a reputation in town. This resulted in more than a little trouble for Uncle Sam. The little girls in the area, looking far older than their tender years, went for the bluejackets in a big way—a few of them so enthusiastically so that they became pregnant. It was all hushed up, of course, but it resulted in the "hot skinny" being given to all newcomers as soon as they stepped down from the train. Anyone who ignored or forgot the warning faced instant disciplinary action and a transfer to some of the worst duty to be found. The "boot" was a reference to the old standby government-issue condom.

Once having received the official explanation, we were told about the school routine and our training schedules. There would be some classroom instruction, but most of our time would be spent in the Ford Company shops where we would be working alongside the regular apprentices. Journeymen tradesmen would be our instructors. We would be learning our trade from experts and would be graded by them as well, with the same standard we had faced in our first month of school still holding true. The idea of being sent to sea as some kind of punishment didn't make sense at first. After all, being at sea is what the Navy was all about. It turned out, however, that if we went to the fleet after having been dropped from our class, it would be entered in our service record, along with a recommendation that no further application to any school be considered for the balance of the enlistment. That made more sense. It was still peacetime and they could afford to be selective.

Once we began work in the shops, there wasn't much chance of anyone being dropped. We very quickly realized that we were getting training that no other service school could provide. Being taught by civilians who were all experienced in their specialty, we were actually learning a trade the way it was followed in civilian life. Real nuts-and-bolts instruction from men earning their living in a trade we wanted to follow when our hitch was up. And we also learned a lot of little tricks that no school would ordinarily teach, like, "When you complete a job in sheet metal, quickly give it a coat of red lead to cover up any mistakes you may have made," and, "The best place to crap out and sleep off a drunk is over in the lumberyard. Nobody ever looks for you there." Then there was, "If you're welding thick plates that require six passes to fill the groove, lay a welding rod in it and make two passes instead. It looks good and will probably do the job." But the most valuable lesson I learned was that a seventeen-year-old kid is not man enough to chew tobacco!

Not all of our time in Dearborn was tied up in work or study. Every weekend there was liberty for those who had money to go ashore. It was on September 1st that the guys from our boot company were promoted to the rank of seaman second class with a grand increase in pay from $21 to $36 a month. We could now grab some of that R & R—Rest and Relaxation. Some of the boys relaxed so much they had to be carried back to the base. It was a good thing the folks back home were not able to see their teenaged boys growing up.

Boots, Gun Grease, and I Turn Eighteen

Liberty was usually up at midnight, but with most of us hitchhiking back and forth from nearby towns we would invariably get back late. That was no problem, however, because a couple of hamburgers or a bottle of beer for the seaman guard would get us through the gate with no one the wiser. Those first two or three weeks in Dearborn had everyone so happy after our boot camp restrictions that some of the boys got carried away. That resulted in their going before captain's mast (the disciplinary review before the base commandant), which in turn brought them loss of future liberties, extra duties, and sometimes a fine. Worse, an entry would be made in their service record that brought down their school average. About a dozen guys went too far, and they suffered permanent restriction to the base until orders could be cut, sending them to sea.

The real problem, I suppose, was that security was so lax there was always the temptation to break the rules. But with school so important, and the weekends being free, hardly anyone would jump ship for their pleasure. There were other ways to take advantage of the situation. More than once girls were discovered on school grounds, down by the river.

Several professional ladies were caught plying their trade on the base, and one night two in-training bluejackets were stopped coming in the back gate rolling a small keg of beer down the road. The guards sent them off to their barracks and the station police confiscated the beer. That seemed in the best interest of all concerned.

Generally, the Navy tried to take care of its own. Every time we would pass through the gates on liberty, we were offered what was called a prophylactic kit. This consisted of a condom, a small tube of medicated ointment, a big sheet of waxed paper, and a piece of string. These were to be used according to enclosed instructions if and when we were exposed to the services of females of doubtful character. We called these little packages "shooter's kits" or "boots and gun grease."

But if used correctly, the kit would protect the romantic sailor against any so-called social diseases, and prevent the local girls from getting pregnant. Upon returning to our dormitories, we were then expected to take a shower and, if we had been "exposed," to "log in," placing our name, rank, and service number on the list found in every crew's head. Then, if at a later date it was necessary to report to the sick bay with symptoms of the disease, the Navy would take care of the offender, with no penalties being imposed. But woe to the sailor who turned in with a louse and it was discovered he had not logged in as required. He would be subjected to at least a captain's mast and be placed in the hospital "clap shack," the venereal disease ward. Any time lost would be added to his enlistment. He might even be required to pay for specialized medical care.

Needless to say, just about everyone took the proffered

kit, whether he intended to use it or not, and when he returned from liberty he logged in. That way nobody had to admit going ashore without making a score. It was a matter of being salty. Today I suppose it would be called being macho. Trying to follow Grandma's advice to be good, I played the salty game like all the others and kept out of trouble. Until my birthday, that is.

On September 27th I turned eighteen, and to celebrate, went out for a binge with a couple of my newfound buddies. The leader of our little group was a fleet sailor named Bob LaJoya. He had come back to the States for school, and he insisted he knew his way around Detroit. What did we know? We followed him. To this day there is some doubt in my mind as to exactly what happened. I do know I developed a fondness for Tom Collins punch. At least that's what Bob told me. He also assured me it was a great liberty, and even made sure I was logged in on the exposure list. But I still ask myself, was it necessary? My shooter's kit was gone, and I had grease stains to contend with. But there was no recollection at all of what might have transpired. I vaguely remember taking a shower that night as LaJoya pounded me on the back, yelling, "Atta boy, Lonnie! Atta boy!" Nothing further ever developed, so it can probably be written off as another case of "all's well that ends well." Still, I wish I could be sure that my eighteenth birthday celebration was as good as my classmates told me it was.

For most of us, the three months at the Dearborn school went pretty smoothly, and we ended our time as qualified strikers (apprentices) in our chosen specialty, entitled to wear the striker's patch on our sleeve denoting our newly acquired skills. Graduation didn't amount to much. There was the usual congratulatory speech by the base commandant, and a similar one by a representative of the Ford Motor Company. There was a disappointing explanation that our certificate of course completion would be forwarded to us because they had not yet been printed. They did manage to give us our final grade and class standing. I didn't do too badly. My 3.345 out of a possible 4.0 put me 23rd in the metalsmith class of 36.

On October 31st, our gang was once again on the train, heading back to Great Lakes to await reassignment to our next duty station. All the way back, everyone talked about what a great time they had at Dearborn and how much fun the liberties had been—especially in Detroit. Everyone talked about that. Everyone but me. I couldn't remember.

For Further Transfer

Arriving back at Great Lakes once again, we were beginning to feel as though it was a home port. Our entire draft of recently graduated strikers was housed in transient barracks to wait for new orders. There wasn't much required of us except the mandatory dormitory clean up. We spent most of our time at the hostess house, on liberty, or hanging around the dormitories washing clothes, writing letters, going to the base movies, or just sitting around telling one another lies. And, of course, there was a real effort to keep out of the sight of the base petty officers looking for work parties.

After a couple weeks of this routine, we were all climbing the bulkheads, anxious to get moving again. On November 14th we were underway. A large number of us were ordered to get packed and ready to move out. We were being transferred to the Puget Sound Naval Base in Bremerton, Washington, FFT (for further transfer). Our draft was sent by train, and after a tiring three-day trip, pulled into the station. Then it was a bus ride to the base, where we were quartered in wooden barracks that seemed to be the same everywhere we went. The chief in charge made a point of telling us not to get too comfortable, because our orders were already being cut for yet another move. Until then, we had liberty every day from noon until midnight.

Liberty was usually spent in nearby Bremerton. A real sailor's town, it could be reached only by taking a ferryboat across the bay. The ferry, the MV *Kalakala*, was extremely modern for its time, all streamlines and highly polished aluminum. Powered by diesel engines, she made the trip in short order with a "bone in her teeth," a heavy bow wave cause by her speed. There were so many ships in the harbor, and water traffic was so heavy, that the trip was exciting to those who had never seen the ocean, or who had not seen warships other than in story books or in the movies. There were a lot of things of interest in the area with a foreign flavor. For one thing, the British battle cruiser, HMS *Warspite*, was in the Navy yard for repairs, and her crew was making their liberties in nearby communities.

Warspite had an enviable record as a warship going all the way back to the Battle of Jutland in World War I, and as might have been expected, the Brits had to play the part of the rollicking, rough-and-tough jack tar seamen. They did it very well, offending many people as they did so. All in all they were a royal English pain in the "arse" until they ran into the Yankee bluejacket. We tried to accept them as fellow seafarers and all that, but they pushed our hospitality to the limit and beyond. They would go into town, get boozed up (the English obviously could not handle their liquor!) and begin to berate American servicemen and civilians alike for failing to do our part in the war. As they put it, we were "letting the English do the fighting" for us. This was not the smartest thing they could have said. We colonists became more than a little upset.

A couple of us were walking down the main drag in

Bremerton one evening and heard what sounded like a full-scale riot coming our way. In a minute or so, running down the middle of the street and looking somewhat the worse for wear, came an English sailor. He was waving his arms and screaming for help. About fifty feet behind him and coming on strong was an American seaman swinging a fair-sized length of two-by-four. And behind him came two local cops calling for them both to stop. The entire parade vanished around the corner with the Brit still screaming. I've often wondered if the police caught up with the Yank before he caught up with the Englishman. As they rounded the corner the guy with the two-by-four was gaining, so I'd bet on him.

A similar incident took place on the *Kalakala*. Two American sailors were hanging over the rail, drunk as could be, heaving their innards out. A big Brit came swaggering down the deck and pushed them aside as he roared, "Make way for a real fightin' mon!" Before anyone else could make a move, the two Americans had picked the bully up and unceremoniously threw him over the rail. I imagine he was able to swim. At least I hope so, because no one called out "man overboard!" or even threw a lifering.

Ah, Bremerton was a good liberty town. We were kind of sorry to leave when we received our orders to pack our gear and prepare to board ship. We were going to sea at last. A chance to develop our sea legs!

On November 25th we trooped aboard the USS *Harris*, bound for San Diego. The *Harris* was an old Lurline cruise liner that had been taken over by the Navy after being rescued from "red lead row." She had been tied up to a dock, slowly deteriorating despite having been given a heavy coat of red lead primer paint to protect her from the elements.

The Navy, deciding they needed transport vessels, would remodel and recondition a ship to suit its purpose. *Harris*'s engines had been overhauled, and she was ready for sea. As long as her captain had to take her on a shake-down cruise, it might as well be to San Diego where our draft was headed. Our transportation was assured as long as she survived the voyage, something that scuttlebutt said was doubtful.

The run to "Dago" took about five days, and I can't remember a more miserable time in my life. I was seasick most of the way, and the old salts aboard were no help with their suggestion that I swallow a piece of half-cooked salt pork with a string attached. The idea was that after the fat was down, you pulled on the string. As the fat came up, so did your guts. Just thinking about it as the ship bobbed up and down...up and down...ychhh!!

There was a lot of work to be done on board to make the *Harris* suitable for the duty that would be assigned to her. Ordinarily, most of it would be done by the regular crew or ship's company. But so long as we were being carried as passengers, somebody decided we ought to work for our passage. I found myself on a working party out on the weather decks.

Like most of the early pleasure liners, the *Harris* had wooden decks. Long years of exposure to the weather, coupled with neglect, had reduced the once-glistening surface to a mass of warped boards and splinters. They had to be returned to their original condition, and we were just the boys to do it with a technique known as "holystoning."

Holystoning a deck was an age-old seafarer's way to keep it nice and smooth and easy to clean. What you did was to take the stone, usually a common house brick, and chip a small indentation on the flat surface. Then, jamming a broomstick into it as a handle, you rubbed that stone back and forth, back and forth, back and forth on the deck, which had been wet down with water and sprinkled with sand. It's hard work, but in time the deck is smoother than a baby's butt.

I thought it would be smart to work hard and wear out my stone. Maybe then the bos'n would let me go lie down in peace and be sick in relative comfort. It did not work. When my stone was worn down and broken in half, he handed me a new one. He had plenty. Eventually, we had those decks so smooth we could run on them in our bare feet. We then scrubbed the holystoned surface with more sand and seawater, using stiff-bristled brooms. I made the mistake of complaining about the hard work. The bos'n, without a word, gently took my broom from my hand and replaced it with a toothbrush. It was real good to get into corners and along the deckhouses to dig out the wet sand. It also taught me not to smart off to a bos'n mate.

Being so sick and hard at work during my first sea voyage, I didn't have much opportunity to enjoy it or experience what being at sea was really like. I've often regretted that, because one's first time at sea ought to be a pleasant memory rather than one of blistered hands and dry heaves. But I survived. By the time we made landfall in San Diego, my stomach had settled down somewhat, and I was able to turn to with the rest of the work party without heading for the rail every few minutes. Maybe one of the things that helped was advice received from the bos'n, who really wasn't a bad guy at all. He said, "Go ahead and puke it all up, but if you feel something fuzzy in your throat, you better swallow it again 'cause that's your asshole." Good advice.

We dropped anchor in San Diego on December 1st and were immediately put ashore to be taken by bus to the San Diego Receiving Station at the Destroyer Base. My orders called for me to be later transferred to the USS *Whitney*, a repair ship then stationed in Pearl Harbor, Hawaii. I could just see myself spending my entire enlistment in the beautiful Hawaiian Islands: gently waving palm trees, soft breezes, hooley-hooley dancers, pineapples, and...boy was I going to like this kind of duty! I might even make it a career.

San Diego, Pearl Harbor —and War!

The Destroyer Base in San Diego was a small installation designed to provide repairs, fueling, and provisioning for small ships like destroyers, tug boats, patrol craft, and the like. Bigger ships needing more elaborate facilities were taken to Mare Island Navy Yard in San Francisco. In San Diego there was also a small transfer center for personnel who were assigned to the DESBATFORPAC, the Destroyer Battle Force Pacific. That's where we ultimately would be sent, but for the time being it was temporary duty in "Dago."

We were put up in the usual wooden Navy barracks that by that time I was convinced were stamped out by machine and shipped as kits to wherever they might be needed. In a way, this was a good idea, because it made getting acclimated a lot easier. Once again there were bunks for us, rather than hammocks, with mattresses provided. With our own bedding dropped on top it made for pretty comfortable sleeping. There were lockers, which made living out of seabags unnecessary. It was also taken as an indication that we would be there for a while.

Our suspicions were correct. Our gang would be stuck there until our orders came through. Beautiful Hawaii would have to wait. Until we left we would be assigned to various work parties. Some to the dry dock to scrape old barnacles from the hull of a tug boat, others to swing a paintbrush with antifouling paint, still others to general labor crews for wherever they might be needed. Me, I lucked out and was ordered to the galley in the chiefs' mess hall. When I first learned of it I thought, "Oh, no. Not pot walloping again!" But my fears were quickly laid to rest when I found myself working with the cooks, peeling vegetables, slicing bread, making coffee, even flipping hotcakes and frying bacon. And the best part about it, there was no need for me to go to the regular mess hall. Working in the galley entitled me to a chief's rations. I made a vow not to smart talk anyone. It was too good a deal to lose.

My efforts apparently caught the attention of the chief cook, because he almost immediately mentioned that he was looking for a couple of cook strikers. If I was interested, he could probably arrange it, he said. Of course, I had to tell him I was already a metalsmith striker, and assigned to the *Whitney*. He seemed pretty sure that with no war on there was not going to be much call for artificer ratings, but there would always be a need for cooks. If I went out to the fleet it would probably be as a deck seaman with no promise of anything else. On the other hand, if I were to become a cook striker and did a good job, he would recommend me for cooks and bakers school.

Well, that called for a lot of cogitation on my part. What he said made a lot of sense, but if he was only running a con on me, my hitch would be screwed up. But I had a gut feeling he was being square with me, so the next morning I told him I'd go for it. We shook on it. Then I wiped the egg mixture from my hand. That was December 6th.

The next day was Sunday, December 7th, the day of the Japanese attack on Pearl Harbor. Immediately upon getting word, the chief cook apologized and said all deals were off. The Navy would want all the repair rates it could get. Pearl was apparently a real mess. In a matter of hours, the destroyer base was an armed camp. Sentries appeared as though by magic, and no one could go near a ship or building without being challenged. All work in the yard was revised as priorities changed. Several destroyers stood out of the harbor in a big hurry, going who knows where. Our draft of strikers was ordered to pack our gear and stand by for immediate transfer. I would be going to the *Whitney* after all.

It was another week before we boarded ship for the crossing to Pearl Harbor. During that week, the base was a frantic, almost scary place to be. At night there was a total blackout except for a few strategically placed and shielded lights. Even in the barracks we had to move about by flashlight until blinds could be rigged on windows and doors. There was no walking around outside in the dark for fear somebody might get shot. All liberties were canceled and guys on leave were recalled. America went to war footing very, very, fast.

On December 13th, our draft was moved back aboard the USS *Harris* for the trip to Pearl. We weren't too crazy about making the voyage on that particular ship, but considering the circumstances, we kept our mouths shut. Instead, we tried to get squared away in our designated quarters and make ready for whatever was to come. There was no such thing as work parties for anyone on our second passage by sea; we had little to do other than various drills for fire and rescue, battle stations, and one that shook everyone's confidence in the *Harris*—abandon ship! Once the transport sailed out of the harbor to join the convoy, we knew we were going to war.

There were six, maybe seven ships all told, including the *Harris*, plus the three destroyers for escort. Those little tin cans were constantly racing back and forth with signal lights flashing as the convoy was herded into formation. After a while things seemed organized as we headed west. By nightfall, we were already into a routine of doing nothing except waiting for chow call, or some kind of drill. Nobody wanted to stay in the sleeping compartments. In fact, nobody went below decks except to eat. We tried it the first night, but it was so noisy we couldn't sleep if we had wanted to. Not only was the engine pounding and rumbling, but we could hear the steam and water as it pulsed through the many lines, and the hull plates as they groaned and protested the strain of plowing through the sea. It was as though the old girl just didn't want to go to war. Maybe she knew something we didn't. Anyway, rather than stay in our bunks and listen to all that, we went up on deck and settled down for the entire crossing. We even slept up there using our lifejackets for pillows.

Sitting around on deck or standing by the rail, we began to get an idea of what being at sea was really like. The *Harris* was continually rolling and pitching as we zigzagged back and forth. The weather, while not really bad, was overcast most of the time, with both sea and sky a dull, leaden gray. The only break in the drabness was the white-capped waves and the blinking signal lights of the escorts. Surprisingly, there were no complaints of anyone getting seasick. I was light-headed the first day out, but this first serious trip for us was too nerve-racking for anyone to think about his stomach.

Every morning at dawn we went to battle stations because that was the time the enemy submarines were supposed to attack. At dusk it was the same thing. And at night the entire convoy would darken ship. No lights topside whatsoever. Just smoking a cigarette on the open deck could result in a court martial. A wartime mentality was developing and it was understandable. We heard all kinds of rumors of the destruction of Pearl Harbor and everyone was jumpy.

Several times the convoy went to general quarters as the destroyers went racing off to cover a sub contact. We would line the rails, watching as they made a run at flank speed to drop their depth charges. We could see them roll off the stern, and see others fly through the air as they were thrown from the "Y" guns. They hit the water with a big splash and it was only seconds before they would reach a preset depth and explode. Gigantic columns of water would reach up to the sky and fall back into the boiling sea as we anxiously scanned the surface for any debris or oil that might indicate a hit. But there was nothing. Instead, it was more observation of the cans cutting through the waters to drop still more charges on a suspected enemy. Maybe the destroyer skippers were as nervous as we were, and who could blame them? It was our introduction to war. In any case, we didn't like it one damned bit. Sure, it was exciting, adventurous, just like in the movies. But it was no movie. It was all very real. Guys could get killed this way.

Early in the morning on December 24th the convoy made landfall at the Hawaiian Islands. When we saw it in the distance, there was a like-minded sigh of relief. We had made it. Still, we were very tense, realizing we were in waters where the Japanese had been so successful just two weeks before. But, along with the other ships, the *Harris* stood into the harbor. What we were to see was absolutely unbelievable. We thought, "This can't have happened to us. This is America. Nobody can hurt us." But we found out that somebody could, and they damned well did!

Pearl Harbor and a Merry Christmas

As the *Harris* sailed into the harbor, we stood dumbfounded at the sight that met our eyes. Everywhere we looked there was only destruction and the ravages of the December 7th attack. The water in the bay was covered with thick, black, tarry oil that appeared to be several inches thick, mixed with floating debris resulting from the explosions and fires. Articles of clothing, lifejackets, and a lone white sailor's hat that had somehow remained snowy clean gave mute evidence to the loss of life. Here and there smoke still rose from smoldering wreckage. When we passed what used to be known as Battleship Row, there were gasps of disbelief. We saw nothing but the burned and sunken hulks of our once proud Pacific Fleet. The USS *Oklahoma* had capsized after having been torpedoed. The *Maryland* and *Tennessee* were both heavily damaged. The *Nevada*, victim of both bomb and torpedo attack, had been beached to prevent her sinking. The *California* and *West Virginia* had gone down at their anchorage. Even the aged *Utah*, an unarmed target vessel, had been destroyed. But worst of all was the USS *Arizona*. Struck by both heavy bombs and torpedoes, her magazines exploding, the gallant old battlewagon was totally demolished. What had remained had sunk to the bottom of the harbor with over 1,000 members of her crew trapped inside her hull. The only evidence of her ever having existed was her foremast jutting from the murky waters, twisted and burned, albeit with colors and pennant still flying from the masthead.

The entire harbor reeked with the stench of death. We were to later see other damage. The destroyers USS *Cassin* and *Downes* were nothing but burnt-out shells in a dry dock they had shared with the battleship *Pennsylvania*, which miraculously received little damage. The aircraft, building, and equipment losses were still being assessed weeks after the attack. The Pearl Harbor Naval Base was almost completely destroyed.

It was almost dark by the time the *Harris* dropped anchor. Immediately, we were transferred to the repair ship USS *Whitney* by whaleboats. We couldn't see much of her as we made it to her landing stage. The only illumination was a few red-colored battle lanterns. We moved up her ladders in a state of uncertainty, trying hard not to stumble. Anyone who might fall into the mucky, polluted waters below, burdened with all his gear, would become a statistic. In spite of the awkwardness of moving around in the dark, our draft did get up to the main deck without losing anyone. Given lifejackets with quick instructions in their use, we were told to sack out right there on deck for the night. Somebody would come around later with hot coffee and sandwiches. Considering the turmoil and confusion that existed at the time, it was no surprise that the chow never appeared. We went to sleep hungry that night, but I heard no complaints.

As we arranged our seabags and lifejackets along the deck, trying to stay out of the crew's way, it dawned on us that it was Christmas Eve—for many of us our first Christmas away from home. We were a bunch of teenaged kids, scared to death and trying very hard not to let it show. I doubt if many of us slept that night. There were a lot of whispered prayers, and every now and then you could hear a muffled sob. One of the guys down the line called out softly, "Good night guys, and Merry Christmas." There were a few more sobs to be heard, and I think one of them might have been mine. Still, despite everything, we did have something to cling to. After all, as our buddy had said, it was Christmas. I guess as we lay there in the darkness on our first wartime Christmas Eve, we were all truly hoping for peace on Earth, and good will toward all men.

The next morning, Christmas morning, we were awakened by the growl of airplane engines as the dawn patrol was preparing for takeoff. Everyone jumped up to line the rail and watch. Several consolidated PBY patrol flying boats were taxiing through the oil-covered waters to finally rise and head out to sea. It didn't seem likely the Japs would be hanging around for a return engagement, but we were all very new to the business of war, and no chances were being taken.

There was still a holiday dinner of turkey, ham, and all the trimmings, and church services were held for those who wished to attend. Not many guys showed up. I don't know if it was a lack of faith or just a strong sense of survival. The chapels were all located below deck, and it somehow seemed a lot safer topside. We remained on deck, watching the base as best we could and talking amongst ourselves about what we had seen and what our hopes were for the future. It was not the sort of yuletide we were used to, but one we would get to know well in the years ahead.

Whitney to *Rigel* to *Trever*

Our draft stayed aboard the *Whitney* for several days, not doing much more than keeping out of the way and waiting. By keeping our eyes and ears open and our mouths shut, we learned much more of what had happened on December 7th. It wasn't encouraging. A few more guys would leave each day, being transferred to their final duty station or ship. On December 27th it was our turn. About thirty-five of us were told to pick up our gear and move over to the boat stage for loading into those big motorboats that seemed to be everywhere. It didn't take long to disembark—and that without anyone falling over the side. With a clang of bells we shoved off, and within a very few minutes pulled up to the landing stage of the USS *Rigel*, another old—very old—repair ship where we would again wait for further transfer. The reason for all our shuffling around was unknown, other than its being typically Navy.

I would have rather spent that extra time on the *Whitney*. The good ship *Rigel* gave every indication of not being long for this world. She hadn't moved for several years, and there was some question if her engines would even turn over. As I said, she was a repair ship, although limited in services she might offer. We were very quickly shown to our quarters and told to stay there except for chow call, to use the head, or go to the washrooms. There was no going up on deck to see the sights. With some considerable trepidation, we all settled in.

There were two things about that ship that have stuck in my mind all these years. First, the food was great! That was a surprise, considering that even in our inexperience we knew she was a hulk held together mainly by her rust and corrosion. As you filed into the mess compartment there was a big sign staring you in the face. "Take All You Want—But Eat All You Take." To make sure you remembered that, there were petty officers stationed by the exit hatch to watch what you might scrape from your tray. I remember one guy who tried to throw away two fatty pork chops. He was told to sit down and finish his meal. There was no wasting of food on the *Rigel*.

The other memorable feature was my bunk. There had been so many overhauls and modifications to that ship that nothing fit right any longer. My bunk frame was at least six inches higher at the foot end than at the head. I remedied that by simply turning around. Still, it was like trying to sleep on the side of a hill. The bedding supports on the bunk above mine were broken, and the guy who slept there was what we could only call a lardass. He sagged far into my space. Complaining did no good because everyone had problems.

The *Rigel* had gone to wartime conditions and all unnecessary hatches and scuttles had been closed down. Fresh air was almost nonexistent. With the burden of all the extra people on board, shower facilities were not always adequate. So along with all the normal bad smells of an old ship, we had one more to contend with—ourselves. Our only escape was to the mess hall. Consequently, we spent most of our time looking forward to chow call and hoping for early orders to ship out.

After four days of sweating it out, orders were cut for three of us to our permanent assignment. We wasted no time grabbing our gear and reporting to the gangway for transport. At the bottom of the ladder, a greasy little sixteen-foot motor whaleboat was bobbing up and down in the choppy water. It was the work boat of the USS *Trever*, whatever that was. Throwing our bags down, we saluted the quarterdeck and colors, and climbed down. With its crew, the three of us, and our seabags, that little boat seemed dangerously low in the water. But when the *Rigel* officer of the deck cried, "Shove off!" we were under way.

The cox'n, with his arms folded across his chest, stood astraddle the long handle of the tiller, which jutted from between his knees. He apparently was going to steer with no hands. The engineer crouched over his wheezing, coughing engine, beating it with a hammer as he pleaded with it not to die. The remaining member of their little trio was forward, huddling under a piece of dirty canvas; why became very obvious to us, very quickly. Boat and crew were all pretty grimy. I couldn't help but think that if this was any indication of what lay ahead, those pictures on the walls of the recruiting office of men in clean uniforms were lies. All lies!

As we pulled away from the tender, the cox'n called for full speed and headed our boat toward its destination. How he knew where that was, I had no idea. There was, as far as I could see, no boat compass. He steered by instinct. I found out that boat cox'n were all like that. They not only possessed a lot of boat savvy, but an overabundance of self-confidence and arrogance. The waters of the harbor were, as mentioned, very choppy that day, and the boat rolled and pitched, causing huge waves of filthy, stinking, oily water—filled with garbage and assorted debris—to break over our bow and drench us all. Even the bowman who hunkered under his scrap of canvas did not escape. In a few minutes our white uniforms were ruined. Somehow, the only one who was not touched was the cox'n who stood in the stern, protected, I suppose, by his attitude.

The trip to the *Trever*'s anchorage took about a half hour, during which we tried to get information from the boat crew as to what she might look like. But they were preoccupied with trying to keep the boat afloat and running. So we took advantage of the time to introduce ourselves. Besides myself as a metalsmith striker, there were two gunner's mate strikers. A guy named Harth, and a rather strange character that answered to the name of "Sheepshit." How or why he ever got a name like that was never really explained. His name actually was something like Hitterhousenberger, but no one could remember that, let alone pronounce it. For all the years we knew him, it was always Sheepshit. That made for some very interesting roll calls. Particularly with a new officer who might not know the crew.

Having made done with the introductions, we began to look for the ship that was to be our new home: the USS *Trever* DMS-16. It wasn't too long before our less-than-friendly cox'n yelled for our attention as he pointed across the water.

"There she is," he called out. "The rusty, round-bottomed son of a bitch you're going to live on for the rest of the war. If she don't sink, that is."

Permanent Duty

The boat cox'n was right about one thing. The *Trever* was rusty. And she was dirty, with scabrous-looking sides where the paint was flaking. If you were downwind, as we were in our approach, you could smell her as well. There was an odor of old steel, stale grease, paint, cooking food, and people—a smell that I would get to know very well, yet learn to ignore. Those of the crew that were on deck reminded me of a bunch of pirates in a storybook or an old-time movie. Wearing dungarees, boon docker shoes, less-than-clean skivvie shirts, and a variety of hats ranging from dirty white hats to khaki-colored pith helmets, they were, to say the least, an unsavory-looking bunch. Particularly since almost every one of them wore a fair-sized sheath knife at his belt. All this, I found out later, was the result of their belonging to the "Hooligan Navy," a group of small ships that drew the worst duty imaginable. Jobs that others could not, or were very reluctant to, carry out. Add to this the living conditions aboard, and the fact that the *Trever* had been kept pretty busy since December 7th with no time for clean-up or maintenance, and it becomes easier to understand. But I was not about to let my smart mouth get me into trouble again. For better or worse, she was my ship.

Originally built as a first line combat destroyer, the *Trever* had been converted into something called a high-speed minesweeper. She was a flush deck, four-stack destroyer type similar to those given to England in 1940 when that friendly country was being threatened by the Axis powers and was urgently in need of destroyers for antisubmarine and convoy escort duty. About 314 feet long, she was only about thirty feet at her widest. When carrying a full load of fuel and ammunition, the *Trever*'s stern was only about three feet out of the water. Armament consisted of four main guns and a bunch of .50 caliber machine guns, plus a few .30 caliber guns wherever they might be mounted. Her torpedo tubes had been removed during the conversion, and the space given over to an assortment of heavy minesweeping gear. This made her top heavy and even more inclined to roll in heavy weather. On the stern could be seen the usual racks of depth charges, plus more minesweeping equipment. Except for torpedo attack, the old tin can could still carry out destroyer duties in addition to her new role of minesweeping.

The whaleboat pulled up to her sea ladder, which was nothing but a few steel rungs welded to the side. We tossed our bags up to the main deck, and then scrambled up ourselves to be greeted by the officer of the deck. Throwing a leg over the lifelines, I gave a salute to the colors and to the quarterdeck, according to tradition. The gangway petty officer took our records and entered our arrival in the ship's log. That was it. We were henceforth members of the USS *Trever* DMS-16 ship's company.

Using the ship's public address system, the gangway petty officer called for the chief water tender to make it to the gangway to take charge of yours truly. And he did it by walking past me, growling, "Follow me." I picked up my seabag and did just that—I followed him. All the way aft to the deckhouse over the crew's quarters. There he turned me over to a burly guy jammed into a tiny cubicle with an old-fashioned wringer washing machine. I found out that he was "Boilermaker Bracken." He was master-at-arms and petty officer in charge of the after crew spaces. He was also operator of this ship's laundry. Bracken was a first-class boilermaker with a good thing going. He had found a used washer and started a crew's laundry service—for a price, of course. It was also enough to keep him from any other regular duties. It was my first exposure to shipboard politics, but certainly not my last.

The chief water tender took off, telling me to lay up to the chiefs' quarters after getting squared away. And "for chrissake, change that crummy uniform!" It took a few minutes for the boilermaker to finish his load of laundry, and then he said, "Okay, let's get you taken care of." He stepped to the top of the ladder going to the compartment below, and literally dropped out of sight. Not knowing where I was going, it seemed smarter to take it a little easier. He did not see it that way. He reappeared and, grabbing my seabag, he disappeared once more. From the darkened space below came a growl. "What are you waitin' for? Get your ass down here!" I did. Once below it wasn't all that bad. There were lights, although most of them were turned off. The spaces were used for both living and eating meals.

Bunk frames were hinged against the bulkheads, with lockers below forming seats at the mess tables on either side of the compartment. The master-at-arms gave me a bunk way in the back, about six feet off the deck, and told me to unpack and to "change that shitty uniform. Bring it up to me, and I'll wash it for you." I quickly changed, thinking how nice he was to offer to wash my crummy whites. It wasn't until later that he told me what it would cost. My bedding was tossed on the bunk, and I was stowing the rest of my things in the locker when I heard it. My name was coming over the loud speaker. "Now hear this. Dawson, lay up to the chiefs' quarters now!" Scooting up the ladder, I raced forward, asking the first guy I saw where in hell I was going.

The chiefs' quarters were found easily enough, and dashing in I found my man sitting at the table drinking coffee. The first thing he did was hand me his cup. "Take a shot. You won't find better coffee anywhere on board." After a quick gulp of his coffee I handed the cup back, taking his offer to be a sign of acceptance. Maybe it wasn't such a bad start.

Then I found out that he was Chief Water Tender "Doggie" Delmar, senior engineering chief aboard ship, and my boss. He also told me that the *Trever* did not carry a metalsmith, so I would be assigned to the fire room. His fire room! He would be responsible for my initial training, and I would be standing steaming watches in his section. I wondered just what in hell a steaming watch was, but figured that was not the time to ask.

Next it was up to see Mr. Shee, the engineering officer. A full lieutenant in the Navy, he was responsible for all engineering spaces and department operations on board. He welcomed me to the ship with a handshake, and I immediately formed a liking for him. He explained to me the US Navy Bureau of Ships and Personnel (BuPers) determined what rates would be carried on which ships. And in their infinite wisdom (his very words!) they had decided that four-stack destroyer minesweepers did not need metalsmiths. With the war going on, however, that would probably change. Meanwhile, I had no choice but to accept assignment to the fire rooms. Metalsmith ratings, he continued, were considered to be engineering and repair qualifications, and had their beginnings below deck anyway, so there was still a chance to go for my striking rate. The Navy wouldn't want to lose advantage of my training. If BuPers was to decide that metalsmiths would be allowed on destroyers, I would be in a good position for promotion. If they did not, once I had acquired a fireman first class rating, transfer would be possible. It was all very confusing, and quite frankly, I didn't believe all I was being told. But at the time, there was little choice.

Lieutenant Shee also informed me that my seaman second rate would be changed to fireman third. Asking why the step downward, I was told the pay grade was the same. On deck there were third-class petty officers where there were none in the Black Gang. Black Gang? That sounded ominous, although it was really just slang for fire and engine room crews. What it came down to was that fireman first class was equivalent to third-class deck petty officer, so I wouldn't really be losing anything. Still confused? You can bet that I was.

Having given me the official Navy explanation, the lieutenant turned me back to Chief Delmar. By that time it was late in the day, and Doggie told me to get my chow and finish settling in. He would leave me free for that night but I was to report to the forward fire room after breakfast. I would meet the rest of the firemen, get a tour of the ship, find out what my work details would be, and where my general quarters station might be found. After that, my training would begin on how to operate a ship's boiler. That, at least, sounded promising.

From a Greasy Hole in the Afterdeck

There was no doubt about it; I was going to become a fireman, along with all the other tin can sailors who put their time below decks making the ship run. What the Navy referred to as a snipe. And I would probably never see the day when I might sew a metalsmith rating badge on my sleeve. But that was the Navy for you. First I was a metalsmith striker, then almost a cook striker, and finally a boiler-tending fireman. Well, I decided if that was the way it had to be, at least I would be a good fireman. So after breakfast the next morning I headed forward, looking for the entrance to the fire room as ordered.

It wasn't hard to find, being the top of an air lock about two feet in diameter, jutting up out of the deck about two feet. The hatch was open, so I just threw a leg over and hit the ladder. Climbing down I found another hatch, more door-like, at the bottom. It was also wide open. If the fire room had been in use, both hatches would have been closed tight. Fire rooms normally operated under pressure, and if the air lock was opened under those conditions it would allow the air to rush out, literally sucking the fire from the boiler fire boxes. That could result in a room full of flames and serious injury or even death to the watch standers. It also meant that without steam the ship would stop.

Entering a fire room was always impressive to me. It was hot, smelly, and crowded with two boilers and all the pumps, blowers, and other machinery to make them work, as well as the four watch standers. The boiler fronts were a deck below where the firemen tended the fourteen burners in each as well as controls for the pressurized air to keep them breathing. Known as the floor plates, the area was really the heart of the operation, because it not only produced the needed steam on demand, but it was the location of the annunciators, the telegraph communication switches to the bridge and engine rooms.

On the upper level were the controls for the water so vital to making the steam that was the *Trever*'s life. That was the bailiwick of the water tender of the watch, who was also responsible for cutting in or shutting down additional blowers should more air pressure be required. On the upper level you might also find a workbench for emergency repairs, the ever-present coffeepot, and a big chair for the chief of the watch. He spent most of his time reading and making or drinking coffee, or just watching his people do their jobs. About the only time a fire room chief came to life was for emergency high-speed or rapid-speed changing runs when chasing down a submarine contact. When that happened, he wasted no time getting down to the floor plates to back up the two firemen working the boiler fronts. On those old cans things had a tendency to get hectic when they got warlike.

Doggie was there and introduced me to the rest of his watch. The two firemen, one first class and one second, had come out to the fleet when they did not score high enough on aptitude tests for school. The water tender was a second class named John Kayler or, as he called himself, "Kayler the Tailor." He owned a small portable sewing machine and operated a tailoring service. John had learned the art from his father, a regular tailor. He specialized in custom fitting of regulation blue uniforms for those guys who could not afford tailor mades. He was one more guy with something going for him. I could see possibilities growing aboard the *Trever*.

It was Kayler who gave me a full rundown on how everything worked, and how I would be operating a boiler when we were underway. Just as soon as I could qualify to Chief Delmar's satisfaction. The extra fireman would then be transferred. After my introduction to my new world, it was a tour of the ship with Kayler doing the honors. We started on the bow and worked our way aft. What he didn't actually show me, he talked about, not missing a thing.

Up on the bridge, down in the radio and sound shacks, were the forward crew's quarters, and the electrician's shack. We went through the galley where we got in the cook's way while we poured some coffee for ourselves. Then it was to the shipfitter shop—construction and repair. It was the closest thing to a metalsmith to be found aboard. When I was introduced to those guys an idea began to form in my mind. The shipfitters' gang was top heavy with rated men, and had no strikers of any kind. Some of the guys were scheduled for transfer to other ships. It seemed to me that a metalsmith was just what they needed. Making sure I was friendly to everyone, I also made a mental note to myself to talk to the first class in charge.

My tour continued on to the after fire room, which was a duplicate of the one we had left. It was in use so the air lock was dogged down tight. There was a single fireman on duty standing what was called a "cold-iron" watch. In port, only a single boiler was kept in use at reduced steam pressure to maintain electricity and other basic operational needs. It was a simple job from the looks of it, but a vital one if the ship was to be on instant alert for any emergency. Kayler told me that I had the midwatch that night and would be shown how to stand a cold-iron watch by myself, and that I had "damn well better learn quick," because the next day I would be doing just that—standing it by myself.

Then it was on to the gunner's mates' shack where I found Sheepshit going through much of the same "getting acclimated" routine I was. After that it was to the engine room and gun decks. That was about it. From thereon I could prowl around by myself so long as I kept out of people's way. My tour was over. That was a good thing, because once again my name was called over the ship's speaker: "Dawson, lay up to the gangway." Aha, this time I fooled them. I knew where it was!

I found Chief Delmar waiting for me with additional dope. He told me where I would be stationed for abandon ship, fire and rescue, and most important of all—general quarters. My battle station was the after ammunition party, where I would be helping to pass ammo to the guns on the afterdeckhouse and depth charges back to the dropping racks. At least it would keep me on deck when the shooting started. I was also issued a lifejacket, steel helmet, and a gas mask. That last item was kind of scary because it made me think that only a few months earlier my boot company had been taught how to use such equipment, never thinking that we might ever have to. The rest of the day was fairly easy. I hung around the fire room talking to the guys and learning a little more about how things were done. There was the right way, the wrong way, and the Navy way. Guess which way we followed.

We knocked off early enough to hit the showers and washrooms before chow. That was quite an experience. The entire shower and washroom compartment was in the afterdeckhouse. Roughly six by ten feet overall, about a third of it was shower room with only four showerheads hanging from the overhead. You never saw fewer than six or eight guys under the water at one time, with everyone shoving and jostling for water and furiously scrubbing their own or someone else's back. The place was so crowded that if you dropped your soap, you just let it go. I think it was just such a situation that led to the idea of "soap on a rope."

On one side of the room there were four stainless steel sinks with three mirrors. I never did figure that one out. On days when the washroom was jammed you had to fight your way in, lather up, and, grabbing your razor, you looked into a mirror and shaved a face. If you were lucky, it might even be your own. On the other side of the room was a shelf with holes to hold three buckets to wash clothes. At the end of the day, or just before liberty, the place was bulkhead to bulkhead with sailors. Everybody buck naked and soapy. Believe me, on a tin can you learned to trust your shipmates!

After chow that night I hit the sack early because of my midwatch. I had that cold-iron watch. I wasn't too crazy about having my sleep disturbed, but was still kind of excited about learning how to tend a boiler. So when someone shook me and said, "Okay, Dawson, down to the fire room," I was awake immediately.

Cold Iron and a Steaming Watch

I crawled out of my fartsack and dressed quickly. Then, climbing the ladder, I headed along the deck in the dark to the hatch of the fire room. It wasn't as easy as it sounds. The deck of an old four stacker was, of necessity, studded and cluttered with valves, pipes, ducts, bitts, boat cradles, and hatch combings—all of which jutted up underfoot to trip the unwary. Add to that the crew members who chose to sleep topside on cots or just flaked out in some convenient spot, and you had an obstacle course to run each time you walked the decks at night. Lacerated and scabbed-over shins and ankles were the mark of a newcomer to destroyer duty. After a month or so you learned how to navigate those hazards without even thinking about it. It was merely a matter of bobbing and weaving, hopping and skipping, and from time to time leaping into the air like an olympic hurdler. After two or three months you would find yourself doing it in a rough sea while carrying a full cup of coffee in each hand—and never spilling a drop even as you climbed a steep ladder to the gun deck, or an even steeper one to the fire or engine rooms. If you saw a destroyer man with his legs all nicely healed, you could bet he was an experienced tin can sailor. But for me that first night, even in the relative quiet of being anchored, it was unadulterated horror. In my hurry to get on watch I think I tripped over everything, including a couple shipmates who were very disturbed at being stepped on. Fortunately for me it was a moonless night, otherwise I may never have made it to the fire room.

But make it I did, and even managed to follow the proper procedure of going through the air lock without sucking out the boiler fire. My trainer was already on watch and proceeded to chew me out for being late. My watch said I was still some ten minutes early, but a junior fireman did not argue with a lofty first class.

The watch turned out to be an easy one. At night there is not much emergency steam drain on the system, so the single burner we had going handled the job. The other fireman, Deghan (whom we called Deke), was very experienced and really not a bad guy. I had lucked out in drawing him as a partner. He showed me how to insert extra burners, how to pull them for cleaning, how to watch the water level in the boiler, how to increase the air flow of the blowers, and a zillion other things. Then he made me do them all under his watchful eye. When he was satisfied that I understood it all, he turned me loose on my own while he climbed to the upper level to go to sleep in the chief's chair. I'm proud to say he was able to sleep soundly because I felt no need to call him for help. He did wake up a few minutes before we were relieved and checked everything. Then he pounded me on the shoulder and said, "You got it kid; I'm going up to sack out." So for the final moments of my first duty watch I was on my own. I don't think Deke would have left me if he had any doubts. Besides, if anything had gone wrong, Doggie would have had his ass for breakfast.

When my relief came down at a quarter of four that

morning, I very, very nonchalantly gave him all the vital information as was standard practice. "She's steaming on number three boiler, one burner, 150 pounds pressure, water level constant, all burners polished, and the log is up-to-date. You got it, pal...I'm going up to sack out." With that I headed up the ladder. My relief, a second-class fireman who would be transferred as soon as I qualified, couldn't believe it. "Hey, Mac, you sure everything's okay?" I didn't bother to answer. I knew everything was okay! And so did Deke, who was sitting on deck in the dark with a cup of coffee. Going to sack out, hell! He just wanted to see what I would do.

He handed me his cup, and as I took a swallow he asked, "Everything go all right?"

"Sure, Deke, just like you showed me."

He took back his cup and smiled. "Okay, kid, let's flake out. If we're lucky, Doggie will let us sleep in for an hour or so." He did.

The next day at noon, after eating chow, I was scheduled for another four-hour stint on the floor plates. It was my first solo cold-iron watch. After relieving the other fireman, I was down there about an hour when I heard the hatch open. Looking up through the grate I could see Chief Delmar come and go over to the workbench. He pretended to look through the log books, and then made a pot of coffee. I knew damn well what he was really doing was watching to see if what Deghan had reported to him was correct. When the coffee was ready, the chief poured a cup and, walking to the top of the ladder, yelled down to me, "Hey, Dawson, cuppa joe?" I looked up and pretended to see him for the first time. "Oh, hi, Chief. I didn't hear you come in." I took the coffee and turned back to my boiler. But I did keep an eye on him as he relaxed and drank his own coffee.

After about an hour he left, apparently satisfied, I suppose, that I could handle the watch by myself. There were a couple more cold-iron watches for me before the *Trever* went out again, but there is no recollection of any more checks of my performance. However, Deke did let me know how to have the gangway petty officer find him in a hurry if there was any real trouble. It seemed that firemen had an unwritten code to keep each other's butt out of the sling. Short of a major blow out we would report nothing to anyone. Instead, we handled it ourselves. He didn't know it at the time, but Deghan had made a friend for life; or at least for the time we were both on the *Trever*.

After a couple more days in port, the *Trever* made ready to get underway once more. It was back out to patrol the waters of the Hawaiian Islands against any attack by Japanese submarines, to escort incoming and outgoing convoys, and to carry out any other duties that might be assigned to us. These were long, weary days, and even longer nights. When we were not standing watches, we were cleaning and repairing equipment, chipping paint, and doing general maintenance. The most important job for me was learning how to stand steaming watches.

A steaming watch is a regular four-hour turn in the fire room while at sea. With both boilers operating at full capacity, the fire room was under a lot greater pressure than in port. Until you got accustomed to it, you had some painful ears. Each boiler had fourteen burners, and normal steaming speeds used about five or six all the time. For high-speed runs and fast maneuvering, usually all fourteen would be cut in. A fireman literally climbed up the boiler front to handle it quickly. The burners all fouled very rapidly from the burning oil, and had to be constantly changed for clean ones. It was my luck to pull the watch as we steamed out of the harbor. With constant speed changes, all the backing down and going ahead, and then increasing speed as we raced through the channel, our fire room was very busy. But with Doggie, Deke, and me on the floor plates, and Kayler the Tailor on the grates, everything went smoothly. We did have the extra fireman second standing by in case I couldn't handle the rush. But Deke was so good at his own boiler he was able to step over and back me up a few times when I just wasn't quick enough to keep up. By the time we got out to sea and settled down to patrol, I think I sweated off about five pounds. But it made me feel good when Doggie told the extra fireman he could take off because we wouldn't need him. When he said that, I looked over at Deke and saw him give me a "thumbs up" before he turned his attention to changing burners. I thought to myself, "Damn, if the family could only see me now. I'm doing a Man's Job."

I wish I could say that all my Black Gang experiences were that smooth and productive, that I never made a mistake, and turned out to be the boy wonder of the fire room. But it didn't work out that way. Like every new snipe, I goofed up now and then. Fortunately, not bad enough to get me reassigned, just enough to make me an average fireman. With Doggie, Kayler, and old dependable Deke to steer me straight, I managed to learn from every mistake I made, and not to repeat them. That was a good thing, because Kayler told me, "Kid, you make the same mistake twice with Doggie, and your name is Shit!"

Battle Stations, Fire Room Frustrations

We fell very rapidly into the routine of patrolling the waters around Oahu, the island where Pearl Harbor was located. The code name for that kind of duty was "easy," and easy it was, most of the time. It was a matter of standing watches, keeping up with ship maintenance, and waiting for the word we would return to Pearl for a few days. The routine was about a week or ten days out, and then into the Navy yard for two or three days, during which time we would take on fuel, provisions, get a little liberty to Honolulu, and an opportunity to do some ship's work that could not be dealt with at sea. That last task alone kept us jumping, because the *Trever* had been scheduled for a return to the States for a major overhaul when the war broke out and everything was postponed or canceled.

At sea we went to general quarters every day at dawn and dusk, those being the hours when enemy submarine activity might be expected. Occasionally, we were called to our battle stations during the day or in the middle of the night when our sound shack would report a contact on what might be a Jap sub. Most of the time it turned out to be a blackfish, or even a whale. In those early days we seldom had any real indication of a submarine, but we still dropped our depth charges and stood by our guns. I've often wondered how many sea creatures were destroyed by our eagerness to close with the enemy, but we were new at the business of war, and had to learn our trade by experience.

My general quarters station, as I mentioned earlier, was with the after ammunition party. What I had to do was stand by on deck over an open hatch to the storage magazine. The shells for the four-inch guns were packed in wooden cases, and weighed over seventy pounds each. They were far-too-heavy to be passed up by hand; they were usually strapped two or three together and taken up by chain hoist. Once up on deck the boxes could be broken open and the shells passed up to the gun deck. Ammo for the .50 caliber machine guns was in metal cans and could easily be tossed up to the guy on the next level, or even up the ladder to the guns. But the guy on top damn well better catch it because the man below didn't look up once he let go of it. If we missed catching a can, or dropped it, we knew they were heavy enough to seriously injure anyone being hit when it fell. Fortunately for all of us, we did not have to do any fast ammo handling during the days of easy patrol. We relied upon quantities of ammunition normally kept in what were called ready lockers on the gun deck. Still, we regularly went through drills every day at general quarters to develop a system and speed.

One advantage patrol duty had for some of us was the time it provided to study and improve our skills. Chief Delmar told me that promotional exams would be coming up before long, and if I was ready he would recommend me for the fireman second class exam. That meant I had to put in a course of study to be eligible. I was determined to be a good fireman, so getting the necessary material from the engineering officer, I went to work. With Kayler and Deghan helping me it didn't take long. On February 20th of that year I completed the course with an average grade of 3.01, which, while not exactly outstanding, was enough to make me eligible to take the test for my rate. I found out that actual course grades were not all that important, anyway, because much of what we did to operate the fire room was not to be found in the book. Deke advised me to keep reading over the course, however, until the day of the exam, because it would be important to be able to provide the answers they wanted, rather than describe what we might actually do.

Cramming for the second-class exam was almost my undoing. With all the newly acquired information in my head, I couldn't wait to let somebody know how smart I had become. One day, during our watch, we were suddenly called on to deal with a lot of rapid speed changes as the captain went after a sub contact. Doggie was slow getting down to the floor plates and I was having a hell of a time covering my boiler and handling the annunciator as well. When the chief dropped down the ladder I made a smart-ass remark about how hard a time we were having and where the hell had he been? He didn't take kindly to my comments, and as he raced over to his position he backhanded me across the mouth. It was hard enough to knock me off my feet to slide under the drip pan at the bottom of my boiler. I was surprised and angry when I started to get up. Deke stepped over, grabbed my arm, and whispered, "Shut your mouth, you stupid ass, and just do your job!" As it turned out, and a good thing for me, the action got hectic and there was no time for further argument. After a while, when things got back to normal, Delmar swung back up the ladder without another word.

As we were pulling and cleaning the burners we had used, Deke really chewed my ass. He made it clear that I had been out of line, and Doggie might very well get me rated second class just so he could transfer me off the ship. I sure wasn't doing myself any good. I figured he was all-too-right, and that gave me more to worry about. The fact that the chief had hung one on me was all over the ship in no time. Even the wardroom had to have heard about it, although nothing was ever said to me. I came to understand that Chief Water Tender Doggie Delmar was not the kind of gang leader to put anyone on report. He preferred to deal with disciplinary matters his own way. Painful, maybe, but at least it kept a man's record clean. I sweated that situation for a long time. I tried to do a good job both in and out of the fire room. Nobody seemed angry with me, not even the chief. In fact, he told me that as long as I had my course for fireman second completed, I ought to start studying for first. He had me completely confused by that time, but taking his suggestion, I started cramming for first class, even though I had not even taken the exam for second as yet.

The day finally came to take the written exam for promotions. Down to the forward crew's compartment we went, and under the supervision of one of the officers, we attacked the test papers. At first it went easy, everything learned in the course and from the guys on my watch came back to me. But there were two very basic and tricky questions dealing with lighting off a dead fire room. I was crawling the bulkheads. I knew that failing just those two questions could ruin me. As

I struggled with them, a deck seaman came in to the crew space to get something from his locker. I happened to be sitting on it, and as I moved he whispered, "Trouble? Give me the question numbers." I wasn't sure what was going on but figured I'd take a chance. So I gave him the numbers and he left. A few minutes later another seaman came down, and as he passed me, he flipped over a tiny, folded-up scrap of paper. Keeping one eye on the ensign, I took a quick look. There were the needed answers. So, finishing up, I turned in all papers to the supervising officer and headed topside. I found Doggie and a couple other chiefs sitting on the well deck having coffee, and apparently waiting to see how their guys made out. As I walked past, Delmar stopped me. With my heart pounding, I turned to face my boss, expecting my world to fall in on me.

"Everything go okay?"

"Yeah, Chief, everything went fine."

Then he dropped it on me. Setting his coffee cup on the deck, Doggie stood up and stepped in front of me. A pretty bulky guy under most circumstances, at that moment he looked positively immense. He glowered at me for a minute and then said, "Damn it, Dawson, if you had come to me earlier I could have helped you to better understand those parts you had trouble with. Hell, you've helped light off a dead fire room. You know how it's done. You damn well better not have that kind of trouble when you go up for first. I ought to transfer you to a goddamned honey barge! Now get the hell out of here."

I couldn't believe it. After all the hassle, after belting me in my big fat mouth, after letting me sweat all those days, he was the one who helped me when I needed it most. Sure, he had chewed me out again. But as far as I was concerned, Doggie could do no wrong. If he wanted me to be a fireman first, that's what I'd do. Meanwhile, like everybody else who had taken a test that day, I would be waiting and watching for the promotion list.

Honolulu Liberty—Tourist Style

Liberty in Honolulu was a far cry from what it used to be prior to the war. For us, it started when our ship was tied up, engines shut down, and when the motor whaleboat no longer needed berthing. Once ashore, there was the problem of getting from the shipyard into town. Trucks and buses were usually available, as well as the ever-present taxicabs. Few sailors availed themselves of the taxis, however. For most of us it was a matter of being jammed into the more common mode of transportation, hoping our uniforms would not get ruined before we hit the streets.

Once in Honolulu, liberty started in front of the Hawaii YMCA. A lot of the younger guys never went any further, being content to spend their few free hours with hamburgers, cold milk, ping-pong, and a pool table. The company of a few of the patriotically inclined wahines[1] helped to make it all worthwhile. Most, however, preferred to go around the city and take their chances on having a good time. In any case, the first stop was across the street at the Black Cat Café. Because of its convenient location, it was the obvious place to go for a cool drink before heading across town, and a last drink before finally returning to the ship.

The Cat was legendary throughout the Pacific Fleet.

---

1. Hawaiian word for "women."

Housed in a rickety old frame building with a heavily stuccoed false front, the Cat had apparently been around forever. It was decorated in a kind of tropical style, but had huge wrought-iron gates closing it off to the street at night or when liberty was over and there were no more liberty men to crawl in. The bartenders and waitresses had one thing in common—insolence. In prewar days the drinks were said to be heavily watered, especially near closing time when the prices were inflated. The place did have a certain ambiance, however, one that could best be described as...malignant. After December 7th, the Black Cat changed. No longer allowed to sell alcoholic beverages, they were reduced to watering the Coke. But it was still the first and last place to hit on liberty.

After that first drink of Coke, we would head down Hotel Street to see what might develop. The street was narrow, with sidewalks just barely wide enough to permit three people to walk abreast. This meant that to pass others somebody had to step into the street and take their chances with traffic. The buildings generally were old, decrepit, and seemed to lean on each other for support. Of dull browns for the most part, some seemed to resemble battleship gray in color and tone. It was rumored that the official Navy paint was available in return for "services rendered." It was anybody's guess what those services might be. Here and there could be found a sort of oriental decoration, obviously intended more for the tourists than the natives. With so many new kids in the services by 1942, there were plenty of tourists ready to be impressed.

All along the street were narrow-fronted businesses catering to the liberty men. Most of them emitted some kind of Hawaiian music with an American accent. Like the music itself, these places were called *hapa haole*, meaning "half foreign."² Supposedly, they appealed to sailors and marines looking for a good time. For some reason the Army was not much in evidence. Maybe in our excitement, we just didn't notice them.

There were souvenir shops where one could buy all sorts of things from a simple grass skirt to the ever-popular pillow cover bearing a picture of famous Diamond Head, with the inscription *Souvenir of Hawaii*. There were photo studios where a guy might have his picture taken in the arms of a dusky local belle in native costume. For a couple of bucks over the regular price she would pose bare breasted. If she were offered a few dollars more the customer would be taken into the back room where the picture might be taken of her in the altogether while passionately clinging to his manly body. They were definitely not the kind of photos to be sent home to Mother—Father, maybe, but not Mother.

For those interested, there were jewelry stores, clothing stores, and barbershops operated by pretty little wahines. If needed, some of the parlors also provided a massage service in the back for those fleet sailors who might be suffering from tension brought on by the pressures of war.

For the more adventurous type wanting a more permanent reminder of his service days, there were tattoo parlors where, for a few bucks, some big, fat, Chinese man would take his needles and ink in hand to create a battleship and anchor, a skull and bloody dagger with the inscription *Death*

---

2. *Hapa* is a Hawaiian word used to describe a person of mixed Asian or Pacific Islander racial/ethnic heritage. *Hapa haole* is someone who is half Hawaiian and half Caucasian/white. *Hapa popolo* is someone who is half black.

Before Dishonor, or, for the more sentimental, a big rose with a flowery-lettered *Mother*. A big favorite, as I remember, was an American flag with a scroll carrying the message *Remember Pearl Harbor*!

Here and there you could find a respectable restaurant where a hungry GI could get delicacies like sweet and sour pork, candied chicken served on high mounds of rice, and other dishes cooked in strange and wonderful ways. All of it in an atmosphere of pungent, mysterious, and spicy fragrances unknown to kids just a few months out of boot camp and away from home for the first time. For those with food on their minds, there were also grocery stores offering both oriental and American goodies—things you never saw aboard ship. There was peanut butter, strange jellies and jams, Vienna sausages, crackers, and cookies. Of course, it was always a chore to carry your purchases around as you wended your way through Honolulu. But being the ingenious sailors that we were, this was a problem easily solved. You see, whenever we left the ship, we were required to carry our gas masks. But what we would do was to leave the mask itself on board ship and sling the empty container over our shoulders. It made a dandy shopping bag and didn't detract from our military appearance.

All things considered, even if a young sailor were to behave himself in a manner that might be approved of by his loving mother, liberty in Honolulu could be a pretty exciting thing to write home about. Of course, for those not too concerned with personal behavior or good conduct, there were other attractions offered by the city and its residents.

Honolulu Liberty with the Old Salts

"Who's going ashore, who's going ashore, who's got the price of a two-bit whore?"

So went the words to the age-old liberty call blown by buglers in the US Navy for generations past—at least the unofficial words. On smaller ships like destroyers, tugs, and minesweepers, where no bugler has ever seen duty, the bos'n mate of the watch might sing the first line to let the crew know that the boat was about to leave, or that the gangway was open. Whether or not he sang the second line depended on his nerve, the temperament of the deck officer, and, of course, the attitude of the captain. Aboard the *Trever* we had so many different skippers that the gangway petty officers played it safe—no second line.

Honolulu was always a good liberty port, especially for the older, more experienced men—the old "Honolulu Hands." When they headed into town they knew exactly where they wanted to go. Their first stop after the Black Cat was one of the short-time hotels that had rooms to let. Going by fancy names like The Rex, The Anchor, The New Senator, and The Service Arms, they all operated in a very discreet, almost secretive manner. Never admitting to even existing when raided by the local police or the MPs, they all advertised themselves with garish electric signs and hawkers by the front door.

Inside, they were all pretty much alike, with a big sitting room furnished with chrome and leatherette settees and chairs that had all seen better days. There would be a small bar for those patrons who still had a drink on their minds after climbing the narrow stairway. Every place was guarded by a 300-pound gorilla in the compulsory flowered Hawaiian shirt. His job was to uphold order and to persuade the occasional sailor or marine who didn't feel he had gotten his money's worth and attempted to leave without paying to do the right thing. But there were very few disturbances to be found in these places of sin. The last thing they needed was a brawl to attract attention—not that they were concerned with anything as mundane as being fined, but an inconvenient bust would cut into business. And the girls had a hard time keeping up with demand as it was.

Oh, yes, there were the girls. That's what the establishments were there for, to provide a quick cure for that oriental disease feared by sailors after long periods at sea—lakanukie! The girls came in all shapes and sizes, from age seventeen or so to shop-worn forties. Blondes, brunettes, and red heads. I'd been told that there were one or two that were gray, and even one that was bald! And you could find them white, oriental, black, and sometimes even Hawaiian. It was reported that the better houses were regularly inspected by the military medical people. Still, there was always a chance that a guy might pick up something if he was careless upon visiting a hotel in Honolulu.

Generally speaking, the places were all very professional. A serviceman would hardly settle back in the chrome and leatherette before a string of ladies would be paraded before him so he might make his choice. Most wore only a flimsy peignoir held in place by a single hook or button. Some preferred even less. Whatever the choice, it had to be something that could be shed in a hurry. Time was money. Not for nothing was the time spent in the other room called a five-minute romance. Some of the girls, in an effort to make the most of a short working day, would usually use two or three rooms with connecting doors. When she came rushing through that door into your cubicle, you had better be ready. To them, foreplay might have been some kind of football strategy. It was strictly bim, bam, thank you man, with the next customer already hammering on the door. And all these earthly pleasure were available for two to five dollars, depending upon a guy's taste and sense of immediacy.

There was one pair of enterprising young ladies that I don't think I will ever forget, mostly because of the novel way in which they conducted their business. Not for them were the restrictions of working in a commercial house with its crowded competition and the need of giving a share of the profits to the proprietor. Oh, no. They used a different approach. They sold hot dogs! They not only sold hot dogs, but they did it right in front of the YMCA! They had the usual steamer to cook the wieners and to heat the buns, and they offered all the trimmings, including mustard, ketchup, and a variety of oriental sauces that did wonders for the ordinary dog. There they would stand, wearing short skirts and silk blouses strained to the breaking point as they chanted their call to passing sailors and marines. "Hot doggie, doggie, doggie...get something here to make you remember Honolulu. Hot doggie, doggie!" Every once in a while some guy would walk up and buy a hot dog, offering a ten- or twenty-dollar bill in payment. Of course, the girl would not have the change, so she would say something like, "You come corner with me, hotshot, I get you change." Then the two of them would disappear around the corner. A bit later they would return and the serviceman would go off with his change, his hotdog, and a smile on his face. I noticed, however, that there was usually a three- or four-dollar tip on a 30-cent hotdog. Yeah, those girls were something else. And those oriental-style hotdogs weren't so bad, either.

By four or so the buses and trucks would be picking up the boys for the return to their ship or the shipyard. A few sailors were now willing to take the waiting taxicabs for the long ride back—the same cabs that cost eight or ten dollars to ride into town earlier. Ten dollars was a lot of money in those days, but the cabdrivers were always young, pretty, and talented. They were extremely proud of their ability to professionally "serve the servicemen."

Liberty, whether for the tourist or the adventuresome old salt, was always up at 5:30 PM in those days. So by five o'clock the police and shore patrol would be out in force to clear the streets of military personnel. By six in the evening the town would be deserted except for a few merchants still locking up for the day, and the MPs still going about whatever MPs do. Liberty in Honolulu during the war was short, intense, and expensive. Yet, it was memorable in its own very special way.

"Hot doggie, doggie, doggie, doggie, doggie..."

And We Watched Her Die

With liberty over and everybody back aboard, the *Trever* got ready for a return to sea and another week or so of easy duty. Our fuel bunkers filled, food lockers jammed with supplies, and our crew refreshed by their few hours ashore, we headed out of Pearl Harbor wondering what the days ahead might hold for us.

The Japanese battle fleet had long since returned to their home islands. However, we knew that their submarines would still be lurking in our waters, waiting for an opportunity to observe our fleet coming and going, and perhaps with a bit of luck, slam a torpedo into some unwary tanker. Generally, they would steer clear of warships unless the odds were all in their favor. But sometimes they miscalculated, and then they paid the supreme penalty.

We had been assigned to escort a small transport and a tug towing a barge full of supplies from Oahu to Hilo on the big island of Hawaii. The transport was carrying a considerable number of Japanese internees to be landed in Hilo, and then taken to an internment camp. Most of them were *Nisei*, or American-born Japanese Americans.[3] A few, we

---

3. *Nisei* is a Japanese-language term used in countries in North America, South America, and Australia to specify the children born to Japanese people in the new country. The Nisei are considered the second generation; the grandchildren of the Japanese-born

were told, had been identified as spies or subversives to be investigated. In any case, they were all considered security risks to be detained. Those were hard days for anyone even remotely thought to be of Japanese origin.

The voyage to Hilo, for the most part, was slow and uneventful. But as the convoy arrived off the big island, things began to warm up. The *Trever* was doing the customary slow patrol of the area as the tug and transport began to head into the harbor. Suddenly, our general quarters alarm sounded as our sonar operator picked up what he thought to be a submarine. The crew raced to their battle stations and in a matter of minutes the ship was at full alert, the skipper taking her on a fast run toward the bearing of the contact. The tug, in an effort to gain better maneuverability, dropped her tow and, together with the ship carrying the internees, headed for safety. The captain, knowing that a single ship was at a definite disadvantage fighting an unseen sub, nevertheless tried to provide cover for his charges.

There was no way of knowing which of the ships might be the Jap's objective, so traveling at flank speed, we ran circles around them, hoping that the submarine would have trouble getting an accurate bearing through our boiling wake. At the same time, our sonar operator was trying hard to pinpoint the Jap's position so Captain Agar might take action of his own.

The tug, being in the lead on the run to the harbor, seemed to be of lesser importance between the two vessels, if our guess was correct. That meant the enemy would be after the transport, or us. His choice became clear when

---

immigrants are called *Sansei*. (In Japanese counting, "one, two, three" is *ichi, ni, san*.)

a lookout reported a periscope off our stern. As the *Trever* swung around to meet the challenge, someone shouted, "Torpedoes off the starboard quarter!" Our unseen opponent had decided to take us out first, and then he could sink the others at his leisure. Turning hard to starboard, our skipper pointed the ship directly into the path of the oncoming fish,[4] hoping to present a smaller target and allow them to pass along our sides. But we were turning too slowly, and those of us on deck stood transfixed, hanging onto the lifelines, watching the white streaks reaching out for us. I closed my eyes, held my breath, and waited for the explosion. It never came. There was a shout from a gunner, who reported torpedo wakes going away from us off our port side. Set too low, they had passed under us. We were still in the fight, only now it was our turn to attack.

The *Trever* raced over the last known position of the enemy submarine, which had disappeared, and Captain Agar gave the order to drop depth charges. Two of them—at 300 pounds of TNT each—rolled out of our stern racks and splashed into the sea. There was a double roar as our K-guns threw two more over our port and starboard rails. In seconds they exploded. Wham—wham—wham—wham! Towering water spouts geysered into the sky to fall back into the boiling waters around us. Turning as quickly as possible, we made another run and four more charges were let go. Wham—wham—wham—wham! As we watched, the ocean was again thrown skyward to fall back with a resounding crash. When our explosive patterns went off, we could feel the power of their destructive capability. It was as though some aquatic giant had swung a super sledgehammer

---

4. Torpedo.

against our hull again and again. For a ship as old as the *Trever*, it would be enough to pop rivets or open seams in our bottom. I could imagine what it had to be like for the Japs in the fragile, enclosed submersible—no less than sheer hell.

Then the enemy changed tactics. Instead of making another attempt at us, the sub directed its attention to the transport. The ship was between the *Trever* and the harbor entrance, so the sub had to make its attack through more dangerous, shallower waters. But he did just that, and our lookouts reported four torpedoes on a path to the old cargo vessel. As slow as she was, it was impossible to take evasive action, and even as she turned, the white-water trails reached her quarter. Two of them were hits. There was a great explosion and the ship reared up as though yanked out of the sea by some supernatural force; then it fell back with clouds of black smoke and immense red and yellow flames rising, coming to a dead stop in the water. We could see men on deck frantically running to launch lifeboats, but it was too late. She shuddered as another explosion shook her entire length. Shuddering as though trying to shake off the pain of her fatal injury, she settled first by the stern. Her bow suddenly rose high into the air and, with a final convulsive spasm, the old cargo ship slid silently beneath the waves. Moments later there was a muffled underwater rumble which we knew would be her boilers going. We could only stand, horrified, as we realized her passengers were doomed to death by drowning, or worse. Ironically, they had to die for no other reason than the fact that they were of Japanese descent. Yet, their deaths had been caused by other Japanese.

We had no time to search for possible survivors. There

was still a submarine to deal with. With another report from our sound shack, our own skipper ordered yet another attack. "Drop charges!" he shouted. They rolled from our stern and arched high into the air from our K-guns, throwing columns of water to great heights as they exploded. But this time, as the water fell back to the surface, it mixed with bits of debris that were already rising from below. Circling the area, we saw still more debris and oil-soaked trash come to the surface. On our gun decks the gunners waited with anxious fingers on the firing keys, scanning the surrounding sea for the damaged sub to break surface. There was no question of accepting surrender. We wanted that pig boat[5]...bad.

On the bridge, the captain raced from one wing to the other as he received reports from the sound shack as to the submarine's whereabouts. He was as determined as we were; maybe even more so, because he bore the responsibility for having lost the transport. If our guns couldn't do the job on a surfaced Jap, "By damn, I'll ride over the son of a bitch!" But there was no enemy boat coming to the surface.

As the *Trever* circled the last known position of the sub, the crew carefully looking over the oil and trash on the surface, the sound operator called out, "I've got breaking-up noises, Captain. I think you got 'em." In a short time even more trash floated up and there was a resounding cheer from all hands when Captain Agar passed the word. "We got 'em, guys. That's one slant-eye that will not sink any more Americans. We got the bastard!"

Once having assured ourselves the sub was no longer a threat, the *Trever* searched for survivors of the transport.

---

5. Navy slang for "submarine;" the term first became popular in the 1920s.

None were to be found. Except for a lifejacket or two and some splintered remains of a wooden raft, there was nothing to show the ship ever existed. The tug, which had made it to the harbor safely, returned and once again picked up her tow. With our mission completed, albeit with a far different result than what we had expected, the *Trever* pointed her bow back to Pearl. It was a very silent trip back for all of us.

In the overall picture of the war, our fight with the enemy had been nothing. Probably not even worthy of a footnote in some obscure history book. But to us it was very important. We had clashed with the Japanese Imperial Navy, and although he had hurt us badly, he paid the price. Captain Agar had said, "We got the bastard." Yeah, we got 'em. But not before one of our own had been fatally torpedoed. And we had watched her die.

Old Salts and the New Breed of Sailor

Contrary to what a lot of civilians think, war is not a continuous clash with the enemy or a struggle for survival. It is not all blood and guts, with death and destruction all around. For the most part, it is endless days of boring patrols, training, hot and dirty equipment maintenance, standing watches, and taking part in endless drills to hone battle skills for the time when action might be called for. In the Navy, a sailor's free time, when he found any, was usually spent washing clothes, studying for promotion, writing letters, and playing many, many games of cribbage and acey ducey. When he could do it without getting caught he would gamble. Officers and enlisted men alike would gamble on anything. Like most ships, the *Trever* had its running poker, blackjack, and craps games. Hell, we even played bingo for a change of pace!

Another thing that took up a lot of time aboard ship was getting to know your shipmates. Even on a small ship like the *Trever*, there was a big difference from one guy to the next. Despite being thrown into such close proximity, each man retained his individuality. There were old salts who had already been in service forever when the war broke out and who had been retained for the duration. They thought anyone with less than twenty years or so was a red-assed boot. To them, it was unacceptable to violate the old custom of not spitting into the wind, whistling aboard ship, or calling a ship a boat. Their careers were steeped in tradition and ritual.

Then there was a new breed of sailor who was seen more and more as the war dragged on: The young guy who came into the Navy to learn a trade, to avoid the draft, or simply because he had nothing better to do on the outside and thought a four-year hitch might be fun. Invariably having no use for tradition, such a sailor had trouble sticking to any kind of system. Things like bell-bottomed dungarees, tailor-made dress blues, equator-crossing ceremonies, and games like acey ducey meant nothing to them. They were civilians putting in their time, waiting to get what they could and get out.

Finally, there were the new people, like myself, who were ready to accept the fact the Navy was hidebound in tradition, even to enjoy it as we began to talk like the older career men. It was fun as well as educational to listen to the old salts, those 20- and 30-year men who had seen service all over the world. Their stories were a lot more exciting than any book in the ship's library, and if a new boy showed an interest they were quick to teach him the old-time tricks and skills. For me, it became a matter of "go with the flow" and benefit from knowing the "lifers" before they transferred off the ship to take their knowledge and experiences with them. Besides, I was Regular Navy. I was no "feather merchant reserve Pearl Harbor avenger!" This boy had been wearing blues *before* December 7th.

One old guy who had been aboard longer than anyone

else was Chief Gunner's Mate Gold. He had been in the Navy so long that some of the other chiefs swore he had been the gunner aboard the *Monitor* when it fought the *Merrimac*. When they kidded him about it, Gold would roar back at them, "Yeah, and if they'd listened to me, we'd have sunk that tin-covered sumbitch!" The gunner was senior man on board, and everyone knew it. If they didn't, he wasted no time telling them.

Another rough-and-ready character was Jack Ryan. A bos'n mate first class when I first reported aboard, he made chief not too long after. Ryan was another man who had been in the Navy forever. It was rumored that he was the senior bos'n on Noah's Ark. Nobody knew much about his background, only that he had come aboard as a cox'n and knew his seamanship. With a tendency to scream his orders to his deck force, Jack accepted nothing less than excellence where his division was concerned. He had no family that anyone knew about, and the Navy and the *Trever* was truly his home. I've often wondered what happened to him when the war ended and he had to retire.

The ship had more than its share of oddballs. Men like Q. J. Brown. His name was really Quentin John, and he had seen considerable duty in the Far East before the war. He was very strange. He was more generally known as "Queer John." A bos'n mate first class, he was known for the fact that he would drink just about anything liquid. Not just coffee, or occasionally tea, but any kind of booze he could get. Quality scotch, bourbon, and rum were fine. But if they were not available he could make with Aqua Velva, Lucky Tiger, lemon or vanilla extract, torpedo alcohol strained through a loaf of bread—anything. I remember one night when we were tied up to the British light cruiser HMS *Leander*, he slipped over to drink alcohol from their boat compasses. Next morning the Brits were crushed, unable to run their boats. Q. J. was sprawled out on our fantail, unconscious. We thought he might be dead and called the pharmacist mate. Before Doc arrived, Jack Ryan got to him first, reviving him with a kick in the ribs and a bucket of cold seawater. "Get your gold-brickin' ass off the deck and turn to; get drunk on your own time, not mine!"

In those days tin cans did not usually carry a doctor. Medical needs, emergency and otherwise, were attended to by a chief pharmacist mate. In our case it was one Chief Van Kirkland, another of the more senior crewmen. Nobody remembered when he came aboard. He was around 45 or 50, and sort of reminded you of your grandmother. Van was roly-poly, pink cheeked, and cherubic. Always worried about the state of our health, he was apt to call for a routine short-arm inspection when we had been out to sea for six months or more. "Preventive medicine," he called it. We wondered what he thought we might catch out there, and from whom—ichthyosis from some friendly mermaid?

One evening, a bunch of us were sitting around on the fantail, shooting the breeze, and the question of Doc's professional acumen came up. We all agreed it would be difficult to find a situation that Van Kirkland could not deal with. Everybody agreed. Everyone, that is, except for Queer John. He was ready to bet that he could throw the chief for a loss. His bet was covered, and he jumped up and ran down the deck, headed for sick bay. As he raced forward, he tore open his pants and began to fumble inside, screaming for the Doc all the while. Dropping down the ladder, Q. J. had his pride and joy in hand by the time he got to the sick bay. "Doc, Doc, look at it, look at it!" Van, up to his elbows in test tubes and bottles, turned a serious face and asked what was wrong. "Nothing really, Doc, but ain't it a beauty?" The chief, showing nothing but sheer professionalism, looked at the organ in question, picked up a glass slide, and said, "I'm not so sure, Q. J.; maybe you ought to skin it back, milk it down, and we can take a smear." Well, that was the end of it. Q. J. paid off his bets as the Doc went back to whatever it was that pharmacists mates do in the confines of their sick bay. But I'll bet that story was still being told on board the *Trever* until the day she was decommissioned.

Not all the characters were among the old-timers. The younger sailors also had their share. Like the guy who climbed the sea ladder carrying his clarinet because he'd heard that every ship had a band. And the kid we called Cotton because of his soft, fluffy, almost-white hair. About sixteen years old, he was a great favorite with all the girls whenever he went ashore. We hated him. And of course there was Arky. Like the kid I knew in boot camp, he was from Arkansas. Despite being a real ridge-runner who had never seen saltwater before, he took to the Navy like an old salt. His only problem was his inability to learn Navy phraseology. To him a rope was a rope, small white line was heavy string, and everything that floated in water was a boat—even the *Trever* herself.

Yeah, there were a lot of different kinds of people on board the *Trever*. As I write this, I can't help but wonder what those guys looking back, as I am, are saying about me: "I remember Dawson. Not a bad guy; a pretty good shipfitter, too. But I remember the time he..."

Soupy, Soupy, Soupy

After liberty call, the most popular bugle sound in the Navy was mess call. Some long-forgotten bluejacket wrote words to it: "Soupy, Soupy, Soupy, Soupy, Soupy..." Not very original, or even catchy, they nevertheless describe the food in those days pretty well—soupy!

The cooks way back then were usually sailors who could no longer work on deck or in the rigging. Cooking skills had nothing to do with it. Ridiculed by the crew, often threatened with bodily harm, theirs was not an easy lot. Among the nicer things they were called were "Slum Burner" and "Belly Robber."

As time passed, the food, like other things in the Navy, improved. By the time I joined, cooks were given special training to equip them to do a better job of feeding the sailors. Those old names hung on, however, although today they are said with a lot less animosity. Generally speaking, the food in the armed forces is pretty good. The soldiers and marines, admittedly, are forced to subsist on field rations from time to time. But on the bases and aboard ship there is really no cause for complaint. No question about it—the Navy feeds the best of all the services.

My first exposure to Navy chow was back in boot camp in 1941. Aside from that hellish, lukewarm, saltpetered glop they called coffee, we were fed very well. With the country still struggling out of a depression, to many of the recruits it was some of, if not the best, food they had eaten in a long time. Three square meals a day was just not a regular occurrence for many civilians, and dessert twice a day was almost unheard of. Navy soup was always a lot closer to chunk-style than broth, and there were always pieces of chicken or beef that could be identified as such. One thing we could always be sure of, there was enough of it. The best food I tasted in my entire enlistment was in the chiefs' mess hall on the Destroyer Base in San Diego. Stationed there just prior to the outbreak of the war, my assignment was in the galley. Consequently, I was having chief's rations. And for them it was like a restaurant with a menu. For breakfast there was a choice of dry or cooked cereal, eggs any style, bacon, sausage, fried potatoes, and hotcakes. To finish up we had coffee cake, doughnuts, sweet rolls, and milk, coffee, or tea.

Lunch and dinner were much alike. There was salad, soup, a choice of entrees, several vegetables, a choice of desserts, and the usual selection of drinks. The cooks were all old-timers who had years of experience and were proud of their culinary art. When I lost my chance to apprentice to those guys, I also missed a turning point in my life.

Most of my time in the Navy was spent aboard the *Trever*, and it must be said that when supplies were available, we ate pretty well. Despite the shell and shrapnel holes in our smokestacks and superstructure, the *Trever* was officially classified as a non-combat and we frequently were the last in line to draw supplies of any kind. But whenever we could send a working party to pick up galley stores, we did okay.

Our cooks followed the traditional Navy menu most

of the time. Wednesday and Saturday breakfast offered us thousands of things to eat—most of them beans, also known as "Navy strawberries," along with stewed prunes and hot biscuits. Holidays usually brought turkey or ham. On Saturday night we could be sure of cold cuts. Although there was a variety to choose from, by far the most plentiful was bologna and some kind of unidentified rock-like yellow cheese. The sausage came in two-foot links about six inches in diameter. Known to one and all as "horse cock," we ate it raw, fried, baked, and boiled. The cheese, although it didn't taste too bad, was impossible to slice. Instead, it just crumbled into chunks. If you ate too much of it, well, not for nothing was it called "choke ass."

The poor watch-stander who had to wait to be relieved before going to chow was sure to get leftovers and catcalls of "horse cock and choke ass for you, mate!" Every day at lunch we could expect soup. It was invariably made from whatever we had for breakfast. Morning beans meant bean soup for lunch. S.O.S. for breakfast called for a kind of loose hamburger soup at noon. The idea was not bad until we might have creamed chipped beef on toast in the morning. You can only imagine what kind of soup that made.

To be honest, there were some food items that were less than palatable. We used to get gallon cans of sweet butter that no one would eat. But it worked real well as cap grease on our towing winch.

Canned grapefruit juice was so sour nobody could drink it. But it was great for swabbing the galley deck, so acidic it cut the old grease and grime right down to the bare steel. Coffee from Australia was so heavily mixed with chicory that it was life-threatening to drink it. And the British mutton...

well, the less said the better. After all, they were our allies.

Now and then the commissary department of a tanker or cargo ship would feel sorry for us and send over real gourmet goodies like ice cream, mixed nuts, or cases of fresh fruit. Once we were given a big wheel of real, honest-to-goodness cheddar cheese. Another time there were cans and cans of whole milk from a refrigerator ship. With limited freezer capacity of our own we had to consume the stuff right away—a real pig-out time!

Good bakers were hard to find on smaller ships, and the *Trever* was no exception. A man might be a good cook or a good baker; very seldom would you find anyone in the galley who could do both. So if a baker were to be sent to a can like ours, it was kept a secret for fear some four-striper or admiral would steal him. We had just such a guy for a while. Although he was an honest-to-goodness baker (his dad owned a string of bakeries back home), he was rated as a ship's cook. As he hated to cook, he was left alone to do his thing with no interference, and his baking was something out of this world. He didn't make pie in those big two by three foot pans like anyone else might. He made forty or so regular pies to send down to the crew's mess tables. His hot biscuits, cakes, and cinnamon rolls were something to kill for. If he needed anything to work his magic, we'd buy, build, or steal it for him.

There were times, however, when a new man transferred aboard who was something less than his service record revealed. Such a man was Del Muggioso. He claimed to be a baker. He must have known something or someone, because he was rated third class. But all I can say about him would be to repeat what some wag wrote and posted on the bulletin board:

> "We all have met with Muggioso's bread,
> Rolled out of putty, and weighted with lead!"

He was aboard less than three months when our chief cook, by way of an agreement with the captain, arranged for Muggioso's transfer to a new destroyer escort just out from the States. The escort needed a baker, and we had an extra! He was even promoted to second class before leaving in recognition of "outstanding culinary abilities." We never ran into that destroyer escort again, and it was probably just as well.

It has been a long time since I've eaten Navy chow, but there are still memories. When we heard the bos'n mate pass the word to "chow down, chow down," we headed for the mess tables. Beans, choke ass, turkey, or ham, it was a high point of the day.

"Soupy, soupy, soupy..."

A Sailor Goes Home

With the first few months of the war behind us, the *Trever* was given an opportunity to return to the mainland for the long-overdue overhaul and refit. On April 14, in company with our sister ship, the *Hopkins*, we escorted a six-ship convoy back to San Pedro, California. The trip was uneventful, with a crew preparing the work that would be done in the Navy yard, getting their uniforms and personal gear ready for leave, and talking about the time-honored "anchor pools" that were shaping up. An anchor pool, for the uninitiated, was a lottery based on the time the anchor was dropped when arriving at a given destination. Sometimes the winner would be determined by the official time the ship might make a specific navigational point. On that first wartime voyage home, it was to be decided by our passing under the Golden Gate Bridge. The official time as entered in the log was to be determined by the navigation officer and the chief quartermaster, neither of whom would take part in the betting. The quartermaster usually ran the pool, so he got his cut anyway.

On board the *Trever* there were always three such pools. One for a dollar, one for five, and the biggie at ten bucks a pop. For your cash contribution you had a chance to pick the exact time the anchor would drop, the gate would be passed, or whatever the determining factor might be. Only one number to a player was allowed to keep things even. Prize money came from that received from the participants. The more players, the greater the payoff was. The chief would take a percentage for handling the game. As I said, he always made his. The one-dollar pool usually paid off $100 to the winner, while the ten-dollar pool was good for a cool $1,000! It was all illegal, of course, according to naval regulations, but that never stopped anyone. The ship's officers held their own pool, and everyone was happy. I played every pool held during my long thirty-nine months on board, but never hit it once.

We made landfall on the 25th of April of that year, and passed under the Golden Gate to the pleasure of all the winners, and the grumbles of everyone else. It was all quickly forgotten, however, in the rush to get the ship in and the gangway over to the dock so leave and liberty parties could get ashore. That didn't take long, and soon both *Trever* and *Hopkins* were heading into the shipyard where our overhaul and refit would take place. I didn't get to ride the ship into the yard, because when the first leave party stormed the gangway, I was leading the pack.

That leave wasn't very long. Only ten days. But it was a welcome change from what had been our daily routine. Some of the boys, having too far to travel to get home, opted to spend their time in California. But for me, it was back to Chicago. With time being so short, I decided to fly one way. That in itself was a new experience for me, but to tell the truth, it wasn't all that super exciting. Not having a window seat, there wasn't much to see, and as a result I slept most of the flight. When the plane landed in Chicago, I grabbed a cab and headed for home.

Back in the old neighborhood there were all the obligatory visits with the family who, as expected, didn't seem very interested that I was home. I spoke with a few friends, and even made a quick trip to my high school to say hello to some of my teachers and the kids I knew there. I was immediately drafted to speak to a couple of classes, telling them what the war was like as I saw it. What Pearl Harbor looked like upon my arrival. There were even a few "sea stories" to liven things up—those old standby Navy stories that are much more legend than fact. There was a temptation to play the war hero, but it was quickly put aside upon learning that I was not the only sailor around school. Besides, everyone seemed entranced with the plain, unvarnished truth.

While on that first leave there was even time for a short visit with a girl I had known in school. She was not really a special girlfriend or anything like that, although we had been writing to each other now and then. But she was definitely more than just another kid I went to school with. Her name was Emma Lydia Kuyat. Almost a year older than I was, she seemed to be more than a little interested in my coming back after the war was over, and what I might be doing then. I promised not to get myself killed, and to write more often. A few months later I had her name tattooed on my arm, without really understanding why myself. Looking at that tattoo now makes me wonder about that thing called fate.

A lot of my time on that first leave was spent with my grandma, telling her about the war, my ship, the guys I had met, and how I was learning how to run a ship's boiler. That last seemed to impress her. She smiled when I told her about that, and said, "I guess you have a real Man's Job now, my boy." It wasn't easy to talk about a lot of my experiences because of the warnings that had been pounded into us before we left. "A slip of the lip can sink a ship!" and all the other security precautions we were supposed to observe. But I got around it like so many GIs did back then—by talking a lot but actually saying very little. Grandma seemed to enjoy it all, even the parts she did not fully understand.

She seemed less worried about what the future might hold for me. Before leaving to return to the coast and the good ship *Trever*, I promised to write and tell her more about what was happening. The first real leave was way too short. I had six days at home, and then it was time to go. I took the train back and that took up three days. Three long days because, although it had been nice to be in Chicago for a time, I was looking forward to getting back to the *Trever*, which seemed more like home than any place I had ever been.

Back to Pearl

When I walked across the gangway to report aboard, the ship was hard to recognize, so much had been accomplished and started in the previous ten days. Most noticeable was the absence of the heavy four-inch main battery, which had been designed for surface action only. With the *Trever* no longer being a first-line destroyer, they were being replaced with a lighter, dual-purpose weapon. Three-inch cannons that could be used for anti-aircraft defense as well as surface targets. The dependable old .50 caliber machine guns that had served so well during the December 7th attack had been removed in favor of the new 20mm gun. Not as quick firing as the old 50s, they had longer range and a lot more destructive power. Our number four boiler was to be removed, and in its place a huge fuel tank would be installed to extend our cruising range. The DMS was becoming "long legged." There were other changes, such as the installation of radar so we would no longer have to sail blind in our travels, improved sonar equipment, better radio gear and more of it, as well as a lot of less-important but very necessary improvements. All of which we would have to become familiar with on our return crossing to Pearl Harbor. There was a general feeling among the crew that our days of easy duty were behind us.

While I was on leave, the promotion list had been reviewed and approved by the Old Man and the exec. With all the rush and rumble of overhaul, it had not been posted right away. But when it was there was a scramble to check it out. I was as eager as anyone else and it was with considerable pride that I saw my name listed announcing my promotion to fireman second class. I had made it! The kick in rank gave me a pretty good increase in salary—eighteen dollars a month! With my new base pay of $54, plus the 20% overseas bonus pay, I was making more money than I'd ever seen in my life. Of course, after deductions, and a bit sent home to my grandma, there wasn't a great deal left for liberty hellraising. But I still tried to hold up my end of the reputation the *Trever* had established over the years.

A lot of the crew was transferred to other ships and stations as part of the Navy expansion program. One of the old hands to go was my division chief, Doggie Delmar, who had become my mentor in the fire room despite our bad beginning. He had left while I was on leave, so there was no chance to express my appreciation and say good-bye. "Kayler the Tailor" was moved up to first class and took charge of our watch. Deke, having been promoted to water tender second class, moved to the grates, leaving me the senior fireman on the floor plates with a new kid to break in. "You got it, kid. If anything happens, call me!"

All good things come to an end, and our time stateside was no exception. It was around June 15th that the *Trever* and *Hopkins* were determined to have completed their prescribed overhaul and refit, and were sent back to the war. We escorted a small supply convoy back to the Hawaiian Islands, and that was about the busiest sea time we ever had. The crossing was really a time of shakedown for the two refurbished minesweepers, and we had a lot of drills and general familiarization to go through. With the new fuel tank and other miscellaneous equipment having been installed, the Black Gang had their grimy hands full. There were new pumps, fuel and water lines, and new procedures to learn because we could not afford the luxury of making mistakes. The deck and gunnery departments had the same kind of problems, and we all faced the difficulties of breaking in a couple new officers, the first of what were to become known as "90-Day Wonders" because they had been commissioned after only ninety days of Officer Candidate School. Most of them turned out to be pretty good. I know of some who even achieved command status during the war. But there were a few that were such screw-ups they caused that entire category of officers to be called 90-Day Blunders. In all fairness, I must say there were some that came out of Annapolis that were pretty sad. But that's another story.

Being limited in speed to the slowest transport in the convoy, it was a long, slow crossing. But we sighted Diamond Head on July 2nd and, turning the supply ships over to the local escort command, the *Trever* and *Hopkins* stood into the harbor for the fuel docks. Then it was alongside the USS *Whitney* for a few small repairs and modifications we found we needed during our shakedown. One of the most important things we had to do was install an electric coffeemaker in the forward fire room. Doggie would have loved it!

Our being alongside the *Whitney* gave me a chance to go over and see some of the boys I had gone through school with who had been permanently assigned to the repair ship. She remained in the war zone all through the conflict, and her crew had little opportunity for leave home. They were dying for firsthand news of the world outside, and we did our best to fill them in. They liked their permanent Pearl Harbor duty, but I think they envied those of us who were more involved in the war itself, whatever our contribution might be.

With our time alongside completed, we spent the next few days undergoing gunnery exercises to polish our skills with our new armament. The difference between the old and new was hard to take hold of at first, but we soon adapted. In fact, some thought too well. Twice the cable between the aerial target sleeve and the towing plane was cut, closer to the aircraft than the pilot cared for. You'd think we'd done it on purpose! The sea sled carrying the surface target was also demolished by direct hits. That did it. The *Trever* was all set to go.

The old can went back into Pearl for refueling, provisioning, and a few more replacement crew members. I remember standing there by the rail watching them as they struggled to get their bags on board. Like the others standing there, I had a greasy sweat rag tied around my neck, a dirty white hat on the back of my head, and the ever-present sheath knife at my belt. Turning to Deke next to me I said something like, "God, they're just kids." He punched me on the arm, saying, "Yeah, just like somebody else I knew. Come on, let's get back to work." As I turned to follow him it came to me, I must have looked the same way, awkwardly clambering over the lifelines, wide-eyed, dumb, and more than a little bit scared. Deke was right. But war forced one to grow up quickly. Not yet nineteen myself, I was a veteran, a qualified fireman able to tell "sea stories" of liberties that I couldn't remember. Those kids would do all right.

Cradle Cruise

The next day, Captain Agar went ashore to get his orders. When he returned we got the word. The *Trever* was pulling out. It was time to strike back at the Japanese. We had waited long enough.

South of the Equator

On July 12th, the *Trever* stood out of Pearl Harbor and, in the company of the minesweeps *Zane* and *Hopkins*, the auxiliary boat *Navajo*, and the general auxiliary ship *Aldebaran*, headed south. Destination: Tonga Islands. The voyage, while uneventful for the most part, was frantic with activity. Lookouts and gun crews were issued binoculars and a newly developed type of goggles that made it possible to look directly into the sun. No way were we going to be surprised by Tojo's planes diving on us out of the glare of old Sol. Every day the men not on watch were turning to for drill after drill. We had drills for gunnery, drills for fueling at sea, drills for fire and rescue, and even for abandon ship with every man jack of the crew for once knowing where his station was in the event of that happening. We all kept lifejackets and steel helmets handy no matter where we were or what we were doing. On the afterdeck there was a dummy three-inch gun where we practiced loading and firing. Over and over each gun captain would put his people through their paces. "Stand by—open the breech, load and fire. Goddamn it, you're supposed to catch that empty case as it pops out. Do it again. Stand by..." Over and over again we drilled until we could do it as naturally as breathing.

Those of us in the Black Gang didn't miss any of

the fun. In fact, we were worked twice as hard as the deck force. Not only did many of us take part in the aforementioned deck and gunnery exercises, but down in the fire room, and back in the engine rooms, we were practicing high-speed runs, fast boiler operation, shifting fuel and water to maintain ship stability in the event we might be hit by enemy action. And we practiced first aid and evacuation for the burned and injured. As time passed we became so proficient at our jobs we almost looked forward to an emergency so we might prove ourselves. All this was happening on every ship in our group.

I said earlier that the trip was uneventful, and it was—almost. There was the time-honored ceremony of crossing the equator. More than just another event, it was a happening. A truly momentous occasion, as any real sailor will be happy to tell you. With its origins lost in the ages, the ceremony is a tradition of the sea that endured for countless hundreds, perhaps thousands, of years. And no mere Japanese emperor and his military minions would be permitted to interfere. For them to do so, or for us to permit it to happen, would incur the wrath of His Royal Highness, Neptunus Rex, Supreme Ruler of the Raging Main of Seven Seas!

So we prepared to receive the royal representative of the King of the Briny Deep. The legends of that mythological god of the seas are so numerous and complex, it would be impossible to go into them here. And needless to say, wartime policies necessitated an abbreviated ceremony for the *Trever*'s crossing of the line back in 1942. This was managed with the royal permission of King Neptune, so old-timers and new sailors alike remained true to the spirit of the occasion, and it went something like this:

Late in the afternoon of the 16th of July, a seaman who had been lounging up on the fo'c'sle came running to the bos'n mate of the watch to tell him that a very wet, weird-looking stranger was up on the bow, looking for someone in authority. The bos'n wasted no time checking it out, and when he went forward he stopped dead in his tracks to come to attention and throw a real boot camp salute to the guy he saw standing there. Weird looking he was, but identified at once. It was Davy Jones (in the person of Machinist Mate 1st Class Red Haines, one of the more senior members of the crew) who had just come from the depths of the rolling sea. Well, actually he had stepped from the hatch to the chiefs' quarters! He was, as the seaman had reported, sopping wet and festooned with a lot of slimy-looking seaweed. He wore nothing but a ragged, stained pair of dungarees and a white sailor's hat that had seen better days. When he spotted the bos'n mate he roared, "I'm Davy Jones, as if you didn't know, and I am here to see your officer of the deck. You WILL summon him, NOW!" The bos'n, playing his part to the hilt, threw another salute and dashed off to the bridge. In a minute or so the officer of the deck appeared and he went into an academy brace as he reported to Davy Jones. The following dialogue took place:

OOD: Lieutenant JG Sanders, officer of the deck, reporting, sir. May I ask what is your pleasure?

Jones: What ship is this? And where are you bound?

OOD: The USS *Trever*, sir. Bound for the war zone.

Jones: Very well. I have been waiting for your arrival. You will please notify your Commanding Officer that I, Davy Jones, have a message to deliver to him from his Royal Highness, King Neptune.

The OOD took off as fast as the bos'n had moments before. He dashed up to the bridge where Captain Agar, himself a shellback of long standing, waited to play out his part. He turned the responsibility of the ship over to Lieutenant Fitch, the executive, and then hurried down to the fo'c'sle. Agar, being the ship's captain, was reluctant to salute Jones, even if he did represent Neptune. After all, they were aboard his ship. But he'd offer his hand as an equal, and continued with the traditional banter:

Captain: Greetings to you, Davy Jones. And welcome aboard my ship.

Jones: My congratulations to you upon your command. It's been some time since I saw you last.

As it turned out, Red Haines had officiated over the line ceremonies when the captain had first crossed it some time before, and they were old friends.

Jones: I have a summons for you, Captain, from his Royal Highness.

Captain: I will be most happy to receive it.

With that, Davy Jones pulled a sodden scroll of parchment

from his water-soaked dungarees, unrolled it with some difficulty, and read it to the captain. In was an order from King Neptune to appear before the royal court and present for their examination all crew members who might not yet have crossed the equator. When he finished, he rolled up the document and tucked it away in his wet pants.

Captain: I accept the royal summons, Davy Jones, and look forward to seeing His Highness and the royal party.

Jones: Very well, Captain. We shall appear on your ship on the morrow as you approach the equator. Until then, I bid you good day, sir.

With that, Davy Jones turned and retraced his steps to disappear into the seas from which he had emerged. Well, actually, Machinist Mate Red Haines, having played his part in the drama, turned and walked away. He stepped through the open hatch and dropped down to the chiefs' quarters. I can well imagine the reaction of their compartment cleaner when Red climbed out of his costume and let it lie there on deck. Captain Agar, upon returning to the bridge, instructed the quartermaster to enter the proceedings in the ship's log. Fun and games it might have been, but it happened aboard a US Navy ship, and so became part of the official record.

All of this might seem like so much foolishness of a lot of child-minded adults. The new breed of sailor I've described sure thought so, and made their opinions quite clear. But the Navy is built on tradition, and the younger seamen who spoke out of turn lived to regret it. Little did they know that their ridicule and contrary comments would be reported to

His Royal Highness by shellbacks in the crew acting as bears. These poor unfortunates were to learn that the Ruler of the Raging Main is not to be trifled with!

Crossing the Line

The following day, July 17th, found the *Trever* fully prepared for the festivities. The officer of the deck had ordered the bos'n to the fo'c'sle to await the appearance of the deep-sea imperiality. To aid him in his watching of the waters, he had two experienced seaman shellbacks constantly scanning the ocean before the ship. Each had binoculars made of two Coke bottles taped together. About four o'clock that morning one of them let out a screech. "There it is! I see it. There it is—the line!" Sure enough, when "Boats" took a look he could see it for himself. And rising out of the sea to climb aboard ship was Davy Jones. With a squeal of his pipe, the bos'n alerted the bridge that things were about to begin.

Upon hearing the pipe, the officer of the deck reported to the captain that the ship was on course, and the royal representative of the king had been sighted. Agar acknowledged, and determining that all was in readiness for the royal visit, ordered that the program commence. The captain, the exec, and the bos'n went forward to stand together on the bow with Jones to wait for the royal court to appear. All this was told to us later, of course. When it actually took place, only those who had previously crossed the line were permitted to come forward. The rest of us were not considered worthy of being in the presence of such supreme individuals.

There are only two classes of beings when a ship crosses the equator: The Honored Shellback, who is a member of the Ancient Order of the Deep, and by virtue of that title, deserving of entering the royal domain along with "mermaids, whales, sea serpents, porpoises, sharks, dolphins, skates, suckers, crabs, lobsters, and all other living things of the sea." Then there were the others. Pollywogs! Phooey! Stinking, slimy, worthless, and untrustworthy creatures who despoil the sanctity of the deep blue sea with their very presence. Only by crossing the equator on board ship and being duly judged and initiated do they have any chance of salvation. So long as they retain their status of pollywog, they are in danger of being devoured, head, body, and soul, by sharks, whales, serpents, and other denizens of the sea.

Those who may cross the navigational position of the equator by air are not considered to have been made acceptable. It must be made by sea, and preferably on the surface. Submariners, because they move below the surface and through the seas, are in a class with jellyfish, octopuses, and a fish known in the southern seas as a South Sea Island Turdsnapper. Scientific progress in ship design is not always accepted by the royal court and the gods they represent. Submarines, at best, are tolerated.

When Neptunus Rex and his royal group were all aboard and in their proper places, the crew was called forward to take part in the festivities. All of us unworthies went forward and were able to see them in all their glory, dripping wet just as they had emerged from the sea. Actually, a couple of the chiefs had been standing by with a fire hose to add that detail of authenticity. But no one dared to even suggest that, particularly a pollywog. I had to admit that they were magnificent.

There in the center, perched on his bucket throne, was His Royal Highness Neptunus Rex, as portrayed by Gunner Gold, senior enlisted man and the oldest member of the crew. At his best Gunner was an old grouch, so his attitude toward the pollywogs seemed natural. He wore a pair of beat-up shower clogs. Somehow the clogs did not fit the image of royalty, but who had the courage to say so? At his side was his lovely wife, Amphitrite, Goddess of the Sea. Tall, skinny, red-headed, freckled, and wearing nothing but a long skivvie shirt filled out with a couple of soup bowls taped to her chest. In real life one of our signalmen, she spent most of her time giggling and pulling down her dress so as not to reveal her true identity. The sight of a pair of less than clean jockey shorts would have blown her image. There was Davy Jones, of course, in his position of His Highness' scribe; the royal doctor (our pharmacist mate); and royal bears (police) to maintain order with their water-soaked, kapok-filled billy clubs. Dominating the entire group, His Highness included, was the royal baby. No one could have played the part better than our favorite fat machinist mate, a guy named Seberg. Bearded, very white-skinned, he was jelly-belly fat and more than enthusiastic in his role.

Seberg not only sat on his bucket, his big butt enveloped it. He wore nothing but a baby bonnet and an oversized diaper that kept slipping. Between giggles and coos, he would grab a handful of belly and wobble it at the pollywogs waiting to be judged.

With his other hand he would splash in a bucket held between his knees, one filled to overflowing with some evil-looking glop. He acted as though he knew something we didn't. He did!

The captain called everyone to attention, and Davy Jones introduced the royal family. Old Neptune, quite out of character for Gunner Gold, was smiling broadly. Most likely he had been tippling at the Aqua Velva. With the introduction over, Jones let out a roar and called for the pollywogs to be brought forward. As we were herded before the court, the captain asked to be allowed to return to his bridge. Once we were all cowering before the king, the program went forward. As you may have guessed, the royal party, family, court, and group were all one and the same, depending upon the circumstances. It was when they were acting as a court that they were most fearsome, having the regal responsibility of meting out saltwater justice. One by one we were dragged forward by the bears to be judged. If we failed to show proper respect, or dared to laugh at a member of the court, we were whopped with the soggy kapok club of an eager bear. But it was hard to be serious when confronted by the flirtatious Amphitrite or the belly-shaking baby. We tried, however, to stand there with properly downcast eyes as the charges were read against us, and as His Highness pronounced our sentence, taking for granted that we were guilty.

Punishment would invariably fit the crime. A cook might be accused of making his coffee with seawater, and be sentenced to drink it himself. A deck seaman who had washed his swabs in the ocean could be expected to be told he must shower with them henceforth. All punishments were to be carried out at the end of the ceremonies. Once announced, however, they were forgotten. It was all part of the game—a part we pollys were not told about until later. There had been all kinds of sea stories about the violent, almost fatal line ceremonies of the past, and we were none too sure what might happen.

It should be understandable that those of us to be initiated sweat a lot that day. Not only the enlisted men, but also the lone officer who stood with us, realizing that his gold bar was no protection against the impulsive whim of the king and his court. The poor guy looked up to the skipper as though expecting some sort of pardon. But Agar just turned his back and walked to the other wing of the bridge. Probably remembering what he had suffered at the hands of Red Haines during his own line ceremony. The officer, Ensign Bonwell Baker, was accused of flirting with Neptune's wife. In all honesty, it wasn't entirely his fault. After all, she was a red-headed and hot-blooded temptress wearing nothing but a skivvie shirt, a couple of soup bowls, and ragged underwear. And the *Trever* had been out to sea for some time. Still, he had to pay the penalty for his alleged amorous advances.

As for myself, I admit to getting off pretty easy, considering my horrendous crime. According to the scribe, I had visited the crew's head one night and, finding the stalls all occupied, had stepped to the rail and done my thing over the side. As a result, I was charged with peeing into the king's ocean! Deciding to be clever, I pleaded guilty and threw myself on the mercy of the court. It didn't work. The king proclaimed me to be a sea lawyer, sentenced me to be dunked into the crew's urinal, and advised me to keep my mouth shut in the future.

Once sentenced, we were passed along to the royal barber. For the second time in my enlistment I was to lose my hair; not all of it, mind you, just a wide swath down the middle. (The ship's regular clipper made a mint over the next few days completing a lot of skinhead haircuts." Our nifty new hairdos were touched off as we were lathered up and shaved with the dull ax.

Next we faced the royal doctor. We had long suspected that our pharmacist mate was a seagoing quack and our suspicions were confirmed. The doctor stood there with a can of grease and a two-foot length of swab handle marked off with numbers. He insisted it was the standard Marine Life Rectal Thermometer. Only the interference of his Highness saved us the humility of what might have happened. The mad doctor had to be content with prescribing equator pills for every one of us. About as big as a marble, they were pukey green in color and made of what only the sea gods and the doctor knew. He insisted that we swallow one right then and there. Most of us took it into our mouth, gagged, and spit it out to the amusement of the court. One guy, however, actually tried to eat it as ordered. When he bit into it he got the full horrible taste and promptly threw up all over his doctorship. He received a royal pardon on the spot for meritorious service. The rest of us had to suffer, unrecognized.

Having completed the initiation ceremonies, we were required to show there were no hard feelings by kissing the royal baby. It was then we found out why he was giggling and shaking his blubber at everyone. One of the bears would take a big paintbrush, dip it into the bucket of glop, and smear it generously over the baby's belly. The mess was a combination of flour, water, fuel oil, salt, garlic, and nobody really knew what else. We were expected to kiss that slimy, slippery blob on command. All we could do was close our eyes, pucker up, and get it over with. But as the poor pollywog did, the baby would throw himself forward and all that slobbery fat would completely wrap around your face clear up to your ears. With that, each new guy's participation in the festivities was ended.

We were congratulated by the king and his court, and declared henceforth to be trusty shellbacks, having been duly initiated into the Solemn Mysteries of the Ancient Order of the Deep. It all took about three hours. Those pollies on watch were relieved long enough to face the court, after which they returned to their watch stations without the benefit of a shower or change of clothes. One of the young sailors thought he would be smarter than the rest of us and save his clothes by appearing before the royal court stark naked! This, of course, upset everyone. Everyone except Amphitrite, who thought he was cute and almost lost control of herself. Neptune was incensed! When the poor guy reached the end of the line, along with all the other indignities he suffered, his little pink body bore the signature of every member of the royal party. Written in US Navy-issue iodine, which had the permanence of a modern-day Sharpie Marker!

Ceremonies completed, everybody became friends, as all good shellbacks must. It was with great reluctance that we said our good-byes to King Neptune and his party. As they filed down the hatch, Amphitrite, true to her character, even threw a kiss and a flip of the skirt to Ensign Baker and the naked sailor that had caught her roving eye. We had other crossings in the years ahead, but to me they were nothing compared to that first wartime ceremony. As soon as we had an opportunity, there would be plenty to write home about.

Look Out Tojo, Here We Come!

The rest of the trip to the Tonga Island Group was uneventful, yet busy, as we had expected. Still, I found time to finish putting in my course for fireman first class. With a final mark of 3.24, it put me in good shape for the next promotion exams, and I looked forward to that. Thinking what Doggie Delmar had said a few months earlier, I had pretty well decided to stay in the Black Gang and be a water tender. If I was going to be career navy, it could be a pretty good deal.

After a few days of steady steaming, our task group arrived at the Tonga Islands. Entering the harbor of Tongatabu, we dropped anchor and became part of Task Force (TF) 62, the force to make the invasion of Guadalcanal and Florida Islands in the Solomons. We didn't remain in Tonga but a few days. Long enough to top off our fuel tanks, take on a few provisions, and make a final check of our readiness. I don't know when I had ever seen so many ships in one place prior to dropping anchor there. There were light and heavy cruisers, fleet tankers, cargo and troop carriers, seagoing tugs, and destroyers everywhere. Many of them were moving slowly from berth to berth as they took on supplies and needed war material. Lights on their busy bridges flashed and blinked as messages were sent back and forth. Our own signal lamps resounded with a continuous "clack, clack,

clack" as we responded to communications directed to our skipper. All across the anchorage, small boats skittered across the choppy water like so many big, gray water bugs as they raced to their destinations. I could feel a tension in the air, and see it in the faces of our crew. Captain Agar spent much of his time ashore at meetings where the final details of the operation were being hammered out. On that last day in port he returned from yet another such meeting, but this time carrying his brief case and a roll of charts. There was a strange look of determination on his usually smiling face, tempered with just a trace of doubt as to what we might be facing in the next few days. As soon as he had clambered over the lifelines, he directed the OOD to inform all officers and chiefs of a meeting in the wardroom. Immediately! Stillness settled over the *Trever* as we realized what was taking place.

Early the next morning, the ship's speaker issued the announcement we were all waiting for. "Now hear this. Station all Special Sea Detail...make all preparations for getting underway." Nobody wasted any time getting out of their sack. Not just Special Sea Detail, but everybody! On the bridge the lights began to rattle again with our signal to the port director that we were ready to leave. The deck force prepared to pick up the anchor, and our steaming colors were made ready to hoist. There was a rumbling throughout the *Trever* as the second boiler was put into the mainline, and the engineers tested main engines. The anchor ball, that big black sphere that indicated our being at anchor, began to slide down from the yard arm as the captain ordered "hoist the anchor!" Moments later, the hook being free of the muddy harbor bottom and almost on deck, the bridge telegraph jangled as the order by Agar was sent to engineering spaces below decks, and was acknowledged. "All engines ahead one third..." We were under way.

In company with other ships of TF 62, the *Trever* headed out to sea. We all had a pretty good idea of where we were headed, although no official word had been passed. It was Agar's policy in the past to get on the speaker once we were at sea, and tell us what was going on. He didn't disappoint us, and once we were clear of the harbor mouth and the Sea Detail had been secured, the horn came to life. "Now hear this. This is the captain. As most of you know, we are headed for the Solomon Islands where the United States Navy and Marine Corp are going to invade and take the bases that have been set up by the enemy for our own use. I don't suppose Tojo's people are going to be too happy about it, but that's their problem. We are going to occupy the Solomons, beginning with Guadalcanal and Florida Islands. There is an airfield on Guadalcanal that the Japs are building, and it is imperative this operation is successful before they are in a position to use it as an advance base to attack our fleet. Exactly what part the *Trever* will play in the invasion depends upon what we find when we arrive. But you can figure that we will be doing some sweeping, we will shell shore positions, and generally support the landing forces. When the Japanese make their counterattack, as we know they will, you can expect to be fighting off air attacks. I know you will all do your share and more in the coming battle. From here on it's no drill. When you hear the GQ alarm, it will be for real. But if everybody does his job the way we have trained, we'll come through this just fine. I'll talk to you again when it's all over. Until then, good luck, and God Bless each and every one of you."

When the speaker clicked off, there wasn't a sound to be heard. Even the normal sounds of the *Trever* herself seemed muted as she plowed through the seas. Slowly, we all moved off to our respective duties, each of us with our own thoughts. Sure, we had seen action before, but there was something different about hitting the Japs in their own territory. Something that none of us had experienced. I've often wondered how many of the guys felt as I did just then. Not afraid, really, but hoping that when the time came we would measure up.

The next few days were relatively quiet, except for a couple calls to battle stations when we had reports of bogeys in the area, or suspected submarine activity. Nothing came of them, however, and we began to feel that our move against Japanese positions might just go unobserved until we struck. Nobody slept much, and when we did it was in some out-of-the-way corner on deck with our lifejacket for a pillow. That last day the cooks made up a lot of soup and sandwiches, because there would be no time for regular meals later. The captain came in on the horn once more, suggesting that we all get as much rest as we could. We were leaving the next morning and there would be no breaks for anyone for a few days after that.

When we darkened ship that last night the usual card games and lighthearted banter were absent as we all sat around and waited. Those on watch were especially alert and ready for anything. Where it was possible to do it without getting in anyone's way, we tended to hang around our battle station so as to be there when the alarm sounded. A few of the guys were below writing letters by the dim light of a battle lantern, forgetting, I suppose, that

Cradle Cruise

no mail would be going out for a while. As for me, I had the midwatch and went down to the fire room with some misgivings. I wasn't too crazy about being below decks when the balloon went up. Still, it was what I had been trained for, and what I did best. Before my four-hour stint was up we would be there. Until then, I covered my own apprehensions by continually telling my junior fireman not to worry. All he had to do was his job the way I had taught him. "It's funny," I thought, "*me* telling *him* not to worry."

Around three in the morning the general quarters alarm sounded, and as soon as my relief dropped down the ladder to the floor plates, I was up and into the air lock to get on deck. With lifejacket and steel pot in hand, I rushed down the port side to my station with the after ammo party, and took my place by the hoist. In moments the word was passed. "All battle stations manned and ready." Come what may, the *Trever* was ready, indeed. And so, as alert as we could be, we waited. We stared off into the blackness of the moonless night, and waited.

Invasion of the Solomons

It's been said that to the individual fighting man the battle is limited to his own experience. What he sees and hears. What he may or may not do. The admiral may well win a great sea battle, the general an extensive land campaign, and both declare victory. But to the sea captain who loses his ship, or the foot soldier who steps on a land mine, the battle is lost. So it was when the *Trever* took part in the invasion of the Solomon Islands back in 1942. To each crewman, the nature of the battle, and its outcome, related to his battle station. The Black Gang and the ammunition handlers deep in the magazines knew nothing of what was happening topside. They did their job just as they had done it countless times in the past, albeit with considerably more apprehension, and a sense of urgency. Even those of us on deck, while we could see and hear what was going on around us, had a different impression of the action from one end of the ship to the other.

On the bridge the officers and enlisted men were concerned with conning the *Trever* in her maneuvers so as to carry out her assigned duties, and yet give our gunners the best possible opportunities to fire effectively. Signalmen concentrated on keeping in communication with the rest of the task force. Radar and sound operators, tucked away in their little steel boxes, had as their only tie to the action a brightly imaged scope to which their eyes were glued. Gun crews had to keep their attention riveted to that portion of the sea and sky within range of their weapons. Ammo-passers, if they were to keep their assigned guns supplied, had little chance to look at anything else once the shooting started. Even the medical people, who fervently hoped their skills would not be needed, waited in an area that gave them some protection, and consequently were in no position to be observers. All of us, regardless of our station or duties, would have to wait until the battle was over to compare notes as to what actually took place.

As the fleet continued to move toward the islands, our eyes became accustomed to the darkness, and I was surprised at how much could be seen even though there was no moon. The silhouette of the islands was clearly defined against the sky, and it was possible to see the ships of our task force moving into position. We knew it would only be minutes before things began to happen. If the Japanese didn't know we were there, they were about to find out.

Then, suddenly, the world seemed to split asunder as the cruisers opened fire on the beach. So bright was the flash of their heavy guns in the darkness, we were able to see each individual vessel clearly. Between salvos, it was possible to watch the glowing shells pass through the air, only to flash again as they exploded on target, tearing apart the enemy's defenses. Again and again the warships' guns roared, and the stench of burned powder floated across the water. I never realized how much smoke and stink there was to the firing of naval guns. How long the bombardment continued, I don't know, but the horizon was showing streaks of the coming day, and still the shooting went on. Strangely, there was no response from the shore. It didn't seem possible that anything could withstand the savagery of our attack. Surely the island would sink from the sheer weight of the naval shells being dropped on it. As the morning drew on and the sky lightened, we would see the fifteen-gun cruiser, USS *San Juan*, ablaze from stem to stern as her main battery fired again and again. Twice she had to back down to get out of her own smoke to give her gunners a clear view of the beach.

It was about eight o'clock that morning that the *Trever*, *Hopkins*, and *Hovey* were ordered to fire on enemy positions, and to cover the first troop landings. We moved in, and steaming in column opened up with full broadsides. Close enough for even the 20mms to reach the shore. It was then that the Japanese shore batteries began to make their reply. Surprisingly accurate, their first few salvos had us bracketed. One of the guys on our after gun deck was heard to yell, "Hey, we could get killed this way!" The enemy batteries were soon located, however, and under the direction of our own fire control, were soon silenced.

We called a cease-fire, and in the ensuing silence we could hear the word being passed aboard the troop carriers: "Now land the landing parties!" Moments later, the boats were passing our stern, headed for the takeover of the islands. Before long, we could hear the sounds of battle as the marines slogged ashore. It passed through my mind that a lot of good men were going to die that day, on both sides of the war.

Our worst fears became a reality as the third wave was going in, and the boats of the first wave were returning with many of them carrying casualties, men who were killed or wounded before they had even gotten out of the landing craft. That sailor up on our gun deck had been right; a guy could get killed out here.

It was close to ten o'clock when the old DMSs withdrew to be assigned the task of minesweeping. Still at GQ, enough of the crew was relieved so they might get back to the fantail and stream paravanes to find and clear any Jap mines that might prevent further landings. While we were conducting the sweep, enemy planes passed overhead on a high altitude attack. Their efforts were in vain, however, as our combined anti-aircraft fire drove them off before they could do any damage. But just for a few minutes there, the combination of minesweeping and fighting off the attacking bombers made for a hairy situation. As it was, the raid came to an end and sweeping operations continued.

The rest of the first day passed slowly. Except for an occasional enemy aircraft dropping a bomb or two at random, or circling the invasion fleet at a far distance, there was little action that took place other than for the marines on the beaches. We took advantage of the lull to reload machine gun magazines, refill our main gun ready boxes, and take a break for the soup and sandwiches as we compared notes on what we had seen and heard. The skipper came on the horn again to give us all a "well done." In the Navy there is no higher praise you can receive from your commanding officer. "Well done" says it all.

That night was another of considerable tension with no one getting much rest. The cargo and troopships had to withdraw until daybreak, with the *Trever* and other minesweeps going along to provide a security screen. We fully expected the entire Imperial Japanese Navy to come along and make a formal protest to our presence. But the night passed in relative quiet. The morning of August 8th, however, was another matter entirely.

Counterattack!

The next morning we had a leisurely breakfast of more sandwiches, soup, and coffee. Those men normally assigned to the Black Gang took a turn below to allow the snipes who were there during the GQ to take a well-earned break. The captain decided to turn on the showers so they might get cleaned up and refreshed before returning to the heat and pressure below decks. We all would have enjoyed a good shower about then, but knew it could not be. So we continued to sweat and tried to keep upwind of each other.

Around eleven o'clock, we received word that a large Japanese group was approaching. High-level, torpedo, and dive bombers that were obviously determined to sink our cargo ships and belabor the marines on the island. From their point of view it was imperative that they stop the invasion of the Solomon Islands. Around noon they hit us in force. First attacking cargo and troopships, and then going after the sweeps and destroyers on their way out. It's kind of hard after so many years to remember exactly what happened as they flew among the ships of our group. There was a lot of shooting going on. Far too much, too close to be directed by our fire control gang. All guns were working under the local control of battery officers and gun captains. In the ammo parties we were passing up three-inch shells by box, pausing only to rip off the top and then throwing box and all up the ladder to the gun crews. Looking back, and considering that each box weighed about 85 pounds, this was no easy feat. Empty magazine from the 20mm were simply tossed over the windscreen with the hope that the guys on the main deck would catch them and run them up to the clip shack for a reload.

One thing about that air raid sticks out in my mind even now—the passing of a Jap attack bomber along our starboard side. Known as a Betty[6] by our people, he was an awesome sight. Big and bristling with guns, he was only about 35 yards away from us, and less than 40 feet off the water. It took only a second for that Betty to flash past, but it was one of the longest seconds of my life.

In that short time span I was able to see and experience so much. Apparently undamaged by all the ships shooting at him, it was close enough for us to see the pilots and gunners looking out at us. Most noticeable was the waist gunner as he looked over his gun sights right at me. Right...At... Me! There was a sparkle of fire from his gun muzzles, and I remember thinking that he had probably come thousands of miles from his homeland, just to kill me. Why? I didn't even know him. Why was he so damned intent on shooting me? As I write this everything about that moment is crystal clear. I remember his helmet had a furry edge around his face. And his goggles were not egg shaped as one might expect, but round. His goggles were round. And he had a mustache; a big, bushy mustache, which was strange for a Japanese man. All of this registered in my mind in the instant it took that

6. The Mitsubishi G4M was the main twin-engine, land-based bomber used by the Imperial Japanese Navy Air Service in World War II. The Allies gave the G4M the identification name of "Betty."

plane to go past. And that impression remains.

As the bomber streaked by and out of our sight, there was a cheer from the gun crew forward. With all the noise of battle we could still hear them yell. Later, we were told that our #3 gun had put a shell right into the side turret—the same turret from which that gunner with the round goggles and mustache pointed his 7.7mm machine guns in my face. One moment we had been looking at each other, the next moment he was gone. He had traveled his thousand miles just to shoot at me...and then die. The raid only lasted a few minutes, but in that brief time the *Trever* had splashed three of the Jap attackers. A cease-fire was called, and we immediately began to prepare for another visit by Hirohito's flyboys.

When no more raids materialized, we began to worry. Our worries were justified around three in the morning of August 9, when a force of Japanese warships steamed into the area and caught our task force unawares. It resulted in one hell of a sea battle. The first of several to be fought around Savo Island, which lay to the west and between the islands we had invaded. History has since referred to that fracas as the Debacle of Savo Island, because it should never have happened, and when it did it turned out to be one of the Navy's greatest defeats of the entire war. Four Allied cruisers were sunk—the USS *Quincy*, *Astoria*, and *Vincennes*, along with the Australian cruiser *Canberra*. The American cruiser *Chicago* was heavily damaged, as were the destroyers *Wilson* and *Ralph Talbot*.

The *Trever* and the other sweeps were still providing a screen for the transports and did not take part in the battle, although from our position we were able to watch it taking place. Had the Japanese admiral decided to press his advantage and come after us, there was no way we could have stopped him. Even suffering losses of his own, he could have destroyed the effectiveness of Task Force 62, and annihilated our marines fighting inland. While we did not know just how bad things really were at the time, we did know that our fleet had been hurt, and we were in danger of being sunk if the enemy came our way. A lot of perfectly good fingernails were chewed up on that warm August morning.

For his own reasons, the enemy admiral and his forces withdrew and we were left to lick our wounds and search for survivors. There weren't too many. The damaged USS *Chicago* and the cargo ships received orders to withdraw and head for Nouméa, New Caledonia. The *Trever, Zane, Hopkins,* and *Hovey*, along with a couple of newer destroyers, sailed with them to provide the necessary screen.

And so it was that the first stage of the Solomon Island campaign was over for the *Trever*. The old converted destroyers had done their job well, and were destined to return to Guadalcanal in the near future. But for the time being we headed to safer waters.

So Wave to the Pretty Ladies

New Caledonia was a French island in the southwest Pacific. Its capital city of Nouméa was a sizable seaport, and the anchorage provided an excellent supply and staging base for the war against the Japanese. Unfortunately, the residents of this jewel of the Pacific resented the presence of the Allied powers. They gave the impression of regarding the war as an inconvenience to be ended as soon as possible, so they might return to their civilized world of decadence and self-indulgence. Especially irritating to them was the attention being given to their womenfolk by the barbaric American sailors. The fact that the ladies loved it was to them sufficient reason to complain to the port authority, and many a ship captain, personally.

We tried very hard to be good allies, to be polite and courteous in our dealings with the locals. Honest, we did. A good example of how far we were willing to go to show our friendliness would be our reaction to their regular Sunday outings, which often conflicted with the war effort. You see, every Sunday afternoon the harbor would be filled with a variety of sailboats cruising up and down the sparkling blue waters. With glistening waxed woodwork, shimmering sails, and dazzling brass work, these beautiful craft would tack back and forth between the military and merchant marine ships, sometimes passing as close as 30 or 40 yards away. And there on their afterdecks they would sit in all their finery, sipping cold drinks handed to them by their native servants, and generally showing us a view of a lifestyle we would never knew. It would have been easy to resent their good fortune, but instead we would wave in a friendly manner. After all, in their own way they were contributing to our high morale. We thought the ladies were especially beautiful to see, dressed as they were in their thin summery frocks, protecting their loveliness with lacy parasols. Rather than getting angry, we found it all to be stimulating, inspiring. Leading to our having wonderful dreams at night, which, when we talked about them later, gave our pharmacist mate reasons to consider putting saltpeter in our coffee as they did in boot camp.

Now it must be mentioned here that just about the time the French regatta would begin to appear, the ships in the harbor would be undergoing a change of watch, and people would be knocking off work for the day.

Aboard ships like the *Trever*, there would be a rush by crew members to get back to the shower and washrooms to do our daily laundry and take a well-earned shower. Our facilities would not accommodate everyone, so most of us would sit out on the fantail with buckets of soapy water, scrubbing our clothes. Including those we had been wearing that day. Consequently, we would all be in the nude. Sometimes as many as 15 or 20 of us would be gathered here.

The fantail of an old four stacker is pretty bare of equipment, with depth charge racks and minesweeping gear located along the sides. Although we were naked, it would not be obvious to the boats sailing by. We, on the other hand, could see over all that gear, and we would wave cheerfully at each sailboat as it passed by. It was the sort of thing that offended the French. It finally brought a complaint to the port director, who sent an unofficial note to all ships present, demanding the practice to cease immediately.

When the message arrived at the *Trever*, we were hurt. It was unfair; hardly what we might expect from an ally. But what could we do? We had specifically been ordered not to draw attention to ourselves, and not to fraternize with royalty. On the other hand, we were Americans, and had a reputation to uphold.

We agreed that the governor and his party would be our target. He had the biggest, most luxurious yacht of all, and he always had a lot of guests and their ladies sitting around in deck chairs, partaking of dainties and sipping champagne.

The following Sunday, when we were back on the fantail attending to our laundry and such, the opportunity presented itself as we knew it would. For some reason, there were more of us back there than you might ordinarily see. With a couple of chiefs who had no need to use the crew washrooms because they had their own in the chiefs quarters, there must have been about 35 guys hanging around, washing, scrubbing, and waiting. One boat after another passed with no reaction from us. Then the word was passed from a lookout we had posted that the governor's yacht was approaching, and from the way he was tacking in the wind, he would pass quite close.

In just a few minutes the luxury craft swept by, and as it did the girls on deck waved. It was all we needed to justify our actions. At the command "now!" we all jumped up, climbed to the top of the depth charge racks, clung to the paravanes, and even stepped out to the propeller guards. Pushing and jostling for a choice position, two or three guys fell overboard. And there we were. Everybody buck naked! We proudly stood to our full height and energetically waved to the passing sailboat. For a moment there was no reaction aboard the yacht. Then the men exploded into action, hustling the women and girls below deck. But even as they vanished down the hatches, some of them could be seen trying frantically to continue waving. In the moment or two it took the boat to pass our ship, its afterdeck was empty of anyone wearing skirts—except for one grey-haired old grand dame who continued to struggle in the arms of the men trying to carry her away—all the time with a gigantic pair of binoculars held to her eyes. It all happened too fast for our own officers to become aware of what was happening and react. By the time the OOD came aft, we were all back to our normal activities of washing clothes and showering. But he was not to be fooled. "Okay, you men just had to do it. You're all in real trouble now." With that, he turned and headed back to the quarterdeck. But he could be seen fighting laughter every step of the way.

He was right, of course. We were in trouble. Within the hour there was a message from the port director's office requesting our captain's presence at once. As his boat pulled away, we wondered what would happen next. In about two hours we knew. When he returned, the skipper looked anything but happy. He stormed past the officer of the deck, saying, "Muster the ship's company on the fo'c'sle. Now!" In a minute the word was passed and everybody not on watch fell into ranks up forward. The Old Man came stomping through the hatch and laid in to us.

Cradle Cruise

"You people couldn't listen, could you? You couldn't leave well enough alone. A bunch of clowns standing there bare-assed naked, waving and weenie wagging like a flock of goddamned delinquents. I just came from the port director's office where he ripped me a new asshole—not only him, but a personal representative of the governor, too. They think I have a crew of perverts. And I think they may be right. They think the entire crew should be suitably punished. Well, punished you will be." The red began to leave his face by then, and his eyes began to regain the twinkle we were accustomed to. Still, he raved about what he was going to do to us. How he had no choice. How we would be lucky if COMSOPAC (Commander, South Pacific) didn't get the *Trever* assigned to the Aleutians, where we would have nothing to contend with except the Japanese and an occasional Eskimo.

Then, with his clenched fists on his hips as though daring us to disagree, he said, "As of this moment the entire crew is restricted to the ship for a period of thirty days. No liberty, no leave, no shore parties, nothing. Go ashore without specific orders for a specific official purpose, and you get court-marshaled." With that, he turned and left the fo'c'sle. As he did, he yelled at the exec to dismiss the crew. There was a few moments of dead silence, and then the executive officer called us to attention and dismissed us.

Immediately after we were dismissed, the exec collapsed over a machine gun mount as though his legs just wouldn't support him any longer. He buried his head in his arms and shook uncontrollably. As we filed through the hatch, one of the chiefs stopped and said, "If you could just speak to the captain. All we did was wave. And that old broad with the binoculars..." The exec just raised one hand and waved the chief away.

We suffered our thirty days' restriction. When you consider that we were in the middle of the ocean most of the time or in some island port where there was nothing to do anyway, the restriction really didn't mean anything. It satisfied the French officials, although somehow it never did appear in our records or the ship's log.

Whenever we made port in Nouméa after that, we still saw the Sunday afternoon parade of sailboats, but none of them came within hailing distance of the *Trever*. The story of what happened took a little time getting around the fleet, improving with each telling. Naturally, we denied doing anything immoral or perverted. I guess the girls waving first, and the old lady with the binoculars, helped our cause. In the final analysis, all we were doing was showing a little good old American friendliness. All we did was wave at the pretty ladies!

Fishing from the *Trever*

The USS *Trever*, like so many small ships during the war, was extremely nonregulation. So long as the important things were accomplished, and the ship was operated efficiently, the crew was left pretty much alone to use their free time as they saw fit, with no organized activities to contend with. One favorite pastime among many of the ship's company was fishing. Even city boys who probably never wet a line in their entire life could be found hanging over the side, looking for that "one that got away" from somebody else. When we did fish, it was not in any manner you might expect. Not for us was there the luxury of standing in a swift running stream as we skillfully manipulated an expensive fly rod, or lying lazily in a rowboat with a bamboo pole, trying to catch a few pan fish. For us, it was deepwater, big game fish. And although we didn't do it while strapped into a fancy fishing chair bolted to the deck, wrestling with a super rod and reel, it was a genuine effort. We were much more direct in our approach as we went after fish the average angler would never see. Like shark.

Frequently, when the *Trever* was anchored in the outer harbor of some island or other, the bright sun reflecting from the ship into the water would attract a lot of sharks. As many as a dozen or so could be seen around our stern, splashing noisily as they went after anything that might be thrown overboard. Whenever this happened, the logical thing seemed to be to go shark fishing. Our tackle usually consisted of about fifty feet of heaving line (a rope similar to old-fashioned clothesline, but much stronger), about eight feet of chain, and a big three-prong grappling hook. For bait there was always a piece of bloody meat from the ship's refrigerator. Whirling the thing around our head a few times, we would heave it out into the middle of the circling sharks, and all hell would break loose.

It would only be a second or two before one of them struck, and the fun would begin. We used no scientific or sportsman-like technique to play the beast. For us it was just a matter of having six or eight guys take hold of the line and pull. Usually the shark would be so wild fighting us, as well as his buddies who all wanted a piece of the action, that the chain would be bitten through in short order and we would lose all our gear. But one day our luck changed.

We tied into a real beauty, well over six feet long. By brute force we managed to bring him alongside. Our deck was only about four feet out of water at the stern, and with all his thrashing around it seemed that he was coming aboard of his own free will. None of us had honestly expected to catch anything, but there we were, with a good-sized shark close aboard, not knowing what to do next. Advice was readily available, however, from the rapidly gathering spectators. "Kill it, kill the sumbitch!" was the cry. Sure, kill it. But how do you kill almost seven feet of very angry man-eater? One of the shipfitters' gang, Little Davy, picked up a crowbar and walloped him on the head about forty times, only succeeding in making him even more upset. The gangway watch came back to see what the commotion was all about, and he solved the problem for us. As duty petty officer he was wearing a .45 pistol. He pulled it from his holster, leaned over the rail, and shot the fish in the head six or seven times, scaring hell out of everybody. But it seemed to do the trick. At least, we hoped so.

Once there was total agreement that the shark was dead, he was hauled up on deck. Finally having caught ourselves a shark, there was the question of what to do with it. Now at the time the ship's crew included a Filipino officers' cook who, upon hearing we had caught the monster, came running down the deck, waving a great big galley knife and screaming, "I get it! I get it!" He did, hacking out the entire upper and lower jaw (he planned on making a necklace of the teeth), cutting out a few choice bits of innards, and whacking off a good-sized portion of the fin. "Make good soup!" he explained. The fin, when dried and ground to powder, would also be a potent aphrodisiac. Just the thing we needed in the middle of the ocean. Gathering up the bloody bits and pieces, the cook returned to his galley, singing to himself and leaving us with a lot of bloody, gutsy fish to dispose of.

We scooped up what was left of the fish and pitched it over the side. When it hit the water, the other sharks went into a frenzy, and in moments it was gone. We got into a bit of trouble over that escapade. Not so much because of our unorthodox fishing, but the method used to kill the beast. The skipper was afraid somebody might have been shot by accident. Besides, we had scared the daylights out of the OOD, who thought we had been boarded by a Japanese suicide squad. The captain withheld punishment, however, when we promised not to do it again. "Sure," the Old Man was heard to mutter to himself. "Promises, promises."

For those not quite so foolhardy, there were other fish to catch. True, they were not as big, but they were easier to bring in, and more often as not good to eat. One such fish was called a Red Snapper. It was so easy to hook that a couple of sailors in an hour or so could take enough to feed the entire crew. They were really good eating, tasting a lot like salmon. There was another tricky little devil called the Puffer Fish. Although not edible, he provided us with a lot of entertainment. Pulled out of the water, he would gulp a lot of air, inflating himself to almost the size of a basketball. He was covered with sharp spines like a porcupine, which were so poisonous that if a guy were to stab himself with one or two and fail to get an immediate antidote shot, he could die. We didn't worry about that, however, because we always wore heavy welders gloves when handling them. When we had one that was all puffed up, somebody would stick him with a knife tip, and he would pop like a paper bag.

After a heavy storm jellyfish would be floating by the thousands near the surface of the water. Dark brown in color and not very big, they were easy to scoop up in a fine mesh fishnet. We would put them in a bucket and set them out in the hot sun, where the fish would actually melt down to a slimy, stringy goo. It was just the thing to throw all over a shipmate who might be walking naked on his way to the shower. The only way to clean away the slime was a lot of hard scrubbing with good-old saltwater soap. Fishing could be a lot of fun.

There were some guys who claimed to have been great fishermen in civilian life. One such person was the captain's steward, a kid named Duff. He told us that with his daddy, he used to go down to the river all the time to catch carp and catfish. Now, one day a few fish swimming around our stern caught his eye and he figured to catch a few. Bumming some tackle, our boy went after them. He was pretty good, and in no time at all had about five or six of the finny critters on his stringer. We asked him what he planned to do with the fish when he had caught all he wanted.

"I'm gonna clean them fish, and I'm gonna cook them fish, and then I'm gonna eat them fish. And I'm gonna cook some for the captain and the officers. I'm gonna give them all a real treat. That's what I'm gonna do with them fish."

We thought about that, and figured if he wanted to eat them it was all right with us. But it didn't seem like a good idea to feed them to the wardroom. You see, we knew what kind of fish they were. Taking Duff by the arm, we led him to the starboard side of the ship where there were dozens of them frantically swimming around the overhead discharge pipe from the crew's head. With 120 men aboard, somebody was always sitting in one of the stalls, and everything he dropped would pass through the drain and out the overboard discharge, where it would be snapped up and gulped down by whichever fish could get to it first. We used to watch them fight for it like sharks after a chunk of raw meat. You can understand why they were known as South Sea Island Turdsnappers.

Duff stood there for a moment, watching them feed. Then he turned kind of pale, staggered back to where he had been fishing, and took a good look at his catch. He dumped his stringer of fish and borrowed tackle over the side and threw up. The turdsnappers ate that, too. So much for Duff, Piscatorian of the US Navy.

Somehow, I don't think he ever wrote his daddy about that experience.

There were a lot of fish in the Pacific for those who were interested in that sort of thing. Some were good for a fight, others made good eating, some were a pleasure just to watch. We saw stingrays, porpoises, dolphins, even flying fish, which we ate raw dipped in a spicy sauce. A few old timers had collapsible tackle they had made and carried in their seabags, fishing all over the world. If given the opportunity, they would have more to say on the subject of fishing than any outdoor magazine fishing expert.

Back to the Solomons

Having given the *Trever* and the other old ladies a couple weeks of soft duty and a chance to polish their minesweeping skills, the Navy decided it was time for us to go back to war. Things had been pretty hot in the Solomon Islands, what with the Japanese being very uncooperative in giving up all that territory, and the marines ashore needing supplies very badly. They also needed some replacements, casualties having been very heavy. So on October 10th, we got underway from Espiritu Santo as part of the escort for the transport ships USS *Zeilin* and USS *McCawley*. We arrived at Guadalcanal on the thirteenth, and as the transports off loaded, the *Trever* and *Hovey* were sent to search for survivors of the Battle of Cape Esperance,[7] which had been fought just the night before.

Steaming to the battle area, the two ships separated so as to cover it in a shorter time. Around nine that morning we spotted the first survivors in the water. There were about eight of them clinging to a liferaft; Japanese, as we had expected. Stopping engines, the *Trever* drifted toward them. One of our seamen was ordered to put over a heaving line with a grappling hook, to pull the raft alongside. When the line fell across the bobbing raft, one of the Japs barked

---

7. Also known as the Second Battle of Savo Island.

a command and the hook was thrown off. They all waved their arms furiously, and began screaming something that ended in a shrill "banzai! banzai!"[8] We had no time for such foolishness, and the order came from the bridge to "shoot that man who threw off the hook." With the chatter of a Thompson sub-machine gun, the Nip literally disappeared in an explosion of flesh and blood that splattered over his companions and into the sea. We again put over the heaving line, only to have it once again thrown off. Once more from the bridge: "Shoot that man!" And another Japanese sailor died, torn apart by heavy .45 caliber slugs. For the third time the line was thrown out to the raft, only to have it rejected. All the time the survivors were calling out in some impossible-to-understand gibberish, with a lot of banzais. That was it. They were the enemy, and if they wanted to die for their emperor, we would be only too happy to oblige. The line and grappling hook were taken back in and the Japanese raft with its occupants drifted away. It floated off our starboard quarter, and our engines came to life with a deep rumble as we got underway.

Before the *Trever* had moved very far, the ship's speaker squealed, and the word was passed for the 20mm guns to open fire on the liferaft and the remaining Japs. Only our number three and five guns could bear, and they commenced firing. In a split second their target disappeared in a great splashing of water, turning everything into a bloody froth. When the cease-fire was ordered, the shattered raft and its grisly cargo drifted out of sight.

---

8. "Banzai" was a Japanese battle cry during WWII, and translates literally as "ten thousand years." Japanese soldiers and sailors often shouted "tennōheika banzai!" during suicide charges, meaning "may the emperor reign for ten thousand years."

The *Trever* moved off to resume the search for other survivors. I found myself hoping that if we did find any more they would be more anxious to live. We didn't talk much about what had happened. Despite our put-on bravado, I don't think anyone was very proud of having killed those Japanese. They were, after all, helpless in the water. And even a bad attitude didn't seem like much of a reason to die. Still, they had been given an opportunity to surrender and live. A good example, I suppose, of the fortunes of war.

Around 10:30 or so, we spotted another group of Nips in the drink. Some wore lifejackets, others were clinging to pieces of wreckage, still others just doing what they could to stay afloat. As the *Trever* approached, they waved frantically and called out to us. Unlike the first group, none of them seemed ready to give up their lives for Hirohito. Stopping engines, we threw out liferings with lines attached, and the swimmers eagerly made their way to our sea ladders to be picked up. As each of them came over the side, they were searched very carefully. That was an easy job because they were wearing next to nothing. Shorts, a breechcloth, tattered remnants of underwear; a few were stark naked. Some of them still wore their little cloth navy caps, which were immediately confiscated as souvenirs.

Altogether, there were 37 of them. They were in pretty good shape, actually, for having been in the water for 12 hours or so. Still, they seemed happy to be aboard, realizing, I suppose, that for them the war was over. They were all herded up to the fo'c'sle, where they were kept under armed guard. Sitting there on the steel deck, water soaked, tired, and bedraggled, they didn't look at all dangerous. Yet they were the enemy that had attacked Pearl Harbor—the men whom we had been fighting. The enemy who had manned the ships that had been kicking hell out of our high-vaunted American Navy.

The reaction of our crew to seeing the Japanese up close was as varied as you might expect. Some of our people just stood and stared, not saying a word. Others hooted and hollered, screaming epithets that made no sense. One gunner's mate, who had lost a brother on December 7, was jumping up and down in front of them as he pointed to a tattoo on his arm, yelling, "Remember Pearl Harbor you little yellow bastards? Remember December seventh?" The tattoo was of an American Flag and the inscription "Remember Pearl Harbor." It took some pretty strong orders from the bridge, and quick action by our chiefs, to keep things from getting out of hand.

The first thing we had to do once the prisoners were all in one place was to try to find out if there were any officers or senior enlisted men among them. But with the language barrier that was impossible. So the Old Man, following the Geneva Convention, gave orders to feed them. And feed them we did. The same thing we had eaten for breakfast ourselves—beans, biscuits, and prunes. Hardly the sort of meal you would expect an Oriental to scarf up. In fact, each of them, as they accepted their tin plate and spoon, sat there looking at it and one another as if to ask, "What is this stuff?" None of them would touch it. After a few minutes, the guards noticed that three of them finally tasted, and then began to put away the rations. As soon as they did, the rest of the prisoners dug in and it didn't take long before we had 37 empty plates. With full bellies they were a lot friendlier and cooperative. I remember one of them stood up and with a big smile pointed to his plate and began to rub his belly as though trying to tell us it was good chow. He even had the nerve to ask for seconds—of beans! US Navy strawberries!

At that point the captain leaned over the bridge windscreen and ordered the three Japs who had started eating first to be isolated because he figured they were all leaders of some sort. He was right. They were naval officers. One of them spoke pretty good English. You might even say American English. He asked that their men be protected from the terrible treatment they had been told to expect from the barbarous Yankees. He had figured out, I suppose, that they would not be kept aboard the *Trever* very long, and he wanted to take advantage of what was probably the best treatment they were going to get as prisoners of war. He was trying to speak with the skipper as one career professional to another. That seemed like a lot of gall, but you had to respect him for the attempt. He was looking out for the best interests of his people. Something that we had been told the Japanese would never do. The three enemy officers were taken down to the wardroom and given an opportunity to take a shower. After which they were supplied with clean clothing, and returned to their men, who seemed greatly relieved at their reappearance. In the early afternoon, the *Trever* linked up with the *Hovey* and steamed back to the transport area, where we tied up to the *McCawley* and prepared to transfer our prisoners. As the gangway was being rigged between our two ships, the survivors began to wail at the knowledge they were going aboard the transport. They were looking up at the rail of the *McCawley* where dozens of marines were gathered, watching them with steely eyes as they fingered their weapons. The leathernecks were a sad-looking bunch, having just been relieved from the land where they had been fighting continuously for two months, suffering heavy casualties. When they saw the Japs coming aboard they made their feelings very plain. To the Nips we had picked up, it must have seemed as though all the horror stories they had been told of American savagery were about to come true. Navy guards had to push the marines back to allow the Japs to climb aboard. Some of them stopped halfway up the swaying gangway, looking back at us as though begging to be allowed to remain aboard the *Trever*. But they were hustled up onto the McCawley's deck, and then to the ship's brig. Where they ultimately ended up, I have no idea.

The prisoner transfer completed, the *Trever* and *Hovey* joined the other escort ships, and when the transports came out of the harbor we took them back to Espiritu Santo, where we were then made available for other duties.

Flight Through Nggela Channel

With the Japanese still very much in control of the waters around the Solomon Islands, any Allied efforts to continue the fighting were being made with considerable stealth. Running the Slot[9] and then slipping into unknown island coves and harbors in the dead of night. For a long time the only ships that could get in and out unobserved were the old flush deckers, fleet tugs, and small patrol boats. Even we were experiencing difficulties, suffering damage and loss of life. But the marines ashore needed all the help they could get. Some of that help was in the shape of American patrol torpedo boats.[10] Not much more than super-powered and heavily armed motor launches, they were proving to be a real menace to the Japanese navy. The Nips referred to them as "those American devil boats that run on top of the water and shoot torpedoes in all directions!" So effective were torpedo boats that the overall commander of the South Pacific decided that more would be made operational, based in hidden

---

9. New Georgia Sound, the body of water that runs through the middle of the Solomon Islands. During WWII, the sound was known as "the Slot" by Allied combatants because of its geographical shape and the amount of warship traffic that traveled through it.
10. PT Boats were small, fast vessels used by the Navy in WWII to attack larger surface ships. The PT boat squadrons were nicknamed "the mosquito fleet."

coves and inlets under the enemy's very nose.

The *Trever* and *Zane* were selected to take four of the boats to the Solomons, along with as many supplies as could be carried. So with our decks loaded to capacity with torpedoes, ammunition, gasoline, and other miscellaneous necessities of war, we headed back to Guadalcanal. Each ship towed two of the important PT boats, each one carrying its own crew, so in the event of trouble they could be cut loose to operate on their own. The entire run was made without incident, however, and on October 25, in the wee hours of the morning, we arrived. The boats were cut loose to make their way in by themselves, as the two minesweepers slipped up to makeshift piers to offload cargo. By 0700, we were ready to leave and head for safer waters. But that was not to be. The commanding general of the island operation requested that we hang around long enough to bombard several shore installations prior to a flanking Marine landing. With considerable reluctance, the Old Man, as commander of our two-ship force, agreed.

So, with all hands nervously biting their fingernails, we stood by for further orders. Around 10:00 we were still waiting when we were informed that three Japanese destroyers were standing into Savo Sound, the area between Guadalcanal and Florida Islands; it was also known as Ironbottom Sound because of the many ships, both Allied and enemy, that had been sunk there during battle action. Three destroyers were more than we could handle, and Captain Agar very wisely decided that the bombardment duties were best forgotten, as we executed the classic maneuver known as "getting the hell outta here!" If we were lucky, we would slip out unobserved. With the *Trever* in lead, our two-ship force took a bone in our teeth and headed for Sealark Channel and the open sea. As we pointed our bows between the coral-studded shoals, we spotted the Jap tin cans. Worse, they spotted us. As reported, there were three of them. They were all new, much larger than we were, and fast—very, very fast. As if that weren't enough, the enemy was very heavily gunned. Together, they could put up a sixteen gun, five-inch broadside against our own combined effort of six three-inch cannons. The Japanese opened fire and their marksmanship left nothing to be desired. After just a few salvos, they had us bracketed. Agar gave orders to chase the salvo in an attempt to keep from being hit. We steered into the area splashed by the enemy's last shot, forcing him to correct each time he fired. But even with excellent ship handling by American captains, it was obvious we were lost. Nothing short of a miracle would save our butts. Reaching out for that miracle, Agar signaled the *Zane* to "follow me," and changed course to head directly into Nggela Channel, a pass that was even more coral-studded than our originally planned route. To worsen matters, Nggela Channel was not fully charted. It was a choice of running aground and being blown apart, or being sunk as we raced through Sealark. If we could make it through Nggela and on to the open sea, we would be able to get away, because the Japanese ships, being so much larger, would not be able to navigate the shallow waters. In the time it took them to work their way around the shoals, we would have a chance to run for it. To help us in our escape we called on the Marine air force at Henderson Field for air support. Everything depended upon our safe passage through Nggela.

The Nip cans continued to fire and both the *Trever* and

Zane responded. But the new course into Nggela changed our angle of fire so only our starboard gun, and the one on the afterdeckhouse, could bear. After a few rounds, the midship three-inch suffered a jammed breechblock, leaving only our after gun operating. But that single cannon did more than its designer ever intended it should. In nineteen minutes of action, the gun crew put out 211 rounds, firing everything that was on the gun deck and more—high explosives, star shells, everything—screaming all the while for more ammo from the ammo party below. Down in the magazines we were pulling ammunition as fast as we could. Those 85-pound boxes were light as feathers as they were passed to the main deck and then thrown up to the gun. Between boxes of three-inch, we were also trying to get rid of the depth charges that were stored in the same compartment. If we took a hit while they were in the magazine, the ship would simply cease to exist. The seaman down in the storage room was rolling the charges off the rack onto his knees, and then walking them to the chain hoist to be pulled up. Quite a feat, considering they weighed about 300 pounds each. Later, he said he didn't even notice the weight, although the repeated strain did considerable muscle damage, requiring him to go to a hospital ship.

Up on the gun deck, an officer's cook named Hambone almost lost the use of his right hand as he slammed the heavy shells into the breech. Our three-inch guns were automatic, with breeches that closed for firing as soon as the loader pushed each shell home. An experienced loader would use the heel of his hand to shove each shell in place. But if he was not quick enough, the block would ride up and slam into his hand and wrist. Hambone was experienced, but was tiring and he was taking punishment. Knowing he was injured, he called for relief, but he was so hyped up by the excitement of the moment, he would not leave his position to allow the number two man to take over. When the action was over, and the pharmacist mate was able to check him out, he discovered several broken bones in Hambone's wrist. He later was decorated for his conduct under fire.

Our #4 gun was firing so fast that the breech and barrel were too hot to touch. And we were getting hits on the enemy. The Japs were too heavily armored for us to do any damage to their hull, but where our shells were dropping onto their upper works, they were effective. One Nip destroyer broke out in flames to the cheers of every one of us on deck that could see anything at all. In the course of the battle our sister ship took a hit. One of the enemy five-inch shells hit the *Zane* right on her three-inch gun. As close as we could figure out later, it landed right in the gun layer's lap. Seven men were lost as the gun was knocked from its mount. Two of them were never found. The other five lay dead as the smoke cleared. In addition to being hit by Japanese gunfire, the *Zane* struck a coral reef as we charged through Nggela Channel. Not enough to stop her, but enough to damage one screw and require her to slow down or have her engines torn loose by the vibration.

On board the *Trever* we were having our own troubles. With both ships winding up higher speeds than either of them had made in many, many years, the boilers of the old *Trever* could not produce steam as fast as the engines were calling for it. Our throttles were wide open, and the pressure continued to drop. Drastic action was called for, and the chief water tender provided it. Completely disregarding his own safety, he climbed to the top of the boilers and wired down the safety valves. Had they lifted while he was up there, the escaping superheated steam would have boiled him like a lobster. But he got them tied down and let the pressure rise. The engines received the vital steam they needed. If the aging equipment could not take the strain, he figured "the hell with it!" Sunk by enemy gunfire or blown up by our own boilers. One way or the other, we die. But the chief's trick worked, and the *Trever* squeezed out a few more knots of speed.

With the additional speed, we began to pull away from the *Zane*, which was fighting for survival. Knowing that they could not keep up, the *Zane*'s captain blinked over a message. "I'm okay, man, go—go—go!" Agar hammered his fist on the windscreen, and with tears in his eyes sent back, "Understood. Good luck and Godspeed." It was not a matter of deserting our sister ship when she was in a jam. Our Navy had all too few ships at the time, and remaining to try and help the *Zane* would have resulted in both our ships being lost. A tough decision to make, but that's why they make a man a ship's captain.

Just when things looked their worst, three Wildcat fighters, responding to our call for help, came flashing into view to fight the Japanese ships. One Nip was dead in the water, burning furiously. The other two turned and headed back up the Slot, abandoning the fight. To this day I like to think that our two overmatched minesweeps were responsible. But we did signal a thank you to the marines, who waggled their wings and headed back to Henderson. Our two sweeps continued through Nggela Channel with the *Trever* far in the lead and the *Zane*, heavily damaged and dealing with her casualties, trying valiantly to keep up. Once in the open sea, with the Japanese threat behind us, we slowed enough for the *Zane* to get into company and together we headed for home.

The rest of the day and night dragged on slowly with both ships remaining at general quarters. The two skippers agreed that we would remain together until the next morning when our new orders required the *Trever* to make for Espiritu Santo at her best speed, while the *Zane*, to favor her damaged screw, would proceed as best she could until an escort could meet her and bring her in safely.

And Commit Their Bodies to the Deep

With the coming of the dawn, we made ready to carry out our separate orders. But first, there was something a damn sight more important to all of us. And we slowed even more so we might bury our five shipmates who had lost their lives in battle, and say a prayer for those we never found. We might have carried them back for internment ashore, but it was the unanimous decision of the *Zane*'s crew that they be buried where they had fallen, rather than on some stinking island that meant nothing to any of us. They had died in honor, and they would be put to rest in the traditional manner of sailors before them.

We came to attention on the *Trever*, and faced aft to where the battered and death-laden *Zane* was rolling in the sea swell. We uncovered and bowed our heads as her skipper read the service. Our talk between ships picked up his words and they were piped throughout our ship. The *Trever* herself seemed to be operating unusually quiet, as though she, too, was showing her respect for the dead. Sure, we knew that a lot of men had died in the war, and many more would before it was over. But these were our guys, and that made a big difference. There were a lot of tears coursing down grizzled and beardless cheeks alike as the final words were spoken.

"Unto Almighty God, we commend the souls of our brothers departed, and commit their bodies to the deep." Our two ships were close enough so those of us on deck could look back as we gave a final salute, and we could see the splash as the canvas-wrapped forms slid from beneath their country's colors and dropped to their final resting place. After the barely heard "Amen," there was only the steady, unceasing roll of the sea, with no indication of their having been given to the blue waters around us. Except for an official entry in the ships' logs, and the memories of us who knew them, there would be nothing to speak of their having lived. There are no markers or tombstones for sailors lost or buried at sea. For those who believed in the legends, there was the consolation of knowing that before long they would again be the happy-go-lucky guys we knew when they arrived and took up residence for eternity in Fiddler's Green, the seaman's happy hereafter. In an effort, I suppose, to break the heavy silence and despair that lay over all of us, one of our old chiefs was heard to mutter, "Look out mermaids, those horny bastards are on their way!"

After the burial ceremony the *Trever* bent on flank speed and headed for Espiritu Santo. The captain of the *Zane* very wisely decided to continue at a reduced speed and run on only one engine. The immediate danger had passed and he wanted to make it back with his ship in one piece, damaged though she might be. Before long we pulled away and she dropped from sight behind us.

The *Trever* made landfall on the 28th of October. Upon entering the harbor we were ordered alongside a tanker for refueling. When our bunkers were topped off, the *Trever* was sent to tie up to another tanker, and it became very obvious what was planned for our immediate future. As we pulled alongside, the fuel ship's derricks were already swinging a new load of fifty-gallon drums of aviation gas to be deck loaded and lashed down. In no time at all we had 175 drums in place and were preparing for a return trip to Guadalcanal. Morale took a nose dive. But Sherman[11] was right, "War is cruelty, war is hell." Besides, we all knew that the marines in the bush still needed help, and as always, the old four pipers would provide.

The next morning, as we were preparing to get underway, we were startled to hear ships' whistles sounding all across the harbor. It didn't take long to discover it was because the *Zane* was standing in. Still running on one engine, she nevertheless had a bone in her teeth, and damned if her battle colors were not still flying. Her own whistle sounded shrilly as she let one and all know she was back. Captain Agar, concerned as ever with the safety of his fellow captain and friend, blinked over a message as soon as the *Zane* was in signaling distance. "Good to see you; how you doing?" The reply was quick, with the attitude we expected: "Pretty good for a one-legged gent." The signal referred, of course, to the fact that the old DMS had come in on one engine. The message continued: "See you ashore. You can buy the first round!"

---

11. In April 1880, Union general William Tecumseh Sherman addressed a crowd of more than 10,000 in Columbus, Ohio, where he said, "There is many a boy here today who looks on war as all glory, but, boys, it is all hell." Earlier in 1864, he had written in a letter to the city council of Atlanta, "War is cruelty, and you cannot refine it; and those who brought war into our country deserve all the curses and maledictions a people can pour out."

Cradle Cruise

Everything was okay again. The ancient flush deck cans had pulled off another successful mission, albeit not without paying a price. The Navy must have thought we had done pretty good. Captain Agar was eventually presented with the Navy Cross for his conduct and courage. The chief water tender was given a Silver Star. Hambone and the seaman who manhandled the heavy depth charges in the magazine, because of their conduct under fire and having been injured, received the Bronze Star and Purple Heart. There were a number of individual commendations, and Captain Agar, always one to give credit to his crew, had the following entered in every man's service record:

"You have materially contributed to the successful conclusion of a difficult and dangerous mission; retirement from which was made in the face of and against vastly superior enemy gunfire. During this retirement, this ship and another like her, despite tremendous differences in armament, gave as good as received.

"In accepting the Navy Cross this date for the *Trever*'s action in the Solomons on 25 October, 1942, the Commanding Officer fully appreciates the very great share every officer and man on board played in its earning."

D. M. Agar
Commander,
US Navy

Pago Pago is Real

A few years before the war, there was a popular movie titled *South of Pago Pago*. Starring Jon Hall and Frances Farmer, it told the story of love and adventure in a South Sea island paradise. Waving palm trees, rolling surf, and soft guitar music provided a background for beautiful dusky maidens and handsome native boys as they frolicked in the ocean, rode the waterfalls, and made love beneath a big silvery moon. In 1942, I discovered such a place really existed. It was on an island named Tutuila, in the Samoan chain.

After our near-fatal adventure in the Solomons, the *Trever* was assigned to a variety of escort and patrol duties, during which we made a trip to Samoa. When we sailed into the harbor it was with considerable surprise. Pago Pago—that was really its name!—was so very different from any base or island we had seen up to that point in time.

The island even *looked* different. It was much greener, with the water of the approaches turning color as we drew closer. The deep blue-black of the open sea gradually turned to a translucent green. The breakers along the beaches were pure white as they crashed against the rocks to fly high into the air as sparkling foam before falling back into the heavy ground swell. The sands of the beaches glistened white in the sun, and the waters of the harbor were crystal clear.

You could see thousands of fish of every conceivable variety swimming below. There was no evidence of any garbage or trash floating on the surface. To me, the most noticeable thing was the absence of the usual smell of rotting vegetation we had come to associate with every other island port. Instead, there was the heavy fragrance of flowers.

The *Trever* had no sooner dropped her hook when we were besieged by gunboats from ashore filled with local natives anxious to sell or trade their handicrafts and fresh fruit for whatever they might get in return. They would ask only a dollar or two for the most elaborate carving or piece of handmade jewelry. One enterprising old man was ready to strike a deal for his boat, all of his handicrafts, and even the services of a sociable old wife for a couple of mattress covers and a half dozen skivvie shirts. These kinds of items seemed to have more value to them than cash. The exec put a quick stop to all the dickering, even though the crewmen involved offered him a share of the potential profits.

The *Trever* wasn't there very long before we could see why the harbor was so beautifully clean. No trash or garbage was discarded into the water, but was dumped instead into special boats called honey barges, which would take the offal far out to sea for disposal. When we fueled ship, extra care was taken not to allow any oil spillage. Even recreational parties on the beaches included time to clean up any mess created.

An interesting thing about Pago Pago was something called the "Rainmaker." The Samoan Islands, being of volcanic origin, had their mountains. The largest of which, according to legend, was the home of one of the chief gods, known as the Rainmaker. Even the natives who had become

Christians still clung to many of their old beliefs, one of which was the idea that when the god was angry with what he might see below, he would show his anger in the form of clouds that hid the tallest mountaintop, allowing him to shut out the world. When this happened, it was sure to rain. The rain was his tears of anger and sorrow for his people. A fascinating story the way they told it. Of course, any modern meteorologist would tell you that when the clouds were that low, it would probably rain. Maybe so, but the Samoan version was much more romantic.

In talking to a grizzled old member of the community, I found out that since the war had begun and all the foreign ships were in the harbor, the mountain was more often wreathed in clouds than in the past. It made one wonder if what he saw taking place on his island was reason enough for the Rainmaker to weep.

The ships in the harbor had no need to run their own boats for supplies or working parties. Navy authorities ashore provided the services of what was called the Fita Fita Guard. Native Samoans had been accepted into official US Navy service many years earlier, and they ran a boat operation using 50-foot motor launches. These South Sea native sailors were dressed in their own uniform consisting of a colorful lava-lava—a kind of wraparound sarong—sparkling white tee shirts, and white Navy hats. They were all excellent boat handlers, as good as or better than most Navy crews.

Knowing their own island and harbor made it a lot easier for them to serve the ships in port, and saved us time. They were also extremely knowledgeable concerning official procedure and traditional boat courtesies and protocol. The people of Samoa were the most friendly I have ever known, and the most beautiful. Even the old folks were handsome and personable. The women were unbelievable. It was about the only place I know of where the Navy had set up a base where the girls were still the way we used to see them in back issues of the *National Geographic* magazine—sarongs and bare bosoms. Unbelievable. But it was a matter of "look, but don't touch," so said a direct order of our beloved captain. That was kind of a wasted effort, however, because the local belles were friendly and, determined to please, they were hard to ignore.

The "don't touch" ruling was actually official policy. For many years the good missionaries had been trying to erect a protective wall between the women and the dregs of civilization as represented by American sailors. (Sailors? Hah! Wait until the marines arrived.) For a long time the churchies had been working diligently to get the young ladies to cover up. We were told that at one time they had all been given bras, with instructions to wear them at all times. Well, they were worn all right. Around the waist where they made dandy pockets! No way was the gentler sex going to restrict their natural movements. And I think it was a wise decision on their part. As you might imagine, the "look but don't touch" order was frustrating, and there was always some guy trying to work his way around it.

One such sailor was our own Queer John Brown. The bos'n mate with the unquenchable appetite for wine, women, and sometimes even song. According to Q. J., he met some little island cutie and propositioned her almost immediately. She was agreeable to his advances, but insisted they go someplace "where nobody see." Brown was so primed by that time he was ready to follow her anywhere. She took him by the hand and led him into the bush, and to a small hut hidden by the jungle undergrowth. Inside he discovered some sort of shrine with an idol at the far end. The girl, it turned out, was not a Christian. Consequently, she was freer with her favors. She busied herself in the shadows for a moment, according to Q. J., and then, slipping from behind the figure of the idol, she slapped blobs of mud over its eyes. Her idea, apparently, was to blind him so he could not watch what was about to take place. Just who seduced who after that was never very clear—or if Brown's story was even true. But it made for great bull sessions when the *Trever* was out at sea.

There were a few other such incidents. Not all of the people took offense, although they probably thought less of us because of our poor conduct. Sometimes they would give as good as they received, and cut us down in a hurry. One such cut down took place on our final day of that first visit to Tutuila. We were sadly preparing to get underway, the gunboats waved their farewells, and we called out our own good-byes to those people we had come to know as friends. One of them was a little girl about thirteen years of age named Julie. Although young by our standards, she was a grown woman by theirs. Julie had been out almost every day to sell her fresh fruit, and we all treated her as we might a younger sister. But she could look out for herself, as we all learned that day. She was wise beyond her tender years. Wise in a way we could only imagine.

As the boats drifted away, we called out our final farewells, promising to see her next time we came to Pago Pago. It was really a nice moment for all of us. But then, a foulmouthed chief had to show what a complete ass he was. The girl had been particularly enthusiastic in her waving and calling to us, and the chief responded, "Good-bye, Julie. Next time we come, you and me make foo foo." Well, that did it! Her happy smile vanished to be replaced by a vicious snarl and a look of complete disgust. She shook her fist at the chief and screamed, "Shit on you, summa bitch!" And then, as if to redeem herself in the eyes of her friends, she added, "Not all you nice boys." Leveling a finger at ol' foul mouth she yelled, "Just him!" With that she turned, bent over, and, hiking up her skirt, she wiggled her bare bottom as she thrust it in the chief's direction.

And that is my last memory of Pago Pago, the Pearl of the Pacific. The sun shining down on that little brown heinie as Julie mooned the chief. Not all us nice boys. Just him!

Navy Strawberries for Thanksgiving

It was in November of 1942, while still assigned to miscellaneous duties, that the *Trever* drew the now famous "Turkey Dinner Run" to Guadalcanal. The outcome of the Solomon Island campaign was still very much in doubt, and the Allied Forces at sea and ashore were meeting with strong enemy resistance. American morale was not as high as it might have been, and the area commanders decided one way to give it a boost was to provide a real old-fashioned holiday dinner for Thanksgiving. To make this a reality became the responsibility of old DMS-16. Two large refrigerated fishing boats were found and loaded to the gunwales with turkeys, yams, pies, candy, and all the rest. Then, with the *Trever* as escort, the "Turkey Dinner Run" headed northwest. Not to make the trip empty-handed, our own deck was loaded with ammunition, gasoline, and anything else we could get aboard that the mud marines might use. Fortunately, we had smooth sailing all the way, and we managed to slip into the harbor unobserved by the Japanese, making our landfall at night.

As we were tied up to the dock, off-loading to the very happy leathernecks and Army troopers, two PT boats came gliding silently through the water to tie up on our outboard side. They wanted to make sure they received their share of the holiday goodies, as well as immediate delivery of the ammo and gas. There was really no time to start dividing up the foodstuff and supplies we had brought in, so we did the next best thing. We opened up our own ship's refrigerator and food lockers, as well as our equipment stores. Almost everything we had, particularly in the line of food, went over to the shore party and the PTs. We figured we were going back and those guys were staying in the middle of a bloody mess. When we finally got underway for our trip back to Nouméa, the fishing boats were not the only ones riding light in the water. We found out just how light we were the next day, which was Thanksgiving.

It seemed that when the word had been passed to hand over everything to the PT boats and the troops, we did just that. We passed over everything! So when it was time for our cooks to prepare our own holiday dinner, all they had to work with was beans! Good old Navy strawberries, gussied up as usual with prunes and biscuits. Still, it was a pretty good day. We had done our best for the guys in the thick of the war, and we knew we could restock our own lockers when we dropped the anchor in New Caledonia.

Meanwhile, there was a lot to be thankful for. Three times the *Trever* had directly closed with the enemy, went into harm's way on several other occasions, and each time the old four piper had come through for us. It was pretty well accepted that the DMS-16 was a lucky ship. A common cry was "stick with the Tremblin' T and live!" Guys who had been trying to wrangle a transfer began to have second thoughts about leaving. Those who had been shipped to other assignments left with some apprehension.

Anyway, we ate our beans, prunes, and biscuits, and each of us in our own way gave thanks for our holding good fortune. When we did drop the hook in Nouméa Harbor and requested a resupply, the tender ship couldn't understand what we had done with all the stores we had taken aboard just a week or so earlier. Their supply officer said, "I never saw a ship where the crew ate so much." When he was clued in to where our supplies had gone, he became very understanding. We not only received everything on our requisition, but several five-gallon cans of ice cream and two big containers of mixed nuts, which he said had been part of his own wardroom supplies, but somehow had been "misplaced." As our working party took the last crate and can into our boat, he leaned over and handed our chief cook a couple boxes of cigars. Our Thanksgiving dinner was late that year, but we enjoyed it nevertheless. But as good as it was, it lacked something we had found in those Navy strawberries over which we had bowed our heads a few days earlier.

A Cat Called Gladys

Cats have been going to sea ever since they were discovered and domesticated by man, and a mutually beneficial association had developed. Cats were adopted not only as pets, but as a way to control the ever-present rat and mouse population aboard ship. Dogs, on the other hand, despite their reputation as man's best friend, have never really been accepted as part of a seagoing ship's company. We had a dog aboard the *Trever* for a while, but he was more trouble than he was worth. There is no place on a ship where you can take a dog for a walk. No fireplugs to pique his interest. And the mutt we had was forever falling overboard. The captain did not take too well to the strident call of "dog overboard!" In the end we had to get rid of him. The bos'n took him ashore in Tulagi and gave him to the natives. I think they ate him.

Once the dog was gone, it was only a matter of time before we had another pet to share our close quarters. One day Machinist Mate Red Haines came back from a beach party with a scrawny tabby kitten under his shirt. He made sure everybody on board knew she was his cat. He even named her Gladys, after his mother-in-law. But she had her own ideas about who she belonged to, and adopted the entire crew.

Gladys took to navy life with no trouble at all. We set up

a litter box behind one of the smokestacks, and she slept pretty much where she pleased. With the exception of the engineering spaces, she prowled the entire ship. Playing no favorites, she could be found anywhere from the officer's wardroom to the enlisted crew spaces. She was a true *Trever* sailor, and as such was logged into the records with the rank of WAVE Apprentice Seaman, expected to comply with US Navy Rules and Regulations like the rest of us.

That cat was so little trouble we didn't even put out a water dish for her. When she was thirsty, she would leap to the top of the scuttlebutt and meow until someone came along and pressed the handle for her. When she had her fill, she would meow once more and jump down. She always said "thanks."

When she was hungry, she would go into the shipfitters' shack and jump up on the workbench. There was a porthole at one end that led into the galley. Gladys would poke her head through the open port and politely ask for a handout. The duty cooks would always oblige. Apprentice Seaman Gladys sometimes ate better than we did.

But like pussycats everywhere, she grew up and reached the age where she began having biological urges. When that happened, it led to a tough time for all hands. She took to yowling in the middle of the night, and it didn't matter where she was. Then one night she went too far. Actually, it was about two in the morning. Gladys had been wandering around the bridge when suddenly she began screaming like a banshee. The officer of the deck, thinking that it was unfair for him and the bridge crew to put up with the caterwauling all by themselves, decided to share the misery with the rest of the crew. Pushing her over beneath the voice box for the ship's speaker system, he flipped the switch.

Her shrieks reverberated throughout the ship. Every compartment and work space. It scared hell out of all hands. You can imagine what it had to be like to be suddenly awakened by the sexually frustrated feline—especially when the squawk box might be right over your bunk. But that wasn't the worst of it. When the OOD decided to share Gladys's frustrations with the rest of us, he forgot there was a speaker in the captain's cabin. Right over his head! The Old Man went steaming up the bridge in his skivvies with his .45 in hand. If he could have found that cat, there would have been a burial at sea next morning. But as I said, Gladys was smart and beat a hasty retreat. In the morning we received an ultimatum. We did something with her, or she had to go.

As luck would have it, just about that time we received orders to proceed to Sydney for repairs and R & R for the crew. Red pleaded with the skipper to give us a chance to remedy our cat problem, promising to do so when we reached Australia. Our WAVE got a temporary reprieve. Over the next few days Gladys got a lot of cold showers.

We arrived in Australia about a week or so later, and when we tied up to the dock we saw the answer to our problem, and Gladys's fondest dream. There, stalking his way down the dock, came the biggest, ugliest, most decrepit-looking, battle-scarred yellow tomcat in the world. He came and sat down at the bottom of our gangway, as though waiting for her ladyship to appear. It was almost as though we had sent a communiqué announcing her arrival. It didn't take long for our girl to realize he was out there. She flew down the main deck like a flash, leaping over the seaman lashing down the gangway, and raced down the plank out onto the dock.

She almost knocked down the old tom in her rush. She ran down the walkway about twenty yards or so and stopped dead. Sitting there with her back to the surprised tomcat, she looked over her shoulder and let out a low, earthy and teasing "grrrrrowl!" She batted her eyes a few times and smiled. For weeks Gladys had been driving the entire crew crazy with her frustrations, and when she finally had a chance to do something about them she gets coy!

Well, Old Yellow wasn't having any of that foolishness. He dashed over and kicked hell out of her. Then, biting her in the back of the neck, he proceeded to do as they say in those romance novels—he had his way with her, to the cheers of the *Trever* crew lining the rail. When it was all over, the duty quartermaster entered the action in the ship's log. I still have to chuckle when I think of it. The log eventually would find its way to the US Navy Bureau of Ship's Archives. Somewhere in the dark corridors of official US Navy history storage rooms, there is a carefully detailed record of how one WAVE Apprentice Seaman Gladys, Ship's Cat, lost her virginity.

Woolloomooloo and the *Trever* Too

It was late in January of 1943 that, along with the *Zane,* we were ordered to Sydney for some much-needed repairs, as well as rest and recreation for the ship's company. Arriving on the 27th, we stood into the harbor with a lot of sudden activity on our signal bridge. Lights were flashing like crazy as messages were exchanged with the signal tower ashore. Those of us on deck began to wonder what all the traffic meant. Was our time alongside the repair ship to be canceled? The situation became clear in a matter of minutes. The shoreside signal operators were all women! They were members of the Royal Australian Women's Auxiliary, similar to our own US Navy WAVES. The same action was taking place on the *Zane.* By the time we were tied up, the entire bridge gang of both ships, including our OOD, had dates for that evening. Talk about friendly international relations!

The *Trever* was ordered to berth at the fueling docks first thing. It was there that Gladys had her amorous adventure. After taking on fuel, we proceeded to go alongside the USS *Dobbin.* A sister ship to the *Whitney,* she had been sent to Sydney as a permanent repair facility for American vessels. The Australians were on a metric system, and their dock workers were all union, so they were unable to handle our necessary work as quickly as needed. To the *Dobbin*'s crew, it was like having shore duty in Australia for the duration. As far as they were concerned, Sydney was *their* town. I suppose it was, until the *Trever* and *Zane* arrived.

Our quartermaster had a bit of trouble getting our arrival properly logged until he received some basic information from shore authorities. For instance, we had tied up to the *Dobbin* at the Cockatoo Island Navy Yard, located in a park known as Woolloomooloo. He couldn't even say it, let alone spell it correctly. And talking to the Aussie officials was not much help. They spoke English, of course, but a kind of English we had never heard. In spite of their accent, the Australians were great. They couldn't do enough to help us once the language barrier was overcome.

If we had any difficulties at all, it was getting service from the *Dobbin*. You see, they considered us a threat to their domination of the city as a liberty town. Any requisitions or work orders submitted could be expected to be buried in a morass of bookkeeping and red tape unless our skipper or exec made a direct request to the tender's first lieutenant or executive officer. It was cumshaw work, those extra little unofficial jobs that are part of every overhaul or repair period, that had to be worked out between the chiefs of the three ships. One way or another, however, we did manage to get everything necessary accomplished, even if we had to do it ourselves.

Aside from the expected US Navy wheeling and dealing, our stay in Sydney was fantastic. The people there were the nicest I have met anywhere. One of the things we heard most often was, "God Bless you, Yanks!" We found out why they had such a friendly attitude before the first day was over. When the war broke out, England withdrew whatever forces she had in the area and pretty much left Australia to shift for herself. New Guinea, which was then held by the Japanese, was just a stone's throw from the Australian mainland, and they were afraid of a Jap invasion. With most of their own military tied up in Africa along with the Brits, they felt pretty helpless. So when the US came along to set up a few bases, we were received like saviors, which in reality we were. There was no love lost between the Aussies and the English. But we Yanks could do no wrong. Generally, we found the city to be much like our own home towns might have been some fifty years earlier. The cars, the trams, fashions, stores, and everything else were like something we had seen in our history and geography books.

The money was based on the English system, with about £3.20 to the dollar. American dollars were equal to six shillings and a penny. Considering the prices in town, we could actually go ashore and have a pretty good liberty for a single pound. And that was important as time went by and we found ourselves with less cash on hand. Before we left, we were buying cigarettes in our ship's store, smuggling them ashore, and selling them to a cab driver for a pound. He in turn would peddle them on the black market. But the pound we received paid for an evening's fun and games.

Australian money was kind of tricky at first, but it only took a few days to get accustomed to thinking in terms of pounds, crowns, and half crowns, as well as the shillings, pence and ha'pennies. The pennies were a real nuisance. Bigger than our silver dollars, they were a real pain to carry in our practically non-existent pockets. We would try and get rid of them as fast as we might pick them up in change. There were a lot of tips given in pennies. Also, they were used for telephone calls, and as fare on city trams. The shoeshine boys in the park received a lot of them in payment for their work. We would simply pay for a shine with a handful.

Once in town, transportation was no problem. Besides the trams, there were a lot of taxi cabs. With gasoline in such a short supply, most of them ran on charcoal gas fed from a big burner hung on the rear end. Smelly and smoky, they would get you to your destination, although the smell of burning charcoal would permeate your uniform. But nobody seemed to mind; it was all accepted as part of the hardships of war.

Merchants, cab drivers, tram operators—just about everybody in town would accept our American money, so there was no need for any exchange when going ashore. Between the rate of exchange and the Yank inclination to tip heavy when in doubt, the advantage was with the native. Still, I don't think there was any deliberate attempt to rip us off, especially when we had a sheila with us to look out for our best interests. Or perhaps their own! In any case, after a day or two there were no problems.

There were lots of fun places to go in Sydney. Pubs were plentiful, although it took some getting used to their beer. Stronger than what we were all accustomed to, it was served warm. A lot of the local boys drank it with a large dash of lemon squash added. Squash was a kind of unsweetened lemonade. All in all, it wasn't bad, but it didn't taste like any beer I'd ever had. Their ale was much better. If you wanted any icy cold brew you had to find one of the more expensive establishments that might have icebox facilities. Hard liquor was usually available only in places similar to American speakeasies of the 1920s.

A very popular place to meet girls and have fun was Luna Park. It was very similar to most American amusement parks, like Riverview in Chicago. Always packed with servicemen, it operated long after all the other places in town were locked up for the night. The engineer of the Ferris wheel could always be persuaded to have a mechanical breakdown when you and your date were at the very top. And a good way to get rid of annoying kid siblings was to pass them the admission to a ride on the carousel. It was another place to get rid of those big copper pennies.

A lot of the Americans ended up at the beach in Bondi. Not that anybody was interested in swimming, but it was big, secluded, and sand was a lot easier to get out of our blues than grass or mud stains from Woolloomooloo.

Restaurants were few in number, and not always easy to find open. When you did go for dinner, the menu was very limited. There was a lot of mutton, which I swear was really goat. Beef was plentiful and one of the most called-for meals was steak and eggs. Tea was served all the time. We learned to drink it with a big dollop of milk. Sugar was available, but only if you asked for it. The coffee, half chicory and pretty terrible, was served black with lemon. You could get used to it, but to get a real honest-to-goodness cup of coffee you had to go to the American Center, a kind of USO that catered to Americans. Hamburgers were unheard of other than at the center. What you might get instead was something called a dim sum. Comparable to a stuffed cabbage roll, they were good but no substitute for an American Wimpy with onions.

The most popular of local food offerings was fish and

chips. What you received for a shilling was a mess of shrimp or pieces of whitefish and thin slices of potato—all deep fried. There were no paper bags, and your order was handed to you in a cone or "toot" rolled from the daily paper. After a while, the vendors became Americanized to the point where a kind of ketchup became available for dipping.

The most memorable thing about Sydney, at least to me, was the police. Like the British police, they were called bobbies, named after Sir Robert Peel of Scotland Yard, who organized the first British police force. All about six feet tall or better, they wore high metal helmets and were unarmed except for a nightstick. Called truncheons, they were weapon enough. I once saw an Aussie copper take out after an American seaman who had tried to steal his helmet for a souvenir. The kid got about forty feet away when the bobbie threw his stick and clipped him right behind the ear. The sailor dropped like a poleaxed steer.

Picking him up, the officer apologized for the roughness and called the wagon. I doubt he took the kid to the station. Americans were seldom arrested for anything. It was much more common that they be given a stern warning and a lecture. The Aussies were very big on lectures. If a house party was raided by the police, the girls were taken in, but the Yanks almost never. I guess they were considering that for the most part we were all kids away from home for the first time in our lives and trying to act like men. Any Americans who did cause problems were more likely to receive rough handling from our own shore patrol or the military police.

The girls down under were beautiful and friendly. Aside from their penchant for drinking a combination of scotch and milk, they were very much like the girls we knew back home—the typical girl next door. With most of their own menfolk in the military, fighting and dying in Africa and the Pacific, they were very lonely. But contrary to what has often been written about them, they were not loose. We were surprised how often we were asked to visit their homes and meet the family before dating. Most of the Australian women, including the mothers, were flat-out starved for masculine attention. Even just to talk. At one home I visited the mother said, "It's so nice just to have a man in the house that I can talk to, and to whom I can serve tea." She hadn't seen her husband in over three years. I think a lot of our reception by the ladies had to do with the way we treated them. The way we were taught by our own mothers and grandmothers to be polite to the ladies. Hold the door for them. Hold out their chair at the dinner table. Hold their arm when you cross the street. That sort of thing. And, of course, "yes ma'am," and "no ma'am." I can't deny that along with our general good manners, there was our good pay rate, compared with what the average Aussie received. The few that were back home on a convalescence leave, or maybe home station duty, were receiving about a pound a month. Compare that to even the lowest pay of an American seaman second class, who drew about $36 a month. And most of us could do better than that. It's no wonder that one of them is reported to have said that the trouble with Americans is "they are overpaid, oversexed, and over here!" Still, once we got to know the Australian serviceman, he was a pretty good guy. More often as not, we became cobbers, or close friends.

That was Australia. Land of Waltzing Matilda, koala bears, and boomerangs. Sydney was unquestionably the best liberty port most of us would ever see during our time in the Navy. The *Trever* and *Zane* put an indelible mark on the city that can probably still be found today if you look around a bit. How that came to be is yet another story. On our very first night ashore...

And a Good Time Was Had By All

I lucked out that first night in Sydney. My name was on the liberty list. Not wanting to waste a minute, I was in my dress blues and ready to go as soon as liberty call sounded. "Who's going ashore, who's going ashore? Who's got the price of a two-bit..." Well, buddy, I was, because I did! As soon as the word was passed, we raced down the gangway. Anxious to show just what real American bluejackets we were, our immediate goal was the first pub outside the Cockatoo Island Navy Yard gate. It was pretty much like any American saloon might have been back at the turn of the century. One long bar, with a brass rail and sawdust on the floor. There at the bar stood the biggest Aussie sailor I had ever seen. He looked like a friendly enough guy, so bellying up to the bar next to him I gave what to me was the best possible greeting: "How ya doin', Limey?" He hit me—laid one on me that stretched me out in the sawdust. Then he glowered down to where I lay sprawled and shouted, "Get up!" Well, my grandma didn't raise no dummy. There was no way I was going to get up without knowing why he knocked me down in the first place.

The bartender leaned over the bar top and with a look of resignation, as though he had gone through it before, explained it all to me. You never, *ever* call an Australian a

Limey. Limeys are British, and considering how the locals felt about the Brits, what I had done was offer the ultimate insult. So, still on the floor and looking up at what appeared to be nine feet of very upset jack tar, I apologized, explaining to him that we had not been forewarned of the consequences of such a faux pas.

Once the formalities of apology were over, he reached down with a ham-like paw and picked me up. Brushing me off, he bought me a drink. Then I bought him one. And because I had more money than he did, I bought another round. That was the beginning of a memorable evening. At least I was told it was memorable. I don't remember much. The only thing I can be sure of was waking up in my sack some time later with a hell of a hangover. From what my shipmates told me, that big Aussie walked up our gangway late that night with me cradled in his arms. He said to the OOD, "Beggin' your pardon, sor, but me little cobber here has had a bit too much beer, and he's kind of stinko. No trouble, you understand, sor, but I just thought 'twould be best if he came back to his ship." The gangway watch logged me in as having returned to the ship and the oversized Aussie went his unsteady way. I never saw him again, although I've often wished I had. That was my first night in Sydney. I'd gotten drunk, been punched out by an ally, and became a cobber, whatever that was. It was some time later that the real meaning of the word became known, and it was not one to be used lightly.

The next night was scheduled to be a duty night for me, but by some careful bargaining and the exchange of a few dollars, I was able to get ashore again. That second night I was determined to get further than the first pub. In fact, along with a couple other guys, I headed for Luna Park. We got there by way of one of the charcoal gas-powered taxicabs, and were no sooner in the park gate when we spotted our quarry. A group of girls, among which was the prettiest hazel-eyed blonde I had ever seen. She had to be around my own age and her smile was devastating. We gave them our best pitch. In my case it was the kind of thing Grandma had always taught me: "Be polite, smile a lot, say nice things about the girl's appearance. It's the only way to meet nice girls." I had to use that approach because I didn't know anything else. At my age I'd had no real experience with girls, at least none that I remembered. So you can imagine my surprise when it worked! Her name was Gloria. Gloria Reed. We hit it off pretty well and before long broke away from the others and had a real ball. Ginger beer and biscuits; Ferris wheel and carousel. The evening passed all too quickly. She agreed to a date the following night, but only if I would call for her at her home and meet her family. It was just what I was looking for—a steady date for our time in Sydney, and a chance to brag to the other guys who weren't so lucky. Before heading back to the ship, I got her address and directions how to get there. Then playing the big operator, I put her in a cab for home and I made my way back to the *Trever*.

The next day was spent working, and lying to my buddies. When liberty call sounded, there was Lonnie at the gangway with pass in hand, ready to go. All I needed to do was remember how to get to the pretty girl's house. But I remembered all right. In fact, even now, more than fifty years later, I still do. Why that sticks in my mind so clearly after all this time I really don't know. Maybe old Doc Freud could explain it. But I found my way into town and to Wynyard Station, catching a tram to the suburbs. When I finally knocked on her door, it was opened by her mother. She invited me in, and the family gathered around to meet Gloria's Yank. They were friendly as anyone could want. "Mum" immediately went about serving tea, and with the china cup and saucer balanced on my knee, nibbling on a biscuit, I was formally introduced to everyone. She had an older sister Victoria, and a younger one, Thelma, who was about twelve and had a bad case of the giggles. Her father was in the Army, fighting somewhere in Africa. We carried on a polite conversation concerning what it was like in America, and then what Mum expected from anyone taking her girl out for the evening. Especially how important it was that Glory got home early because she had to get up for work in the morning. Having successfully survived her mum's interrogation and advice, I took Gloria by the arm and off we went. A big night for her, it turned out—dinner at a nice restaurant, the flicks, and a long walk out at Bondi Beach, where I behaved myself. Getting back to her house later, we found Victoria and Thelma had waited up. As we stood on the porch and I kissed Gloria good night, it was with one eye open, looking over her shoulder where I could see Mum peeking out from behind the curtains.

We went together all the time my ship was in Sydney, and got along great. After a few days, nobody waited up for us, which showed, I suppose, that her mother trusted me. A lot of evenings I would arrive early, which gave Mum and me a chance to talk. There was a feeling of family I'd never known much of before.

Some nights Gloria would have to work late, and that didn't allow time for a date. On those nights it was a matter of going out with the boys to see what was happening in town. I learned to like Australian beer, dim sums, milk in my tea, and even steak and kidney pie. Also included in my education was the fact that Aussie police were nice guys, but not to be trifled with; that bartenders would cheat a sailor if they had the chance, but cabdrivers generally would not. If you became falling-down drunk, a civilian could be trusted if they offered to take you home until you felt better, after which they would help you back to your ship. Another important lesson we learned was not to mix the rides at Luna Park with Australian beer and ale.

One ride in particular was great fun if you were sober, but a killer if you were not. It was nothing but a gigantic playground-type slide called the Slippery Dip. All the girls thought it was wild. About a hundred feet long, it had several rises and dips like a roller coaster. You sat on a well-used leather pad at the top, hanging onto handles at the sides, and you pushed off. The first drop was almost straight down, and if you didn't lean back you could make the trip on your head. One of our engine room machinists found that out the hard way. His name was Goshie, and he was older than most of us, so we thought he would know better. But he was pretty much "in his cups" by the time we got to the park, and feeling no pain as he approached the Dip. He sat down on the leather pad, but hung onto his white hat rather than the handles. When we pushed him off, he leaned forward and, falling, he rolled and slid the entire distance. Up and over the dips he went on his head and shoulders with his fat butt up in the air. He slammed into the padded wall at the far end and climbed out unsteadily to his feet. Still holding onto his hat, he yelled, "EEEeeeoowwWWW! What a ride!" We all thought he was so good we wanted him to do it again.

But no dice. Old Goshie liked it well enough, but not enough for a repeat performance. So we had to content ourselves with watching the girls in our party. Screaming, skirts flying, bloomers flashing, they were a joy to behold. One of them, a real honest to goodness English cockney lass more than a bit mellow from drinking scotch and milk, screamed all the way down. "Now don't you Yanks go peekin' at me knickers. EEEeeeoowwWWW!" Peek at her knickers? Watching her go down the Dip, I don't think she was wearing any.

Our time in Sydney ended with a ship's party at the classiest place in town. We wanted to make it a real bash, so a committee went to negotiate with the manager of the King's Cross, which was the closest thing they had to a nightclub. We ended up renting the entire building, all three floors of it. There was a ballroom, two dining rooms, and the otherwise disused private rooms upstairs. A little American cash carefully spread around enabled the manager to get all the food and liquor we could handle, as well as a band guaranteed to play American music. Festivities began around seven in the evening and lasted as long as anyone could stand. Shore patrol, military, and city police came in to persuade us to be a little more restrained, and ended up joining the party. It was quite a thing to see a dignified Australian bobby with a beer in one hand as he called in to report everything under control.

I took Gloria to the party, but we didn't stay long. Her mother knew about those kinds of shindigs, and made me promise not to let her get drunk or do anything she shouldn't. But even then, I do think Glory saw a side of the Americans she didn't know existed. We had been there a while when she asked me what was going on upstairs. That seemed a good time to leave. After I dropped her off at home about midnight, I went back. The party was a smashing success. Even our skipper remembered enough of it to agree to that. In fact, it was so successful, the *Trever* was politely asked by the city authorities not to come back to Sydney again. Just how true that report was I don't know. We could never get the captain to confirm or deny.

When our time finally came to leave, it was with considerable reluctance on our part. So many good friendships had been made that some of our people planned to go back after the war. The crew of the *Dobbin* could not wait for us to throw off the lines and get underway. Maybe they figured they would get their liberty town back. But Sydney would remember the *Trever* and the *Zane* for a long, long time.

In spite of our sailing orders supposedly being secret, the entire town seemed to know we were leaving. The dock was crowded with people young and old waving good-bye as we drifted out into the harbor. There was more than one long face on our deck as we waved back. On our signal bridge the duty signalmen made a last exchange message with the girls in the tower ashore. On the *Dobbin* there were a lot of crewmen lining the rail and cheering, but also giving us that old American gesture known as "the finger." As we stood out of the harbor with a bone in our teeth, we were still looking wistfully back at one of the greatest places we had known. The captain put an end to it, bringing us back to reality as he passed the word. "Okay, people. Let's get back to the war."

Yeah, the war. For a few weeks or so we had forgotten all about it.

New Zealand Stopover

After we left Sydney, the *Trever* and *Zane* made a short stopover in New Zealand. A few days in both Auckland and Wellington gave us an opportunity for a last liberty or two before sailing once again into the war zone. New Zealand was like Australia in many ways, although the people, while friendly, did not show the camaraderie we found so common in Sydney. Most agreed that of the two cities, Wellington was by far the better liberty town. For one thing, the main street began at the docks, meandered all over town, and ended up back where it started. You could go on liberty, get absolutely snockered, and if you could find your way to the main drag and manage to crawl on your hands and knees, it was possible to head in either direction and get back to your ship. That was very convenient for guys like Q. J. Brown or Jack Ryan.

Neither of the cities could boast of any really interesting places to go, although both had their share of pubs and more. The closest thing either of them had to a place like Sydney's King's Cross was a ballroom in Wellington. It was on the second floor with its main entrance at street level. A long, curving stairway took you upstairs, where you went into the ballroom itself through the middle of the dance floor. A bandstand occupied one end of the room with an orchestra right out of the 1920s—old-style tuxedos with wing collars, and a singer who crooned through a megaphone. Dancers traveled round and round in a circle. The place was popularly known to Americans as the Gonorrhea Racetrack; unfairly, I think, because to the best of my knowledge none of our guys ever turned in with a case of the bug. One or two sailors did report becoming infested with crabs and had to resort to the old Navy cure of blue ointment—"Oh how it burns and itches, but it kills the sons of bitches."

The New Zealand police were much like the Aussies, but a lot less inclined to extend professional courtesies to the Yanks. And the service, called Kiwis, were not very friendly at all, much to our surprise. They actually resented our presence; probably because as a group they were all shorter in stature. Our plentiful supply of cash and our popularity with their womenfolk didn't help matters any. Thinking back now, I suppose their attitude was justified.

In some instances, our excellent relations with the New Zealand ladies was to our disadvantage. Take as an example the manner in which we lost our ship's Oil King. On any ship the Oil King is a pretty important individual. Usually a senior chief petty officer, he had the responsibility of keeping an accounting of all fuel and water aboard. Without fuel we would go nowhere. Without an ample supply of fresh water, the ship would simply cease to operate.

When we tied up in Wellington, the chief wasted no time getting himself established in town. The very first night he found a local lady who succumbed to his charm, and immediately took him to her home. The lady, it turned out, was the wife of a New Zealand army sergeant who she thought was off fighting the war in Africa. Feeling quite safe, the Oil

King moved into her bedroom to enjoy her sexual favors. Just as they were at the peak of passion, there was a crash as the bedroom door burst open. And there stood the Kiwi sergeant. Africa, hell; he had come home and wanted to surprise his wife. Boy, did he!

He was kind of a small guy like so many of his mates, and after a quick look at his wife's bed partner, he knew that combat was out of the question. The King stood about six three in his socks. When he was wearing them, that is. The Kiwi did the only thing he could do under the circumstances; he grabbed the chief's pants and ran. Right down to the local police station, where he swore all kinds of charges against our lothario. Alienation of affection, breaking and entering, I don't know what all. It was reported in the papers that the desk officer said, "A Yank, eh? In bed with yo'r missus? And he threatened you, did he? Now that ain't any way for a loyal ally to behave, now is it?" To support his accusations, the sergeant offered the chief's pants. In the pocket was his I. D. and liberty pass.

Our stalwart Oil King, meanwhile, was unable to chase after the little guy; after all, he was starkers, having been caught in flagrante delicto. But after finding a pair of pants somewhere, he headed down to the station to swear out charges against the New Zealand husband. When you think about it, hubby did steal the chief's pants. The civil authorities, not really sure of their right to hold military personnel, decided to call both the New Zealand and American military police, who arrived in short order.

The New Zealand MPs, disinclined to take any action against one of their own, did nothing. The Americans, being shore side marines not particularly fond of the Navy, looked upon the entire thing as a big joke. About that time the wife arrived and began to screech and holler, telling one and all that the Yank had crashed into her house and had his way with her. To hear her tell it, "He broke into me house, grabbed me by the bum, and shoved me in the bed. Then he downs me and he ins me. Right in me own house!" The Kiwi MPs challenged that immediately, claiming they had arrested her several times for "bestowing her favors to military personnel in a commercial manner."

All this was accurately reported in the next morning's newspapers. The front pages of which found their way to every bulletin board on both the *Trever* and *Zane*, and to most other ships in the harbor. We were scheduled to leave in another day or two, and the chief was being held ashore. There was no way the US Navy could hush it up, and had to let it run its course. So when we received orders to sail, the other chiefs aboard packed the Oil King's personal gear and had it sent ashore to US facilities. So much for the chief. We never saw him again, although for a long time a single copy of that front page, yellowed and tattered, remained on a bulletin board somewhere aboard ship. That front page with the glaring headline: American Sailor Caught With His Pants Down.

Mess Cooking and Worse

With our rest and recreation behind us, it was time to get back to the war. For me, personally, it was time for a three-month stint of mess cooking. It was not the most glamorous or exciting part of my Navy service, but it was something that was unavoidable. I had thought that once that week at the mess hall back at Great Lakes was over, it would be the end of that kind of duty. But no such luck. On board the *Trever* it ran for a full quarter, although the nature of the job was a bit different.

I found myself literally keeping house for about 30 guys. As a snipe, my assigned compartment was aft, where I was responsible for half the crew space. This meant keeping it clean and setting up for chow three times a day, because our living quarters doubled as a mess hall. It required going up to the galley and bringing the hot food back to the compartment, where it was served to the thirty chow hounds at my table. You can only imagine what it was like carrying seven big tureens of hot chow and a big pitcher of coffee along a heaving, rolling deck in a rough sea as you hippety-hopped over the assorted valves, bitts, and the like protruding from the deck. After each meal, the mess had to be cleaned up, dishes washed and put away, and the compartment cleaned. Really not too bad, except for the aforementioned rough weather. Then it was a matter of trying to stop the pans of soapy water, all the mess gear, and anything else flying off the table and into someone's bunk, or all over the deck.

Ordinarily, the mess cook on the other side of the compartment would rotate the cleaning duties with me. One week he would do it, and I would take the peeling duty up in the galley. Then we would switch. Personally, I much preferred the galley duty, unless it meant dealing with onions. Sitting out in the sun, even in a rough sea, peeling potatoes and turnips was not all that bad. Although my first day at it was one to be remembered.

There were about a zillion spuds to be peeled and cut up for noon chow. Settling down, I whipped out my sheath knife and went to work. Clippings flew in all directions as I went through that pile of potatoes in no time at all. The chief cook came along, checked my work, and said, "Nice job, Dawson, but we can't afford to peel 'em that thick. Now why don't you try peeling the peelings?" Needless to say, I never made that mistake again. From then on, my potato peelings were damn near transparent.

There was one good thing about that three-month period. It gave me a chance to get to know the chief officers' cook real well. He used the same galley to fix wardroom chow. As a result, it wasn't long before I was eating very, very good on board the *Trever*. Another good thing about mess cooking was the money to be made. If you took care of the guys on your table, they made it worth your while. On more than one occasion somebody on my table would come off watch too tired to eat. I always managed to stash a sandwich or something for him to eat later. Snatching extra butter from the ship's frig, or maybe stealing an extra pie, all helped to ingratiate a mess cook with his shipmates. On payday, they would pass a bowl down the table and everybody would throw in a buck or two as a tip. During the three months of mess duty I averaged about $40 a payday. More than my base pay, it wasn't hard to accept. There were some sailors who volunteered for the duty just for the money to be made. I wasn't about to go that far. There were other things on my mind.

The three months went by fairly easy for me, and I looked forward to getting back to regular duty. Especially since being informed there was a vacancy in the shipfitters' gang. The first lieutenant said the spot was mine if I wanted to transfer from the fire room. They wanted to take advantage of my having been to metalsmith school. Of course, it meant a complete change in my Navy career. At the time I was the senior fireman on my regular watch, and had completed my course for first class. All I had to do was take the exam, which I felt sure I could pass. Going into the shipfitters' gang meant changing my rate to seaman first and becoming a striker all over again. Yet, it was as close as I was going to get to doing what I was trained to do. There was a long discussion with Kayler, who had kind of taken Doggie's place as my mentor in the fire room, and he said that although he hated to see me go after having trained me, if it was what I really wanted, he would give me a good recommendation.

Even Deke said the chance might not come again. After that, it was a matter of talking to the guys in the shipfitters' crew to see what they thought of my joining them. They were all for it because up until then none of their guys had been to school. So in the end I decided to go for it. A shipfitter rate was pretty close to metalsmith. It consisted of construction and repair all over the ship, with the exception of the engineering spaces. It would be an opportunity to get the grease out from under my fingernails and come out of that greasy hole in the afterdeck to see the sun, and maybe even get a little tan.

The lieutenant began the paperwork for the transfer, letting me know that when I finished my time as mess cook, there would be a month with the deck force to gain what he called deck experience. It meant being the most junior of all seamen, even though I was already rated at seaman first class. And I would be working for Jack Ryan of all people. But that didn't seem too bad, because by then I knew that he could teach me a lot in that month. And he sure did. Yeah!

At the end of the quarter, I gathered my personal gear that had been left down in the fire room and reported to Ryan. He smiled, and said he had just the job for me, captain of the head—the guy in charge of cleaning up the crew's latrine and washrooms. On a bigger ship it would mean being in charge of a crew of seamen who would do the actual work. On board the *Trever* it was a one-man operation. I had to scrub, and clean, and polish, and sweep, and swab. Then keep a supply of toilet paper on hand, and whatever else Jack might think necessary to keep those vital compartments operable. Every morning I could be found in my spaces, hard at work.

But it did have its good side. Once finished with the clean up, I was through for the day. By noon chow I was free until evening, when it was necessary to make a fast check after everyone had their shower. During that free time I tried to keep an eye on Ryan and his people to learn as much as possible. And, of course, when the ship was going in or out of port it was necessary to help handle lines and such. So all in all my month on deck passed very quickly and I reported to the shipfitters' shack, ready to go to work.

Shipfitters' Gang

When I reported to the shipfitters' shack that first morning, it was with mixed feelings. I really hated to leave the fire room after finally having established myself as the senior fireman on my watch and qualifying as fireman first class. Having made friends down there and then leaving didn't make me feel any better. Although the guys in the Black Gang would probably be as friendly as always, I would no longer be a member of the clique. All ship's companies are like that. Every gang and department has an invisible wall between them and the rest of the ship. Still, there was an eagerness to get started in my new assignment because being a shipfitter was about as close as I was going to get to the specialty for which the Navy had sent me to school.

The people in the gang welcomed me into their midst, handing me a cup of coffee and showing me where my personal mug might be kept. There were four other men in the department besides me: Red Edmunds, a first class who was in charge; "Uncle Huk" Hawkins, another shipfitter first; Curley Shafer, with the rate of carpenter's mate second; and another seaman striker known as Tex Oliver. I was the only one without a nickname. For some reason, that would be the case throughout my entire enlistment. It was always just, "Hey, Dawson!"

All my work and duty assignments changed with the exception of my battle station, where I remained an ammunition passer aft. Watch standing was considerably different. Whereas in the fire room a watch could be a hard-working four hours, watches above deck were pretty easy going. In my case I became a loader on a three-inch main battery gun. They were not usually in action, so I was really acting as a lookout over an assigned sector of the sea and horizon. If the ship went to general quarters I would stand by my loading position until the regular loader arrived and then beat feet to my own station aft.

Once relieved from a watch standing, it was my responsibility to report to the shipfitters' shack and turn to on whatever job we had going, or to work at my assigned maintenance chores. Our department was responsible for just about all construction and repair, as well as damage control, aboard ship. Like Tex, I would be working with one of the rated men to learn the ropes. On my own there was the responsibility of maintenance of certain fire-fighting equipment and our diving gear. Of course, it fell to Tex and me to keep the shop clean. This last was very important because while it was our shop, it was also the starboard passageway, the traffic lane for everybody aboard.

Open to the weather at both ends, the shop had a hatchway leading into the galley. On the outboard side was the electricians' shack and the storekeeper's office, and several lockers where we kept a lot of our power tools, diving gear, and miscellaneous contraband. On the inboard side of the passageway were a long bench, more gear lockers, and racks for our welding gear.

One new duty I was not particularly fond of was that

of operator of the anchor windlass. Whenever the anchor was raised or lowered, the heavy chain would run around a big steam-powered winch-like affair up on the fo'c'sle. It was controlled by two hand-operated wheels jutting out of the deck. The operator had to kneel or squat there and regulate the speed of the chain as it whipped out and around the winch. Raising the hook was not too bad, because it was done by steam power and was not very fast. All that needed to be done was set the brake on command of the chief bos'n. Dropping anchor was another story entirely. When the order came to drop the hook, the deck crew would simply take a big sledge and knock loose the catch holding the anchor in place. It would drop like a bomb, hit the water, and go straight down. The chain would follow it with a roar, the links zipping out of the chain locker below, up and around the windlass, throwing rust and paint flakes up in a cloud, which usually enveloped the shipfitter at the brake. When it was judged to be out far enough, the bos'n would call for the brake, and I would start spinning those wheels like mad, hoping everything worked before the end of the chain flew out of the hatch. Supposedly, the end of the heavy chain was secured to the reinforced deck below, and couldn't come out. That's what we were told. But with the old DMS being more rust than good steel, nobody was quite sure, so I braked as hard and fast as possible.

We never did have an accident, but it was common knowledge that one of the newer destroyers had. They were engaged in dropping the anchor, and the brake didn't hold. The chain end came right out of the hatchway with the heaviest links flying wildly in a big arc, using the capstan as a pivot, and swinging around until it cleared the deck of the entire anchor crew. Eight or ten sailors went down. Two were tossed overboard, and the others scattered like ten pins. When it was all over there were two dead to contend with and an assortment of broken arms and legs, cuts and contusions. So whenever the *Trever* dropped that big hook, everyone backed out of harm's way. Everyone, that is, except the brakeman. And who was he? You guessed it. Still, in all the months at that assignment, no problems arose. To which I can only say, "Whewwww!"

The other members of my new gang couldn't have been nicer to a new boy. "Red" made a point of seeing that I was exposed to every kind of job that came along. Once they were agreed that I might really have learned something in school, there were jobs involving welding, burning, sheet metal work, and just about everything we had been taught back in Dearborn, Michigan. Uncle Huk saw to it that I learned the rudiments of diving and fire fighting, while Curley hammered at me to become familiar with every part of the ship. Edmunds even made available a copy of the *Trever*'s blueprints with the comment, "You damn well better get familiar with this shit barge, because one day you'll be running this gang!" I didn't know it at the time, but he was right.

Edmund and Hawkins both spoke to the first lieutenant, our division officer, claiming that as long as I had been to school (none of them had!) and already had my course in for fireman first, I ought to be allowed to take the exam for shipfitter third class as soon as possible. They would see to it that I passed. The lieutenant agreed.

All in all, it looked like Lonnie was finally in his proper niche in the Navy. While lying in my sack one night, unable to sleep, it occurred to me how good things were turning out. My Navy record was pretty good, despite my frequent goofs, and there were several guys who could really be called friends. If I didn't get myself killed, it might turn out to be a pretty good career for me. Something Grandma said to me just before I left home came to mind: "You go, my boy, and show them all. Make me proud." I thought that if she could see me at that moment, and understand it all as I was beginning to, she would be proud. With a silent promise not to let her down, I rolled, wiped my eyes, and went to sleep. It was a restless sleep, as I remember, dominated by a very vivid dream. Something about a gawky teenaged kid wearing a third class petty officer's badge as he went about doing a Man's Job. With an old lady hovering in the background, smiling as she whispered, "Show 'em all!"

Two Stars and a Crow

On March 6, 1943 the *Trever* steamed into Nouméa where we were to lose our well-liked captain. Lieutenant Commander Daniel Agar was relieved of command, and sent home on a well-deserved leave. Later, he was given a division of four newer 1850-ton destroyers. Finally, he was getting a command on par with his Annapolis classmates. Agar was replaced by Lt. Commander J. T. Wheeler, Regular Navy. He was, it turned out, a stickler for discipline, a real by-the-book skipper. There was no way we were going to get by with tailor-made uniforms, funny haircuts, or waving at the pretty ladies. He made that very clear at the change of command ceremony. But we took it all very calmly, because we knew that with all the new ships being commissioned, he would be getting another transfer shortly. Meanwhile, we put away our tailor mades, shaved, got regulation haircuts, and stopped looking for French sailboats.

With Captain Wheeler on the bridge, the *Trever* went to routine escort and patrol duties. About the most exciting thing that happened while he was aboard was our taking the Landing Ship (LST) 343 from Lunga Point on Guadalcanal to the Russell Islands, where we unloaded troops to reinforce the Army garrison. We spent the night there and, along with other ships and the shore installations, were subjected to what had become a nightly visit of an old Japanese biplane bomber. He drifted over the harbor about midnight and, after buzzing back and forth for a while, dropped a couple of bombs and went home. We were told that he never did any damage, but was a real nuisance because he kept everybody awake. Then, too, there was a concern that the damned engine might fall out of that ancient crate and land on someone. Not for nothing was he known as Washing Machine Charlie. Except for the single annoying Nip bomber, the entire operation was uneventful. Good thing, too, because our new skipper had no cause for complaint.

On April 24 we received our third wartime skipper when, as expected, Wheeler was transferred, to be replaced by our own executive officer, Lieutenant William H. Shee. Another Regular Navy man, he took command with a flourish, speech and all, to let it be known that it was going to be "his" ship. Understandable, of course; he had been aboard for several years and was thoroughly familiar with the old DMS, and certainly knew its oddball crew. We knew that as long as we performed to his satisfaction, he would overlook a lot. So out came the tailor mades, whiskers began to sprout, and the ship's barber began doing business in strange-looking haircuts. We even began posting lookouts again for any indication of local sailboats with pretty ladies.

By that time I was getting along pretty well in the shipfitters' gang, and was given the word that if I was prepared, I could take the exam for shipfitter third class. Boy, was I ever prepared! When the day arrived, I headed down to the forward compartment with a couple extra pencils and a head crammed full of facts and figures the other gang members had been pounding into it. The exam was long and detailed, consisting as it did not only of questions about what was to become my technical specialty, but a lot of military tradition, Navy customs, and courtesies. Being a petty officer was not going to be easy. But I'm proud to say that the entire exam was covered with no need for me to send topside for any answers. All I had to do after completion was wait for the promotion list to be posted. While waiting, there was a war to help pass the time.

Our next battle star came to us by way of the New Georgia campaign. Along with the USS *Schley*, the USS *McKean*, and seven LCIs (landing craft infantry), the *Trever* made up Task Group 31.3 under the overall command of Rear Admiral C. H. Kort, USN, who selected the *Trever* as his flagship. Coming aboard as he did with his entire staff made for a crowded wardroom, but our own officers made the best of it. They had little choice. After all, it's not every day an old four piper carried a flag admiral.

We departed Wernham Cove in the Russells on July 29 and set our course for the invasion site of Oliana Bay in New Georgia. The Japanese must have been asleep, because our task group was discharging troops before any opposition was acknowledged by the admiral. Everything went well, with none of the escort vessels firing a shot beyond the original shore bombardment prior to the landing. In no time at all we were ready to leave. When we made our return landfall in Nouméa, the admiral and staff debarked, after giving Captain Shee a Navy "well done!"

It was during the run to New Georgia that the promotion list was posted. I was more than a little pleased to see my name with the new rate of shipfitter third class. There was no time wasted sewing that third-class "crow" on my dress blues or in beginning my study for second class. I felt that I was on my way.

On July 5, the Americans struck at Kula Gulf in New Georgia to occupy Rice Anchorage and to prevent the Japanese from reinforcing their own forces at Munda. The *Trever* was part of the task group taking in the invading GIs. Not being a troop carrier, the old four stacker had to do it the hard way. We had over 200 Army personnel and their equipment on our weather decks. Exposed as they were to the elements, all they could do was hunker down and take it. They were not at all accustomed to the heaving, rolling antics of a tin can, and more than one guy lost his lunch over the side. Or in his lap. Or in his buddy's lap. They all eagerly looked forward to the landing. I guess they figured facing an angry, dug-in Jap defense was better than putting up with the continual roll and pitch of the old Tremblin' T! They might get shot at, but they wouldn't get seasick.

While the Army had its troubles, our own people got along just fine, and the operation came off like clockwork. The *Trever* earned another battle star. We were all thankful that the last two had been acquired without being drenched in the blood of our shipmates, or the guys we put ashore. Someone once wrote, "There are no atheists in foxholes." Let me tell you, there are damn few aboard a combat ship!

About a month after the New Georgia campaign, we received orders to go home. The USS *Honolulu* had been hit with a Japanese "long lance" torpedo at the Battle of Kolombangara and, having lost most of her bow, was being sent back to Pearl Harbor for repairs. The *Trever* was to be part of her screening force. We made Pearl Harbor on August 16, and after refueling, taking on provisions, and making a few minor repairs of our own, we went to sea and took our position as escort for a convoy eastward, headed for home.

Fourteen Days' Leave

On that final leg of our voyage back to the States, we had the usual anchor pools. Three of them, as I recall, one at a buck, five bucks, and the biggie at ten dollars a pop. Feeling lucky, I played all of them. The payoff would depend upon the exact time we passed under the Golden Gate Bridge. But a problem developed. When we hit the coast, the fog was so thick we couldn't even see the bridge, let alone check our watches as we sailed under it. We had to rely on the ship's navigator, who would log the time officially. Of course, he was not holding any pool tickets, and was said to be scrupulously honest. And we all believed it. Sure we did! As far as I was concerned, it made little difference, because my time estimates were so far off. The excitement of going home, however, tempered the pain of losing, and the sixteen dollars was soon forgotten.

Inasmuch as I was still the lowest-ranking member of our gang, my leave was scheduled for the second rotation. That was okay, because as it worked out, there was an opportunity for a little Frisco liberty before heading for Chicago. My leave, when it did begin, was only fourteen days, but my decision was still to take the train. Flying had been great the last time, and I did have a bit more money in my pockets, but it seemed more important to save it for spending at home.

I was lucky enough to get a seat on one of the faster trains and the trip only took about 36 hours. Even that cut into my leave time considerably, but there was no other choice. When the train pulled into Chicago, I wasted no time grabbing a cab and heading for Grandma's house. As we rolled through the streets, a million sea stories began to form in my mind. What a time it would be telling the family and neighbors about my war experiences.

What a disappointment! Those members of the family I was able to see didn't seem at all excited or interested in my experiences, or even my newly won promotion. Most of them never even called to say "hi" or "welcome home." There was a bigger glad hand from the people in the neighborhood. But even there things were not as expected. Most of them seemed more concerned with telling me about the shortages they were having to endure, and wanted to know where all the material and foodstuffs were going. It was hard making them understand that I had no special contacts with the officials who made those decisions.

A visit to my high school wasn't much better. It was not at all like the last time I had dropped by. Most of the kids I knew were already in service, or working at some temporary job until their draft number was called. A few of the teachers remembered me, and asked if I might speak to their class as I had done previously. But this time they were all strangers to me, although they seemed concerned with what had and was happening in the Pacific. Especially the boys who were ready to graduate and might very well end up in uniform.

There was one eager audience for my sea stories, however. My Grandma! Good old Grandma. She listened patiently to every tale I had to tell. She shivered at all the right places, asked the right questions, and from time to time would reach out to gently touch my new rating badge. Now and then she folded her hands and thanked God I had made it home. Actually, I doubt she understood half of what I was saying, but she played her part beautifully. I guess she knew that beneath my new-found sophistication, those dress blues with the colorful campaign ribbons, and my third-class shipfitter badge, I was still the scared teenaged kid she had raised and knew so well and still worried about. Her obvious concern saw me through a lot of tough times.

Most of my leave was spent with the girl I had known in high school. Emma Lydia Kuyat. She had changed her name by the time I had gotten home on leave. She was working at Douglas Aircraft, and somewhere at the plant she had picked up the nickname Penny. She let me know in no uncertain terms that I was *not* to call her Emma any longer. Growing up does funny things to people. Anyway, I went along with her, although to me her new name was quickly shortened to simply "Pen."

Pen and I put a big dent in the cash I saved. Shows, dinners, and lunches in nice restaurants, cabs to get around, all the things I had never been able to do before. We spent a lot of time just walking over the bridges downtown, and along the lake front in the park. You could still do that sort of thing back then without getting mugged. There was a lot of hand holding, snuggling, and nuzzling as we talked about our future. By then we had pretty well decided that whatever that future might be, we would face it together. Because of the war, we made no concrete commitments, agreeing to keep in touch and see what that still questionable time ahead of us might produce. As soon as we could see some kind of "after the war" scenario shaping up, we would talk about marriage and a family.

There was no doubt, however, that the time we spent together and the things we said would have a profound effect on any career plans I might have with the Navy. The fourteen days drew to a close very rapidly, and it was time to get back to my ship. Another train trip was in order. Saying good-bye to one and all, especially my new-found interest in life, this sailor got on board the train and headed west. The trip back wasn't too bad, because it seemed that at almost every stop we made, another of my shipmates climbed aboard. By the time we made it to Frisco, our group was ten or twelve strong. The gang stopped in town long enough for a last drink, then reported in. We were about twelve hours early, so after getting the okay from the OOD, a few of the hardier guys took a quick shower and headed back into town. Most of us sacked out for some badly needed shut-eye. The next morning there was just enough time to square away my personal gear and report to the shipfitters' shack, ready to turn to. Leave was over and we had a ship to get ready for whatever lay ahead.

US Navy Fire Fighting School

In the shipyard most of the work was handled by civilian tradesmen. All we really had to do was keep on top of them to see that we were receiving all that was requested, and that it was being done to specifications. Despite the war, a lot of the yard workers were more interested in doing as little work as possible while drawing the highest pay obtainable. Strikes were common, and there was more than one fight that broke out between Navy people and the civilians when the latter sat down and refused to budge because of what they called a "grievance." It was usually something stupid, like a Navy shipfitter installing a piece of pipe rather than waiting for a yard crew, or a signalman fitting his own halyards to meet his way of using them out at sea. Our own gang was shorthanded because Edmunds, upon being promoted to chief, had been transferred. Uncle Huk took charge of the department, and we were all responsible for standing emergency fire watches over yard welding teams, supervising installation of new equipment, and getting as much cumshaw (unauthorized) work done as possible. We ended up with electric coffeemakers all over the ship, special lockers for diving gear we had "drawn" under cover of darkness, and armory lockers for the additional small arms we had acquired. Also, we managed to have a couple extra machine guns mounted on our flying bridge.

It was during our overhaul period that I was assigned to the Navy Fire Fighting School. Because of my third-class rating and the possibility that I might well be in charge of the gang myself in the foreseeable future, Huk decided it would be up to me to get the special training and then bring the expertise back to pass along to the other guys. It sounded great to me. It would be pretty exciting, and would look good on my record when going up for second class.

The Fire Fighting School was located on the far end of the yard, and ours would be the first class going through. All of the instructors were regular city firemen who had been drafted and given a Specialist F (Fire Fighter) rating. Our class was made up of Navy people from ships and bases all over the country, ranging in rank and rate from seaman second class to full commander. Once we were assigned to classes, all rank and privilege was left behind. Everybody wore dungarees with no sign of rank.

The class was broken down into teams, the leaders of which were selected at random. It was kind of interesting, I thought, that our team included a full commander while our appointed team boss was a carpenter's mate third class. But it wasn't long before we were all on a first-name basis, although it was kind of tricky to call a full commander, "Hey, Sam!"

A lot of time was devoted to lectures on fire fighting theory, the various types of equipment we would be using, and how to work as a team. We were cautioned to pay close attention, because there were a lot of tough fires to fight where someone might get hurt or even killed. Nothing in our course was to be simulated. We learned how to handle hoses, a variety of nozzles, chemical and mechanical foam, small portable pumps called "handy billies," and a new type of electrically powered submersible pump that could supply enough water for a ship to do almost anything. The fires we were exposed to included paper and wood, electrical, oil and gas, paint, and the newly developed plastics that were highly inflammable—just about anything the instructors could get to burn, including a jeep and one or two small boats. One of the most frightening and difficult fires to deal with at sea has been that of oil or gasoline on the surface of the water. It was a very common occurrence, because when a ship is hit by enemy gunfire or a torpedo, it might literally be afloat in a sea of flame. Included in training was a method of leaping from the deck of a burning ship into such an inferno. To make the exercise as realistic as possible, we were taken to the top of a fifty-foot tower overlooking a gigantic tank of water, the surface of which was covered with oil. A fireman, using a torch, lit it off, and in a few minutes it was burning furiously. Flames leapt high as black, oily smoke rolled off in clouds. "Oh, come on," I thought, "he's not going to ask us to jump into that!" Slowly I began working my way to the back of our not-so-eager group. Our instructor explained the proper way to jump, how to hit the water, and how to use a breaststroke to push the burning oil away from us as we swam out of the fire area. Doing as we had been cautioned, I listened very carefully. What I heard was how I was going to drown or be burned to death. However, nobody made the jump. After scaring us all to death, the specialist, laughing like crazy, took us all back to ground level.

Dropping down the ladder, I heaved a sigh of relief. But I must admit that when I took my shower that night and washed out my daily change of skivvies, those light-brown stains were just a bit more than the time-honored "hash marks."

By far the most exciting experience in school was getting involved in actual fire fighting aboard a real ship. Well, almost real. It was a ship specially constructed for the school. It was a mock-up of the central portion of a cargo carrier, complete with four decks containing fire and engine rooms, ammunition magazines, storage compartments—the works. For purposes of training, it was fitted with watertight hatches and doors, as well as those steep, hard-to-navigate ladders found on board all ships. Being on dry land rather than at sea, the mock-up was built on pilings and concrete blocks, which led to her official name. Carried on the official Navy lists as the USS *Hemorrhoid*, she didn't go anywhere. She just sat there on her piles! So help me, that is the official explanation, as written in her log.

Our first day on the *Hemorrhoid* was one not easily forgotten. A "few thousand gallons" of fuel oil had been pumped into her bilges, topped off with gasoline. Everything was closed down tight and the fuel was lit off. The necessary air was supplied through vents designed for that purpose. When it was going real well, the main hatchway was flung open, and I swear, the flames leaped out about twenty feet, along with billows of stinking black smoke. Our team was handed a water hose and told to "run on in and put 'er out, will you guys?" Water on an oil fire? Were they nuts?

Our full commander, older than the rest of us and a real fatherly figure, said, "Come on men. They won't really let anyone get hurt. Let's do it!" From the back of our gang came a quiet voice. "If you're so damn sure about that, Sam, why don't you go in first?" The Old Man looked hurt. He jammed his cap down tighter on his head, picked up the heavy nozzle, and turned toward the fire. We had no choice but to get on the hose with him and, following his lead, we charged the *Hemorrhoid*. Of course it didn't work. We had to back out, wet and dirty, to give it some thought. All the time our instructor, standing well back in his nice clean uniform, was screaming encouragement. "Do it! Do it! Damn it, remember what I've been telling you. Do it! Do it!"

Somebody remembered, because he yelled, "Fog, fog!" We knew immediately what he meant. Quickly, we attached a special device to our nozzle and, taking up our hose, we went back in. Only this time we were spraying a fine water mist before us, a mist that would turn to steam in the heat and effectively smother the fire. But again, it didn't work. The technique was correct, but we couldn't breathe in the steam. So out we came again. Our team leader called for rescue breathing equipment. As soon as our guys were dressed in the gear, we headed into the inferno again, pretty sure of ourselves as we passed through the hatchway, with the commander still on the nozzle and our leader the number two man. In due time the fire was out and we emerged from the ship dirty, wet, but victorious, to the cheers of our classmates. Ours was the only team that successfully fought the devil fire and won.

Fire Fighting School lasted a little over two weeks, and when we graduated it was with a feeling we had learned something important that we could take back to our ship. On our last day we checked in wearing dress blues. It was a surprise to see what had been a dirty bunch of smoke eaters suddenly resplendent in gold braid and service ribbons.

Still, as long as we remained on school grounds and had not been handed our certificates of completion, we were still on a first-name basis. After the graduation exercise, when we were shaking hands and saying our good-byes, it was no longer "Sam" but "Commander, Sir." And you know, I didn't mind a bit.

Returning to the overhauled DMS after completing school, it was to see a lot of the equipment I had been training on installed and ready for use. Uncle Huk and I proceeded to work out a training schedule for our gang to follow once we left the yard. To this day, because of that school and its realistic training, I feel a certain kinship to every fireman I see. At least there is an understanding of what they do.

Our yard time drew to a close, everybody was back from leave, and the *Trever* was pronounced in all ways ready for sea and active duty. We received our orders to rejoin the fleet.

National Guard Commandos

Leaving the Golden Gate Bridge to fade in the mist astern, the *Trever* headed west toward Hawaii as one of the escorts for a supply convoy. Our destination was Pearl Harbor, and we made landfall on October 8, sighting Diamond Head early in the morning. After turning protection of the convoy over to local escort vessels, our sturdy old can stood into the harbor, making directly for the fuel docks. Our time at Pearl was short, just long enough to fuel, take on a few provisions and more ammunition, and make a last few adjustments to things that had been installed back at the Mare Island Navy Yard. For those of the crew who still had a few bucks left after stateside leave, there was an opportunity for a bit of Honolulu liberty.

After our time at Pearl Harbor, the *Trever* was ordered to Guadalcanal, where we joined Task Unit 31.55 as part of the screening force. Our main responsibility was the safe arrival of the troop transport USS *American Legion* at Cape Torokina at Bougainville, where we would discharge troops to occupy that enemy stronghold. As we had done in the past, the *Trever* also carried about 200 Army troops on deck for the trip. Actually, calling them Army would not be correct. They were part of a National Guard unit. Or, as they preferred to call themselves, National Guard Commandos! They had seen no combat up to that time, but you would never know it if you listened to them. What a blood and gutsy group!

Dressed in camouflage jungle suits, they were festooned with all the implements of war. Guns, knives, machetes, and even hand grenades hanging from their battle harness. A lot of them wore shoulder holsters with personal handguns. To us it resembled a lot of comic book rice paddy rangers. Quite a few were regularly sipping from canteens which we suspected held something other than water. From the time we took them aboard until it was time to hit the beach, they swaggered about our decks, telling anyone who would listen how they were going to storm the beaches and end the war right there. For the most part they told one another, because we had already "been there" and knew it would not be as they thought. Experience had taught us that the Jap was not the squinty-eyed, bucktoothed little runt as he was so often portrayed on the propaganda posters. He was a courageous, resourceful fighter skilled in the art of war. And most important, he was quite willing to die for his Emperor, screaming "banzai!" with his last breath. But there was no telling that to the guardsmen. So we just let them ramble, puff, and posture. Their moment of truth was yet to come.

Early on the morning of November 13th our unit steamed into Empress Augusta Bay and took position off Cape Torokina. Japanese aircraft almost immediately began to pass overhead, dropping a lot of multi-colored flares. There was no doubt they knew we were there. Still, there were no attacks on our ships. On the *Trever,* our commandos began to get very nervous at the sight of the pyrotechnic display over the ship. Especially when we told them it was probably signals for an organized resistance to the landings.

Cradle Cruise

The *American Legion* moved closer inshore and began to lower her troop-laden landing craft. Japanese shore batteries took us under fire at that point, making the operation much more hazardous. There is something very scary about night action. Heavy gunfire lights up the sky with every flash, and you can actually see the projectiles, white-hot from air friction, flying to their targets. Some of them, like tracer bullets, left a trail of fire behind. Star shells from the enemy guns would periodically light up the entire bay. For some reason, their shooting was ineffective, and no hits were scored on either ships or boats, although in the light of the gun flashes we could see their shells splashing close enough to wet the soldiers in the landing boats as they moved shoreward. But in spite of it all, our people headed in.

As the *Legion* was sending her own boats to designated beach areas, we received the order to "land your landing parties," Navy jargon for "get your troops ashore where they can do some good!" Not having regular landing craft, the *Trever* resorted to inflated rubber invasion rafts. Blown up by compressor, they were put over the side and secured with a single line until they were loaded and ready to shove off. All we had to do was get the blood-thirsty guardsmen into them so they could get ashore and end the war as they had promised to do. But that turned out to be a much greater problem than we had expected. For some reason, after watching all the gunfire taking place and hearing the roar of the shore batteries and seeing the shells splash so close to the inbound boats, our killers in camouflage were having second thoughts. Even their officers were beginning to suspect that all was not as they had been told. As our deck crew was inflating the rubber rafts and putting them over the side, the rest of us were getting the commandos organized according to the way they would disembark. First platoon in this boat, third machine gun squad into another, and so on. The idea was to have them hit the beach ready to fight if it was necessary. But by the time we were ready to get them into their rubber dinghies, they were as screwed up as an army cook in a fire drill. Milling around in all directions, supposedly still searching for some piece of equipment or other, they were ready to go anywhere except into combat. So we took matters into our own hands.

If a given boat was to hold twelve men, we grabbed the closest twelve and put them over the rail. After a few minutes we were actually throwing them over. Once in a while there would be a big splash when one of them missed the boat. We were told later that a couple of them drowned because they hit the water with all their battle gear and sank before anyone could pull them out. Of course, that was all hearsay! We did finally get the last landing craft away and were able to report to the task unit commander that our troops were off the beach. Little did we know.

When the last of them were gone, the *Trever* moved over to her screening position by the *American Legion* and waited for her to complete her own operations. With the first rays of the sun showing over the horizon, we discovered we still had about twelve of the blustering guardsmen aboard. They had managed to stay hidden in the dark of night. Of course, they figured it was all our fault they had been left behind, and would have returned to Guadalcanal with us. They were sorry about that, because they really wanted to go and fight alongside their buddies. What a dilemma! Brave fighting men being deprived of their right to serve their country. Our captain, feeling he ought to do something for the poor guys, called the *American Legion,* which was quick to send over one of her empty landing craft to take the forgotten heroes off our hands.

They were even given a free ride to the sandy beaches of that tropical paradise so they might take a part in ending World War II. What bugged us was that in the end they would get a star for the invasion and defense of Torokina, just as we would.

Once rid of the stragglers, the *Trever* was assigned to check out shoals in the area so Navy charts could be brought up to date. With that completed, the escort ships took turns bombarding the Japanese shore batteries until they were silenced. There was very little fire returned by the enemy, and nobody could understand why we had not experienced greater resistance to the operation.

By midafternoon, the latest Cape Torokina venture was brought to a close as far as we were concerned, and the task unit formed up for the return voyage to Guadalcanal. We received a Navy "well done" from the area commander, and authorization for our fifth battle star. Compared to our former missions, Bougainville had been a piece of cake.

1943 — A Lull in the War

Where the war was concerned, 1943 was a comparatively easy year for the *Trever*. With all the new ships coming out of the shipyards back in the States, many of the older cans were being relegated to such duties as target towing and escort in the area of the Solomon, Ellice, Marshall, and Admiralty Islands. True to the purpose, the DMSs also spent a lot of time sweeping the approaches to those bases and island strongholds under Allied control. There was always the chance of a Japanese mine layer submarine slipping in under cover of night to lay its lethal eggs. But generally, combat duty was going to the newly constructed destroyers, escorts, and auxiliary ships designed for a specific purpose. Where a landing operation did require minesweeping, however, the task force commanders still called for the old flush deckers. Those fancy new ships, for all their modern equipment, couldn't match the high-speed sweeping techniques developed by the four stackers over the years, or the actual wartime experience we had gained the hard way. We had held the line against the Japs that first year to give the American military and war industry the much-needed time to gear up for battle. But for the most part, by the end of 1943, that was all behind us.

Almost daily, we would receive requests from the Navy

Bureau of Personnel for specific ranks and specialist ratings to be sent back for what was called "new construction." All those ships being launched needed experienced men to form the nucleus of their crews. Vessels like the *Trever* were seeing a lot of changes in skippers as younger officers were given first chance at command before being moved on to other assignments. Even our senior enlisted men were moving out so fast that departments that had been headed up by chiefs and first-class petty officers were being taken over by second and third class. The shipfitters' gang was no exception. Edmunds, Uncle Huk, and Curley Shafer were suddenly gone and we found ourselves with no gang leader. I was called down to the exec's office one morning and told to take over the department immediately and to get my course for second class completed in a hurry. To fill vacancies in my crew there would be a couple of carpenter's mates third class coming from the States, and a pair of new strikers from our own deck force. The strikers I knew. "Buttermilk" Brock and "Lil Davy" Davies were both rated seaman first class, and had some civilian experience we could put to good use. The carpenter's mates were something else. One of them, Lanny Lamond Lambert, was coming from a soft stateside berth where he had been rated third class after building a dog house for the base commander. The other kid, "Shorty" Schuler, had at least taken an exam for his rate, but still wasn't much of a mechanic. It was going to be my job to whip them into some kind of a repair crew.

    At first, there was considerable friction between me and my new men. It was hard for them to accept my being the boss when they held third-class rates that were on a level with my own. But it didn't take long to explain to them that my warrant predated theirs, and I had been aboard a lot longer and knew the job. They didn't. After that, things went a lot smoother. We even turned into a pretty good team. After completing my second-class course with a grade of 3.8, my position was pretty secure.

With so many people leaving the ship, some reorganization was necessary. I was pulled from the main battery and, after some basic instruction, went on to stand 20mm machine gun watches. There were three of us to man two guns on the afterdeckhouse, with myself as gun captain. My battle station changed as well, when instead of passing ammunition I was put into a damage-control party. It came as a complete surprise when I found myself in charge. That called for a lot more study on my part.

It was a good thing that the *Trever* was no longer a first-line combat vessel at that time because with the constant turnover of the crew we were really in no position to deal with any emergencies. But we learned to make due with the few experienced people that were left. A few months into the new year I was again called down to the exec's office and informed that it would soon be time for me to be sent back to new construction, and somebody else would have to take over my gang. The only one available just then was Lambert, the builder of dog houses. That didn't seem like too good an idea and I said so. My suggestion was to get someone from another ship already rated and experienced and then kick Brock and Davies up to third class to take some of the pressure off the new guy. Meanwhile, I would push them to get their courses in without saying what was afoot. The exec agreed, but with the understanding that we would say nothing for the time being.

Cradle Cruise

Of course, I immediately clued Buttermilk and Lil Davy as to what was shaping up. They took to studying like you wouldn't believe. Lambert and Schuler began to smell something. They were concerned that the two strikers might be promoted and then given what was rightfully theirs—gang leadership. But my responsibility was to the ship, not a couple erstwhile primadonnas who had been sent to sea because they had screwed up elsewhere.

Once I knew that my turn for a transfer would be coming soon, it became a question of what kind of duty I might want. My division officer took me aside to let me know it might be a good idea to make up my mind before leaving the old DMS. With his and the exec's recommendation, there was a good chance of getting it. So giving it a lot of thought, and feeling that I ought to remain a shipfitter, I opted for a seagoing salvage tug boat, or maybe one of the new, big minesweepers. Either way, it would mean six months of school in the States. I'd had my fill of war by that time, and figured that more of the same might get me killed. I wanted some shore duty, and school seemed the way to get it. The lieutenant agreed with me, saying he would speak to the skipper and exec. Meanwhile, there was still a lot of shipboard maintenance to attend to, as well as the regular shenanigans that were so important. After all, there was a lot more to be done than just fighting the Japanese.

And You're a Gun Captain?

Being captain of a 20mm gun crew had its drawbacks. Sure, I received an extra five dollars a month as long as I held the position and could qualify as a gunner. But there was also the responsibility of making sure my guys kept a good lookout while we were on watch, prepared to take action until the regular general quarters crew could get to the gun deck.

The *Trever* was on an offshore patrol in the Solomons one day, and my team had the noon to four o'clock watch, and as always, we were constantly scanning the seas and sky for any indication of the enemy. We were about a mile or so from the beach when we spotted what appeared to be a low-flying aircraft skirting the shoreline. Painted in green and brown camouflage, it was not easy to see and when we reported it to the bridge there was some argument as to anything being there. But we insisted, and readied our gun just in case. The machine gun crew on the galley deckhouse took the same precautions.

Finally, the bridge located the plane and ordered us to track it as the horn was sounded for general quarters. About that time the aircraft turned and headed out to sea, straight in our direction. From our angle we could see no insignia, and because of the similarity between an American observation plane, the Kingfisher, and Jap planes of the same type, we had to assume it was Japanese. The regular GQ gun crew was late relieving us so we had the ball. The plane was so close by that time we asked permission to fire. I had the headphones, and heard the click as the bridge talker was making his reply. Assuming it would be in the affirmative, we opened fire. The galley deckhouse gun opened up at the same instant, just a split second before actually receiving a "commence fire!" The observation craft flashed over the *Trever* as we fired, raking his wing. Actually, we had both technically fired without permission, but with the order from the bridge to do so, we felt justified. As it turned out, that justification was important for both guns, because as the plane roared over us we could see a white star on its wing. We had fired on a US Navy plane! We knew our collectives assess were in deep doggy doo.

    The pilot climbed high enough for us to get a really good look at him, and his signal lamp was blinking like mad as he identified himself. We found out later that the damn fool pilot had decided to buzz the *Trever* just for laughs. Well, we sure laughed, and showed our shiny 20mm teeth as we did so.

    Our gunnery officer, one Morgan Lefevre III, Lieutenant Junior Grade, USNR, like to went stark raving bananas. Very career oriented, he was sure that it would make the captain see him as irresponsible, unable to control his gun crews. In no time at all he was on my back as captain of the first gun to fire. Actually, we had triggered off at about the same time, but he was having none of it. He had to have a scapegoat, and I was it. Only the interference of the officer of the deck saved us from a deck court martial, or worse. The officer of the deck, fortunately for us, was my division officer, Lieutenant JG William Joseph Moriarity, who quickly informed the skipper that as officer of the deck he had given the order to commence fire, and if anything we ought to be commended for our quick response, particularly since we did hit the plane, which at that time was unidentified.

The incident, not being all that unusual during wartime, died down after a few days, but Moriarity warned me to walk very lightly for a while. As he put it, "Mr. Lefevre is no guy to cross, and I might not always be around to cover for you." We knew there would be dark days ahead. I began to look forward to my upcoming transfer to new construction.

A month or so later the *Trever* was on antisubmarine patrol in the same area and we had been at GQ for several hours chasing down sonar contacts. Lieutenant Lefevre, as gunnery officer, frequently positioned himself on the afterdeckhouse as his battle station. When we finally secured from general quarters, I raced back up to the gun deck to take the regular watch. Lefevre, as he was leaving, said, "Okay, Dawson, secure your guns. Uncock them, but leave them loaded in case we go to GQ again." I couldn't believe it. What he was ordering was impossible. The design of the weapon simply wouldn't permit it. I called after him to bring it to his attention, but he only yelled over his shoulder, "And you're a gun captain? Just do as you're told and don't give me any trouble."

"Damn it," I thought, "don't give you any trouble?" What did he think he was giving me?

My crew and I talked about it and agreed that there was no way we could do what the gunnery officer had called for. So we did the only thing open to us. We had the word passed along for the chief gunner's mate to hie back to the gun deck. Grumpy, crotchety, old "Gunner" Gold was of the opinion that every piece of ordnance aboard ship belonged to him personally. Gold came steaming back in a foul mood. We had disturbed his coffee break. He asked impolitely what in hell was wrong. As gun captain, it fell to me to explain what Lefevre wanted us to do, and why we couldn't see any way to carry out his order. "Gunner" went off the deep end, romping and stomping all over that gun deck, screaming that only a complete idiot would try anything like that with *his* guns. In the midst of this tirade, Lieutenant Lefevre came climbing up the ladder with blood in his eye. He had heard our call for the chief, and assumed the worst.

Getting to the top of the ladder, he headed for me, demanding that I stand to attention and explain why I was not obeying a direct order. Gold just stepped between us and without mentioning any names made it pretty clear what he thought of anyone who would mishandle his guns. How he had personally taught all the crew to use a 20mm, and how he didn't need the help of some self-taught book reader. It might be added here that Lefevre had never been to gunnery school, but had read all the books. The fact that the lieutenant was his division officer was lost on the chief. With his thirty-plus years in the Navy, low-level brass didn't impress him much. Lefevre stood there and turned purple. Finally, he turned and went forward, muttering something about everyone going on report. Chief Gold turned to me and yelled, "Damn it, Dawson, don't stand there picking your nose and your ass! Secure those guns the way you were taught!" With that, he slid down the ladder and went back to his coffee, telling anyone who cared to listen what he thought about green officers with a job beyond their capabilities.

We never heard any more about it other than the scuttlebutt that the captain had given Lefevre a real reaming. A short time later our exec was transferred, and orders were received promoting Lefevre to full lieutenant, along with making him the number two officer aboard. Those dark days we feared were about to begin. As soon as the new exec took over the job, there was a rash of requests for transfers, because we all knew what was coming. Moriarity suggested that I not apply because it would only be turned down. "Wait it out," was his advice, "after all, the exec can't do anything without the skipper's approval, and you're already on the list of people to be moved back to new construction as soon as orders come in." As it turned out, all transfer requests were denied, because the captain did not want to lose any more experienced, rated men than he had to.

It was about that time that the examinations for promotions were scheduled to take place. Lefevre let it be known there was no sense for me to take a test because, in his mind, I was not "petty officer material." This was kind of odd, inasmuch as I was already third class and running a department that ordinarily would be handled by at least a first. I refused to let him scare me off, knowing that if I passed, my warrant would be signed by the captain. Besides, my passing would be on my service record. So when the fated day arrived, down I went to the forward compartment to attack the problem head on. I knew there would be no sending up for any answers I might not know. My only chance was to make it on my own with a respectable grade. It was tough, but worth it. When the results were posted a couple days later, my name was there with a grade of 3.7 out of a possible 4.0—one of the highest scores by anyone that day. It was too good to be ignored, or so I thought. Anyway, it would be awhile before a promotion list would be posted, and until then, along with a few other guys, all I could do was sweat it out, try and keep out of trouble, and do my job.

Dirty Fingernails and Apple Pie

It didn't take long for my new gang to start pulling together as a team. If we couldn't do the job, there would have been some changes made, and nobody wanted that to happen. As long as we produced, we were left pretty much alone. It was my job to determine what work had to be done from day to day, and who would do it. From time to time I would declare a holiday routine (day when we would do nothing at all) for no other reason than I thought we needed a break. If one of my guys wanted to work at a hobby like making jewelry or a sheath knife, I tried to make time for him as well as help find the raw material he might need. Everybody had to learn how to weld and how to use the acetylene cutting torch, our shallow water diving gear, and any other equipment we might acquire. Not letting anyone other than our own team use the gear made us kind of special. All the other departments had to treat us right if they wanted our help on anything.

The shipfitters were the general repairmen for just about anything other than specialized equipment involving fire control, communication, radio, and radar. Even there we were called upon to design and install some crazy fittings. Like a carefully crafted rack for a glass coffeemaker, or to tap into an air duct to provide a cooling breeze for the chiefs' quarters. Important things like that. We also handled mundane jobs like extra mounts on the flying bridge for the machine guns we had "found," awnings on the quarterdeck, or extra boxes for ready ammunition. And we were the ship's plumbers. Boy, were we ever the ship's plumbers.

Once, the captain of the head had been polishing bridge-work, and dropped the can of polish down the overboard discharge pipe. It slid along the line and jammed in an elbow turn, blocking the entire system. The kid didn't say anything about it to anyone and the blockage was not noticed until the system just stopped working. By that time, the line was packed solid with human waste for several feet, and the only remedy was to go below deck and tear it all out, clean it up, and replace everything. That dirty and smelly job fell to the shipfitters. When I got the word, the only man open for a job was Buttermilk Brock. Good old Buttermilk. So named, incidentally, when Lil Davy accidentally spilled a gallon of white lead on him and, laughing like crazy, screamed, "Look at old Brock, he fell into the buttermilk vat!"

Anyway, Brock got the job. He didn't like it, but he got it, and tackled it like he would anything else. The pipes to be ripped out were in the overhead in the after crew's quarters, and it made quite a mess. The people who lived there fled to the weather decks and fresh air as soon as the first connection was broken loose and the wonderful fragrance filled the compartment. It didn't take long to rip out, but when Buttermilk brought all the pieces topside to be washed out, he was a mess himself. He had the stuff all over his coveralls, his hands, everywhere. He was a guy who didn't like to wear gloves on the job, and he even had the glop under his fingernails. Everybody got a big laugh out of that, but my striker didn't say a word. He didn't even get angry, in spite of everything. I began to get an idea that he might have something in mind when he looked up at me and said, "It's okay, Lon. It's okay. I can handle it."

In time, Brock had everything cleaned out, the lines all replaced, and the system operating again. He even rigged a fan to blow the smell out of the compartment because that was not only where the crew lived, but ate their meals as well. The job done, Buttermilk went up to take a well-earned shower. He needed it. When he returned to the after compartment, evening chow was about to come down, and having a regular seat at the mess table, he took it and sat there, smiling, good-naturedly accepting all the razzing he received. He was being called "turd jockey," "poop pusher," and "Mr. Brown." And those were the nicest things being said. He still didn't get upset; he just sat there, smiling. But as soon as chow arrived his plans became very apparent.

We were scheduled to have chili and rice that night. A great favorite of the *Trever* crew, there was never enough where we were concerned. For dessert there was to be apple pie. For Brock, chilled apple pie was his idea of living. Now, it was customary for the mess cook to first bring down a big pot of coffee and then return to the galley for the food. When the word "coffee down!" was passed, the guys would take their seats at the table and be ready to eat when the mess cook arrived with his tureens. As they were drinking their coffee, our boy put his plan into action. He drew his sheath knife and, leaning over the table, began to clean his fingernails, letting the scrapings fall to the tabletop.

Knowing what job he had been working on, and imagining what he was scraping from under his nails, several of his tablemates got sick and headed for fresh air, their appetites suddenly gone. Buttermilk unconcernedly continued to dig out the crud from under his fingernails. Some of it fell into his coffee cup, whereupon he picked it out with a knife tip and took a big drink. A few more sailors left the table. By the time the chili and pie arrived, half the mess was vacant, and for the first time since coming aboard Brock had all the chili and rice he could eat. And pie? He polished off a whole one by himself. Nobody else wanted any.

Of course, there were repercussions. The executive officer wanted to know why he had been scraping excrement from his nails at the supper table, and why, as his gang leader, I did not have better control over my men. It was then we found out how devious the boy could be. He had scrubbed his hands and nails along with everything else when he showered. He was clean, and he knew it. But then, he smeared grease on his bar of soap and dug his nails into it to get the mess of brown stuff under and around them. That's what he was digging out as he sat at the table. Soap and grease. The exec, our old friend Mr. Lefevre, threatened to bring Brock up on charges, but the captain would have none of it. Lieutenant Moriarity stopped me on deck and said, "You guys just won't quit, will you? How much of this do you think Lefevre will take?" He turned away and I could hear that choking gurgle deep in his throat as he fought not to laugh. He was right, of course; we were pushing it. As for Buttermilk, he figured even if he was put on report, it was worth it. From the overall reaction, particularly from Lefevre, I think maybe it was.

Asiatic Earrings

With the *Trever*, like some of the other DMSs, on standby duty rather than sailing with a task force, we were not required to remain at a constant state of alert. This gave us time to think of other things to do. Anyone who has "been there" can tell you that war is usually long stretches of tedium and inactivity interspersed with a period of absolute terror. Those long, boring times can be as hard on a sailor as any battle, albeit in a different way. And very tough on a crew of about 120 living in each other's pockets on board a ship only 30 feet wide and 300 feet long. Sometimes we would get so desperate for something to occupy our mind other than shipboard maintenance and battle drills, our better judgment would be lost. An example would be our Earring Craze of 1943.

One of the signalmen, I think it was Jessie Meeks, got the bright idea of wearing a ring in his left ear. Why his left ear? Why wear it at all? I don't know, and I doubt Jessie did, either. But you can always justify doing something weird if you want to. There were explanations like "it's for crossing the equator" and "we traveled halfway around the world." More likely it indicated we had all been away from civilization for too long and had gone a bit Asiatic. But as I said, you really don't need a reason. You just do it. Meeks started it, and in no time at all half the crew was sporting a ring and a drop or two of dried blood in their left earlobe. The blood came from the way the piercing was done.

There was no using dainty little gold studs with a sharp post that slid through the ear nice and easy, and then kept the hole open as it healed. We knew nothing of such techniques. For us it was a lump of beeswax behind the ear, which had just been swabbed with the same alcohol we drank. Then a buddy would take a three-corner sail needle that was used to sew canvas, pushing it through you ear until you yelled with pain. The needle held a short piece of what might be called grocery string, tied in a little loop and painted with iodine. Each day you added more iodine, and pulled it through the earlobe until it healed. After that the string was yanked out and the ring slipped in.

When the time came for me to join the crowd, naturally the operation was performed by my own guys. My ear was properly washed with alky, and while Lambert held my head motionless, Davy jammed the lump of wax in place. Then old "Doc Buttermilk" took his sail needle and pushed it ever so slowly through my quivering flesh. The sadistic bastard took his damn sweet time about it, too, despite my agonizing moans and groans. Shorty Schuler just stood there, saying, "Aw, come on, Dawson, it don't really hurt so much." How the hell did he know? It wasn't his ear! All in all it came off pretty well, and in no time everything healed with no complications, and from my ear swung a little gold ring. Just like the other guys.

Although the exec wasn't too enthusiastic about it, the skipper didn't pay too much attention to the craze so long as no one turned up with a bad infection. Regular checkups by the pharmacist mate was all we needed to prevent that from happening. But as you might expect, something had to go haywire with the program—old Murphy's Law in action. With us it was Shorty Schuler who wanted his ear pierced so he could join the rest of us. Lanny Lamond, being his buddy, offered to do the surgery. It worked like this.

One evening during a holiday routine, we were sitting around the shack, drinking coffee liberally laced with alcohol, and swapping lies as usual. The subject of earrings came up, and it was then that Shorty decided he wanted his ear punched. That's what he called it, and that's what led to the trouble. In retrospect, I know that if we hadn't been drinking it would never have gone any further. As it was, we figured that if it was going to be done, that was as good a time as any. But instead of wax and a sail needle, Lambert reached for a sheet metal punch. The kid wanted his ear punched, and punched it would be. We all thought it ought to work. So we washed the punch in alcohol, wiped it off, gave the patient another shot of coffee, and got on with it. Lanny grabbed hold of the ear, slipped the punch over the lobe, and bore down. Schuler let out a shriek that set our teeth on edge and sobered up. He was dancing around the shop like a drunken tar doing a wild hornpipe, with Lambert running after him because he still had a grip on the tool, which was hung up in Shorty's ear. He finally let go, and the punch fell to the deck with a considerable amount of the kid's blood. Don't let anyone ever tell you an earlobe don't bleed. His sure as hell did.

In spite of everything, the operation was deemed a success. Even by Shorty. When we finally caught the little guy and checked out the procedure, we could see the desired hole all the way through. Hell, we could see lamplight through his ear. A bit pinkish from the bloody froth, but light just the same. Thank goodness his ear went numb, and we could give him some first aid consisting of a dirty rag to hold to his head as he headed down to sick bay to have the doc do the job right.

When Shorty had screamed, the OOD came running into the shack and asked when in hell was going on. We told him the truth. We had punched Schuler's ear. He accepted that, and apparently thought no more about it. He didn't ask how we had done the job, and nobody volunteered any information.

The pharmacist mate, of course, had to keep a record of all treatments he gave to anyone, even our little bitty buddy. It didn't take long for Mr. Lefevre to become aware of exactly what had taken place. He turned purple, spit all over himself, and put our entire department on report. There was a captain's mast for all of us the next morning. A captain's mast is the lowest form of official shipboard disciplinary action, which can only lead to simple restriction, extra duty, and so on. But it can also carry recommendation for a court martial. The accused appears before the captain with charges read by his division officer or gang leader who made the complaint. The man on report was given an opportunity to explain, and his boss or division officer may speak in his defense. In our case, I was the gang leader! So our defense was up to Lieutenant William Joseph Moriarity, who had so often saved our butts in the past.

Mr. Lefevre was ready to send us all to Portsmouth Naval Prison. He charged us with drunkenness, which was true enough, although so common that the captain didn't pay too much attention to that. We were also charged with "deliberate injury to a shipmate." I was surprised we were not charged with damaging Navy property. That punch did get kind of bloody.

In the course of the mast we all pled guilty because we knew better than not to. Moriarity made a good pitch on our behalf, but it still didn't look good for us. Although I had not taken part in the action, my being gang leader made me the responsible party. I wondered if the incident would have any bearing on whether or not I would get my second-class rate. The captain asked our man Lambert what he thought he was doing, punching the kid's ear the way he had. Lambert, trying to cover his butt, made it very clear that Schuler had asked him to do just that—to punch his ear. "At the time, Captain, I was doing just what my buddy asked me to do." Then the skipper turned to Schuler and said, "Okay, Shorty, suppose you tell us exactly why you wanted a hole in your ear." Schuler drew himself up to his full five feet whatever and, refusing to cop out on the rest of us, replied, "Sir, I wanted to be like the rest of the guys. It seemed like a good idea at the time!"

Then it was the executive officer's turn. He strongly recommended that we all be given a deck court martial. That might have been the easiest for us, because the most we could have gotten as punishment, according to regulations, would have been a heavy fine, restrictions, extra duty, and possibly being refused our next promotion. Lefevre apparently didn't know this, but Moriarity did, and his stern look told us to keep our mouths shut. He might get us out of trouble yet. Well, that might be okay, but I had the feeling I would remain a third-class petty officer for a long time.

Captain Shee leaned back in his chair and looked very

solemn. Then he announced his decision. Because everybody aboard had been drinking now and again with no charges being brought against them, he would officially overlook the alleged drunkenness. But God help us if it happened again! He would also overlook the ear piercing business itself because so many crewmen were already wearing earrings and there had been no trouble to date. But he wanted the practice stopped, right now. He would sit on any decision where our gang was concerned. If our boy's ear became infected, we would all go down the tube. There would then be a deck court martial for all of us, and a transfer to some godforsaken island where we could keep company with the gooney birds as we awaited the end of the war. Lefevre opened his mouth to say something at that point, but Shee waved his arm and the mast was adjourned. That, we thought, was that.

We all went back to work, and were promptly chewed out by just about every man on board who didn't already wear an earring. They insisted we were "earring-happy idiots" who were making life rough for all hands. You might have expected those candy asses to gripe. They didn't wear The Ring! What did they know?

Looking back at it all some fifty years later, I can see how stupid we were. As the gang leader, it was my responsibility to stop it at the beginning before it got out of hand. But with the coffee we were drinking at the time, I had to agree with Schuler. It seemed like a good idea. I really think that the only thing that kept us all from going down the chute was the fact that the captain had a bit of a reputation of his own as a hell-raiser off duty. That and the fact that he had no use for his executive officer. Whatever saved our butts, we had to agree we were very lucky, and we had best apply our energies to doing a better job in the future and to make a point of not doing anything to antagonize Mr. Lefevre.

Misfortunes of War?

The promotional exams had been taken in November of 1943, and after several weeks had passed with no lists being posted, we began to wonder what was going on. I could understand in my case that our little earring caper might be enough to hold up my new rate, but what about the other guys? Something was definitely not right. With so many of the old-timers having been transferred, we had lost our pipeline into the wardroom, and were relying on scuttlebutt for our information. We had even tried to con the officers' cooks and stewards into getting some dope for us, but the people we had previously looked to had been shipped out and their replacements did not know how things were being done in our kind of Navy.

In an effort to get to the bottom of the situation, I turned to Lieutenant Moriarity. Sure, he was an officer, but he had also been a friend and knew that anything he told me would be confidential. So I buttonholed him one night when we were on watch together, and asked for a direct answer. He said that the same thing was taking place on all the ships in the Pacific. Commanding officers and execs were holding off all promotions because experienced rated men were being hijacked for new construction. If they did not promote anyone, they could keep their experienced people longer and maintain the efficiency of their ships. In our own case, although Captain Shee had been on the *Trever* for some time and knew almost everyone on a personal level, he still had his own career to think about, and although he had no use for his exec, he was obligated to support him. As a result, we had a lot of overqualified men on board who were not being kicked up the ladder. For those considering a Navy career, it could be disastrous. If we didn't make our rates during wartime, we might as well give up, because when the fracas was over and the Navy went back to peacetime footing, promotions would be slow and difficult.

As it was, after September 1942 all rates and ranks were being made on a temporary basis, and after the war people would revert back to their permanent rank. A chief petty officer might find himself reduced to first or even second class. A full commander might find himself wearing the stripes of a lieutenant. His records may show that he was capable of performing the duties of a higher rank, but he would have to work his way back up. For those of us looking forward to twenty or thirty years of service, ending the war with a low rank or rate would be a good reason to think of a new line of work.

We managed to get through the 1943 Christmas and New Year holidays without incident. Then, in January, things began to look up. Captain Shee was to be kicked up to lieutenant commander and sent to another command. As we suspected, our exec, Lieutenant Morgan Lefevre III, took over as captain of the *Trever*. We thought that with his new position he might mellow and reconsider the promotion list. No such luck. If anything, he became more domineering and arrogant than ever. During his period of command he made the kind of mistakes we expected. Never really a good ship handler, Lefevre had several very near collisions going alongside a tender for fuel and repairs. His minesweeping technique left a lot to be desired because he simply did not understand the effect the rolling sea might have on our streamed paravanes and other gear. Everybody took the rap for his blunders, including the officers. Moriarity was especially vulnerable because he was the ship's first lieutenant and in charge of sweeping operations. And the fact that he had stood up for the shipfitters at our mast didn't do him any good, either.

Shortly after Lieutenant Lefevre took command, the promotion list was again passed up to him by the newly appointed executive officer, H. K. Ranking, Lieutenant, USNR, and again it was rejected. The skipper refused to sign any warrants, still insisting that we were not of proven ability. It appeared that our only salvation lay in his reassignment, which was sure to come. So we waited, and waited. There was little more we could do.

The Lefevre reign of command lasted almost six months to the day. Six months of bungling, cover-up, and a drop in morale as we watched our hard-won reputation as an efficient ship go down the tubes. Fortunately for us, we had no combat assignments during that period. If we had, even the luck of the old Tremblin' T could not have saved us. We went from day to day just doing our jobs and trying to keep out of trouble. There was no drinking, no earring capers, and no waving at the pretty ladies. Gang leaders, myself included, began to get downright testy. More guys were put on report than at any time since I had come on board. Captain Lefevre began to spend more and more time in his cabin, coming out only for meals, GQ, minesweeping operations, and the like, leaving the actual operation of the *Trever* pretty much up to his exec, Mr. Ranking. Then we discovered through our newly established line of communication into the ship's office that he had actually applied for a transfer himself—almost unheard of for an officer holding his first command.

Things began to take a turn for the better as our prayers were answered. On July 24, Morgan Lefevre III was relieved by one Alfred Hempstead, Lieutenant, USNR. When our former captain left the ship, there was no one other than the OOD and the gangway watch to see him off. It was the first and only time anyone could remember an officer or crewman leaving the *Trever*, for whatever reason, without a friendly sendoff. You could almost feel the tension lift as he got into the boat for the trip ashore. As the boat cox'n rang his bells to pull away and head for the beach, it was as though the ringing was a signal for a pall to be lifted from the old DMS. We had no idea what the new skipper might be like, but anything had to be an improvement.

We found out very quickly what kind of a captain we had in Lieutenant Hempstead. One of the first things the exec did was to present him with a promotion list, explaining that its approval had been delayed because of our hectic schedule. From what we were told later, Hempstead took a quick look at the list and asked, "Are these men qualified?" Mr. Ranking assured him that they were. With that, the warrants were quickly signed. The captain said, "If they can't do their jobs, I'll find out in a hurry. If I rate 'em, I can bust 'em." On August 1st the list was on the bulletin board and I was officially rated shipfitter second class. A new day had dawned over the old four piper, and with the sun we all began to revert to the mob of Asiatic hooligans we were, while the *Trever* returned to being a most unorthodox, but efficient, ship of war.

Back to Normalcy

The next few months under Hempstead's command saw things getting back to normal on the *Trever*. At least to what we considered normal. People began to show signs of the old craziness. Tailor-made dungarees and whites began to show up, as did beards and a few weird haircuts. Some of the guys who had removed their earrings while Lefevre was skipper began to wear them again, and the regular ongoing poker and craps games could be found in the living quarters and the cold-fire room. Not that the new captain was a pushover or anything like it. Actually, he ran a pretty tight ship and expected everything done in the best possible way. But he also knew that on the old ships like the flush deckers, things were a lot more informal and nonregulation than in the Real Navy.

Hempstead was also tough on maintaining discipline where it was necessary. We saw captain's mast being held once a month for defaulters guilty of things like taking a swing at a petty officer, insubordination, constantly being late to relieve the watch, and, worst of all, sleeping on watch. He was very fair in prescribing penalties, however, letting the punishment fit the crime. Even those who were on the receiving end of that punishment would feel that such treatment had been fair.

The skipper also made it a habit of stopping to shoot the breeze now and then with crew members. I remember the day he spent in the shipfitters' shack talking about our job and how we did it. He also extracted a promise from us to build a toy ship for his young son. We did a great job on that. It was Navy gray with all the official insignia, numbers, and even the ship's name and ID. For our part, our little Navy politicking couldn't hurt. He'd heard about the Great Ear Punching Caper.

It was in September of that year that I turned 21, and my cradle cruise enlistment came to an end. Going up to the ship's office, I asked the chief yeoman how this would affect my service. "My hitch is over. Do I get to go home now?" The chief didn't say much, just pulled my records from the file and rummaged around his desk until he found a big rubber stamp. He banged that stamp onto a wet ink pad a few times, and then slammed it down on a fresh page in my record jacket.

After that he turned it around so I could read it. There, in big red letters, it proclaimed: RETAINED IN NAVAL SERVICE FOR THE BENEFIT OF PUBLIC WELFARE. That said it all. I did have the option of re-enlisting if I chose, but for some reason I decided to hold off. As it was, although technically I was still Regular Navy, my enlistment changed to something similar to the reserve. I was in until the war was over, unless I decided to re-up. It kind of rankled me that I was on equal status with some feather merchant reservist. But the chief promised not to tell anyone. Being Regular Navy himself, he understood the stigma attached to being considered USN Reserve.

During the time we had Hempstead as skipper, the

Trever continued to be involved in escort, target towing, and minesweeping. We were originally scheduled to go on the invasion of Saipan, but our evaporators broke down just as the task force was forming up, and we were put on standby duty instead. The USS *Hopkins* took our place. The *Hopkins* was a sister ship, one of what had been Mine Squadron Two. We hated to see the Sloppy Hoppy get the assignment, because we knew we would never hear the end of it. About a year or so earlier, when the *Hopkins* had been getting some pretty soft duty while the rest of us were getting shot at, some unknown sailors had slipped over in a boat one night and painted the letters USO on her side. The culprits weren't from the *Trever*, but most of us did know who they were. But would we tell? No way! The crew of the Hoppy was pretty upset about it and was just waiting for a chance to get back at us because they always figured we were guilty. So as the *Hopkins* stood out of the harbor on her way to do the job we should have been doing, they blinked over a message. "See you after the party. Don't wait up!"

Later on we did get the opportunity to again do something important. The heavy cruiser USS *Canberra* and the light cruiser USS *Houston* had been damaged in surface action and the *Trever* was senior escort vessel to take them back to Ulithi, where they would join a task force heading back to Pearl. The trip back to Ulithi was very tense, because the group was limited in speed to that of the slowest ship, and the danger of Japanese submarines was very real. A good part of the trip was made at general quarters, ready for a fight. But, fortunately, we arrived safely and turned our charges over to another escort command.

In the middle of December, the *Trever* joined a convoy

headed for the Western Caroline Islands, acting as part of the escort screen. We got underway on December 14, expecting a fairly uneventful trip. Instead, we ran into a fight that was more harrowing than anything the DMS had experienced since December 7, 1941. A battle that threatened to put an end to the war record of the *Trever* and her entire ship's company. A battle with an enemy more terrible than the Japanese could ever be. We tangled with Mother Nature herself, in the shape of Typhoon Cobra.

Typhoon Cobra

The quarterly reorganization of regular duties had taken me from the 20mm guns and placed me on wheel watches. As a helmsman, I was in a position to see and hear everything that was happening in the control center of the ship. Standing at the ship's wheel, I didn't miss very much of what was said by the OOD and the bridge crew. I had the eight to twelve watch on the morning of that fateful day of December 15—the day we got caught in a typhoon—and things were going so well I felt uncomfortable.

The sun and sky were so clear and bright it almost hurt the eyes. We had received heavy weather warnings, but there was no indication of anything like it approaching. The sea was like glass and steering was easy. Once the wheel was set to a course, the compass didn't vary more than a degree on either side. It just didn't seem natural.

I was not the only one who felt something was wrong. The captain spent the entire morning perched in his high chair on the port side of the bridge, right next to the wheel. I noticed that he seemed nervous, although he said very little except to occasionally ask me how the wheel felt, or to call for a barometer reading. It was his constant attention to the barometer that gave me a sense of foreboding. If it suddenly began to drop, we were in for a blow.

Cradle Cruise

About ten in the morning it began to slip downward. The sea began to kick up and I could feel the change in the steering the skipper had been asking about. As the morning drew on the wind began to rise and it became more and more difficult to hold the ship on course. Usually the wind or sea conditions would push the ship from one direction to another, but that morning the *Trever* was constantly going to both sides of the designated course. She began to roll and pitch as well. By the time I was relieved at noon, the compass was spinning like a dervish, a bad indication of things to come. My relief, to my surprise, was the quartermaster, rather than the regular stander. The chief took the wheel only at GQ or when we were in extremely heavy weather.

When I went down to chow, the deck force was battening down everything for heavy sea conditions. All loose gear was removed from open spaces, and lifelines were being rigged the length of the main deck, so anyone who might be topside would have something to hang onto. Extra lashings were being put on our two boats and the liferafts to prevent their being carried away in strong winds and heavy seas. Somebody was sure expecting the worst.

The *Trever* began to pitch high by that time, and every time she would slam back into the trough of the waves, white water crashed over the fo'c'sle all the way to the bridge. All topside hatches were being tightly dogged down, and it became very hard to walk on deck because rolling had increased to a point far beyond anything we had experienced in the past. By two o'clock we were in the midst of what was officially designated as a typhoon. Typhoon Cobra, to be precise. It was later judged to be the worst such storm in the Pacific in fifty years.

The convoy was directed to split up, with each ship fending for itself as best it could. Torrential rains began to pound our topside, at times being blown horizontal by 100 knot winds. Visibility dropped to zero, and from the bridge it was impossible to see our own bow, let alone any other ships that might have been in the area. We were all hoping there was no collision, because things had happened so fast we could not be sure the convoy had scattered widely enough to avoid it. The waves by that time were rearing higher than our bridge. The OOD was able to stand on the wing and look straight up at a wave top.

The old minesweeper continued to roll, at times far more than her designers ever intended, or believed, possible. At one time we were held over in excess of 48 degrees, and hung there for moments before finally coming back, only to go in the other direction. With each roll the blackened seas seemed to climb straight up to the lead-colored sky before crashing over our decks. The *Trever* began to protest the pounding as only a ship can. Engines howled as they tried to turn screws in an unforgiving and punishing swell behind us. Fire room blowers whined as though in pain, trying almost vainly to send enough air below to keep our boilers alive. Without them, we would have floundered.

Word was passed for all hands to stay below and off the weather decks unless it was absolutely necessary to be there. With every wild, lurching leap of the ship, crew members were running to the opposite side and actually leaning themselves, as though in some way that might help bring her back to an even keel. All of us were giving thanks for the thirty tons of lead ballast we had packed into our bilges the last time we were in the yard—ballast to counteract the topside weight of our new minesweeping gear. By that time the heavy seas were regularly breaking over the bridge, cracking and breaking windows. Our deck ventilators were being crushed as though by a giant hand, hatch covers were ripped out of the steel plate. Both our boats had been smashed and carried away as their lines were snapped like pieces of grocery string. The massive steel davits were bent and twisted like pretzels. The power of the typhoon to destroy was unbelievable, even to those of us who watched it.

Down in the fire and engine rooms the snipes tied themselves to their stations so as not to slide across the floor plates into the machinery. The *Trever* throbbed and vibrated as though she would tear herself apart when our stem rose free of the water, and the screws, having no purchase, would spin uselessly in the air. The very plates of our hull creaked and groaned from the stress of being twisted by the action of the churning seas, causing all of us to remember that those bottom strakes were only 3/8 of an inch thick. Just 3/8 of an inch of pitted, rusty, overage metal between us and the demanding ocean. Through it all the hard blowing gale shrieked at us as would a demon from hell. Like a fiend from another world determined to possess our souls. It was a noise more felt than heard. "OOOOooooooOOoeeeeEEEeeeEEE!" It never stopped, but kept wailing and keening like a sailor's requiem. We were scared, but we hung on. Gritting our teeth and praying, we hung on.

The captain had been fighting to keep the *Trever*'s bow to the storm, to keep us from broaching if the seas were to hit on beams. It seemed to be working, although the ship continued to suffer a pounding. As we tried to take what shelter we could, there was a heavy hammering, crashing noise on the starboard side of the galley deckhouse. Looking over we could see that while we had lost both boats, the bow section of the gig was still with us. Having torn away from the rest of the boat, it was still secured to the davit by its bow line. The splintered bit of wreckage was flying free to slam against the deckhouse to do more damage. A bos'n mate stepped out on deck with his sheath knife in hand, intending to cut it loose.

He fought his way across the leaning deck and climbed the twisted boat davit. Bracing himself against the onslaught of the pounding waves, he reached out to cut the remaining piece of line. The *Trever* took a deep roll to starboard and dirty, black seawater broke over the side. We heard a scream, and when the waves fell back, the bos'n mate was gone. Several men dashed out and, clinging to the lifelines, looked for him. There he was, supported by his lifejacket and being carried on the crest of a wave some 25 yards from the ship. Immediately the call went out: "Man overboard, starboard side, man overboard!"

As soon as the word reached the bridge, the captain began to swing around to try and pick him up. In the heavy swells the rudder alone was useless for maneuvering. We could hear the engines rumble as they were given full power. Starboard back and port ahead as we began to swing ever so slowly toward the bos'n who was still riding the wave, but being tossed about like a bottle cork. The crewmen on deck began to make ready to pick him up should we be able to get close enough. One seaman shed his lifejacket so as to give himself more freedom of movement. The others tied a line around his waist and, taking hold, stood by as he prepared to go over the side after the bos'n.

Ever so slowly the *Trever* was working her way toward the crewman, who by that time was no longer yelling or waving his arms at us. He gave every indication of being dead, or at least unconscious, as he was tossed about. But we determined to get him back aboard. It took about two hours of maneuvering before the captain could bring us close enough to where we put over a heaving line. Our people continued to call out to let him know we were not going to abandon him to the storm. Then, suddenly, as quickly as he had left the ship, he returned. A high tossing wave threw him into the air toward the ship, as though the sea gods had relented and were casting back what they no longer wanted to destroy. The bos'n arched through the air and slammed up against the sea ladder welded to our side. By some miracle he was still semi-conscious and as his hand fell across one of the ladder rungs, his fingers instinctively closed. In no time at all the deck crew had their man over the side, and they reached down to pull the bos'n to safety. But he still had a tight grip on the rung and wouldn't let go. He told us later that after all that time in the water, he had hold of something solid and he was not about to let go. Finally the seaman who had gone over the side and who was clinging to the ladder with the bos'n stomped on his hand to break his grip, breaking a couple of fingers as he did so. Pulling the waterlogged man on deck, the guys immediately rushed him to the skipper's cabin, which was the only reasonably dry place aboard ship. At the captain's orders, he was placed in the bunk where he was tended by the pharmacist mate for shock, exposure, and his injuries. In striking the ship's side, he had broken his leg in two places. And, of course, he had several smashed fingers.

With our man safely aboard, the old DMS again turned bow onto the storm and we continued to fight our way through heavy black seas with more waves higher than we were, and visibility at its lowest. Looking back, it's strange how we were able to see some 40 yards or so from the ship so long as we were trying to recover our shipmate. As soon as we had him, everything socked in tight again.

By eight o'clock that evening the barometer began to rise and the sky could be seen, although it was still dirty gray and black in color, and the waves began to subside. It was over, and we had come through it, although not without paying a price. Cobra was lowered in status to that of a bad storm, and that was so welcome that, in spite of continued rolling and tossing of the *Trever,* we put our repair parties throughout the ship to check on damage and patch up what we could. I was with my own gang when I heard the word passed. "Now hear this. Dawson, relieve the watch." I passed my responsibility of my gang to Pheeples and headed for the bridge. Arriving there, I relieved the quartermaster at the wheel. He had been fighting it all through our ordeal, and could hardly stand. Taking his place on the platform, I took a look around the bridge. Windows were broken, the deck was awash with water, and even the captain's chair was soaked. But as members of the bridge gang were being relieved, there were a lot of smiles and handshakes all around.

With the regular watch set, the *Trever* pointed her bow onto a course for Guam. We arrived late on the 16th and sent the bos'n to the military hospital on the beach. We took on fuel and made for Eniwetok, making our landfall on December 22. It was there that we were able to get news of what had happened to the rest of the Pacific Fleet during Typhoon

Cobra. It was absolutely unbelievable.

Nearly 800 lives had been lost, and the number of injured was still to be counted. Three new destroyers had capsized and went down with all hands, the USS *Hull*, the *Monaghan*, and the *Spence*. Several cargo vessels had also sunk. Even ships as large as aircraft carriers had suffered severe damage, battling fires in their hangers. Dozens of aircraft of all types had been blown overboard, carried away, or were damaged beyond repair.

Hearing all that, we realized just how lucky we had been. But it had been so much more than luck. Every man aboard had new respect for the old four stack tin cans in general, and the *Trever* in particular. She was indeed a charmed ship. A lot of the guys who had applied for transfer were noticeably quiet. More than one transfer request was torn up.

On December 24 we got underway again, headed for Pearl Harbor as escort to the US Army ship *Santa Isabel*. It was a very bleak, but nevertheless happy Christmas for us that year. The voyage east was quiet and uneventful. As I stood my wheel watches steering for Hawaii, I could not help but notice how smooth and easy the ship responded to course changes or corrections. Although the sea was not really glassy, the *Trever* cut through the water, bone in her teeth, with hardly a pitch or roll. The engines actually purred and the boilers had only their normal, quiet hiss we had become accustomed to; we scarcely heard them. But there was something to be heard for those who cared to listen. All those little sounds of a ship that only a real sailor knows is her way of speaking to those who understand. The *Trever* was proud of her victory over the typhoon. Proud of how she had saved us all. And why not? The old girl had every right.

Lon Dawson

We arrived in Hawaii, sighting Diamond Head on December 31. As we stood into the harbor, sailing through the gates, there was a message from the signal tower ashore. "Welcome Home, and Happy New Year!" There was no doubt about it. It was indeed a Happy New Year.

Pearl Harbor and Home

The *Trever* spent a few days in Pearl Harbor, taking on fuel, provisions, and having a few necessary repairs made to enable us to travel to the mainland with no further problems. While we were there, along with about forty other crewmen, I received orders for transfer to new construction. That left me with mixed feelings. After having been on board my ship for over three years, and having just survived what had been called the worst typhoon in anyone's memory, I felt a real tie to the old bucket that would be hard to break. She had been home to all of us for a long time, and we had come to trust her. The *Trever* had proven to be a lucky ship. Still, we had no idea of how long the war would last and a lot of us were thinking in terms of a Navy career. We knew it would be necessary to move on if we wanted to climb that promotional ladder. There would be school for some of us, and immediate reassignment for others. In any case, we really had no choice because the Navy would send us where it felt we were needed most.

We began to get our personal gear ready to leave the ship upon arrival in the States. In my case, there was very little to pack. I had been living in the shipfitters' shack, and all my possessions had been stored there. My seabag and bedding had been swept away during the typhoon, and all I had left was what clothes I was wearing and what had been kept in a locker fitted into the overhead, safe from the raging seas and wind. Everything could go into a single suitcase. Fortunately, my tailor-made blues had been up in that locker, so I was ready to ship out.

There was the problem of preparing Lanny Lamond Lambert to take over my gang when I left. He was the next senior man and the responsibility would be his. Scuttlebutt had it another shipfitter would be transferred aboard from one of the other DMSs, but nothing was confirmed. Davy and Buttermilk were not too enthusiastic about having Lambert as their boss, but they would be up for their own rates soon, and would probably transfer off to new construction as I was doing. So my suggestion was that they just be patient and make the best of it.

During our stay at Pearl, the ship's signal gang busied themselves making up our Homeward Bound pennant, so that it might be streamed on the trip back. A tradition in the Navy, it would signify that the *Trever* had completed her mission and was going to her home port of call. We knew that with the way the war was going, even if it were to last another year or so, the *Trever* would see no more combat. With the newer ships coming off the ways, and considering the structural damage she had suffered during the typhoon, the old girl would be relegated to easier duties. Most likely she would be operating out of Pearl Harbor. Well, she deserved it. Along with her sisters, the *Trever* had held the line against the Japanese until the Navy was able to regroup. Anyway, for most of us, the USS *Trever* DMS-16 was going home. Hence the pennant of red, white, and blue.

That pennant was a thing of beauty to behold. Actually

a streamer, as I said. Over 130 feet long and about a foot wide, it represented every man aboard. The officers were indicated by a white star on a blue field for each of them. For the enlisted men there was a foot of red and white streamer for each. Upon arrival at our home port it would be cut up and each guy would receive his section. Until then, it would be flown from our mast head all the way back to the mainland. As we steamed out of the channel and headed to sea it snapped and cracked in the wind, its colors sparkling in the bright sun. All the ships we passed on the way out knew what it represented, and sounded a blast of their whistle or siren as we passed through the buoys.

The trip back was uneventful, as we expected. To our great pleasure there was always a brisk wind day and night to keep our pennant streaming overhead. Not once did it fall to deck or get tangled in our rigging or superstructure. But then, we never thought it would. For such a thing to happen to the *Trever* was unthinkable!

On January 9 we sighted land, and by noon we were tied up at the Mole Pier on the San Diego waterfront. The transfer draft was mustered on the quarterdeck and we said our good-byes to the rest of the crew. Then, after tossing our gear onto a waiting Navy truck, we climbed aboard for the run to the Camp Elliott Training and Distribution Center outside of San Diego. It was commonly known as TADCEN. It would be our first stop before going on leave and then receiving our assignment orders.

As the truck pulled away, we were able to get our last look at the ship we had all become so attached to. I must have had a strange look on my face, because one of the guys gave me a dig in the ribs, saying, "Snap out of it, Dawson, it's all behind us now." Sure, he was right. But when he said it he had a tear in his eye.

Probably from the wind.

When the truck arrived at Camp Elliott, it dropped us off at the barracks to which we had been assigned, and then lumbered off to where the rickety old Navy trucks were kept when not presenting a hazard to normal traffic. The barracks were the same old two-story buildings we were all familiar with. Our service records and transfer orders had already been sent over to the base Administration Building and we were left to ourselves to settle in and relax for the evening. We would begin the necessary processing the next day.

Early in the morning, after a rather quick breakfast of shore-side chow, our draft was mustered at the Ad Building and told what would be taking place. There were a lot of forms to fill out, and we were given an opportunity to show our preferences for new duty. We had all been in the Navy long enough to know it was a lot of seahorse hockey because they never really gave anyone their choice of anything, unless it was to the Navy's benefit. But we played the game. We would be allowed three choices for shore duty station, school, and choice of ship. After that was all over with, we would get our authorizations for thirty days' leave plus traveling time. The traveling time was really for those who would be reporting directly to their new assignment. For the rest of us, it would simply be six extra days because we would be reporting back to TADCEN.

For shore duty my first choice was New Orleans. I figured that the French Quarter would make for some pretty first-class liberty. My second choice was the Mare Island Navy Yard, because it would be a good place to gain experience in my specialty rate of shipfitter. My third choice was the repair base in San Diego, for the same reasons. Choices for school were made the same way. My first choice was damage control and repair, second was minesweeping, and third was deep-sea diving. That last was not because of any feelings of heroism on my part, but rather for the extra $50 qualification pay after graduation. All three schools were good for six months of stateside duty, and after three years of continuous sea duty, and during a war at that, shore duty looked pretty good. In all probability I would be going out to sea, despite my announced selections of duty, so I tried to make my choice of ships as wisely as possible. My first choice was a seagoing salvage tug, second a fleet minesweeper, and finally a destroyer. My thinking was that any of them would be a good follow-up to school.

Finally, with all the paperwork completed, we were issued leave authorization, and we trooped back to the barracks to get ready to leave. It didn't take long to get our dress blues brushed and pressed, a little laundry done up, and get what we would leave behind locked up in a warehouse. The next morning we were up early for chow, and then through the gates for a long, long leave. Sharp as could be in my tailor-made blues, walking with a pronounced salty sea swagger, white hat cocked over one eye, and with a gold earring flashing in the sun, I headed for Chicago. Home was the sailor, home from the sea.

A Sailor Ties the Knot

When my train pulled into Chicago on that last leave, things were quite a bit different than in the past. The war had been going on for years and people had become accustomed to it. There was no longer the big hoorah every time a sailor or GI got off the train, or walked through an airline terminal. Our general hero status had become a thing of the past. It was probably just as well, because we could all sense a climax developing and those of us who might be leaving the service would have to return to some kind of normalcy. Still, it was a letdown to be almost ignored.

Back in my neighborhood, a serviceman on leave had become a pretty common occurrence, and nobody was impressed by seeing a uniform. I was still anxious to tell about my experiences, but the audience was no longer there. My family, who had never seemed particularly concerned with my absence, was about as blasé as they could be. My grandma, however, gave me a bear hug that almost broke my ribs, and then hung onto every word I had to say. It was the kind of reception that a guy away from home would think about. And as you might know, in my case it would come from Grandma. Good old Grandma.

Most of the time on that leave was spent with my girlfriend, Penny. I was home one day when we talked seriously about getting married. The future looked pretty good at the time, even with the war still going on, and regardless of whether or not the Navy became a career. So we decided to go ahead and tie the knot. With wartime shortages and high costs, the wedding would have to be fairly conservative. But with a little help from my friends and a family member or two, we pulled it off. My cousin was best man, and a close friend of Pen's was maid of honor. My wife-to-be thought my earring was cute, but made me promise not to wear it for the wedding pictures. I promised right enough. Then turned around and wore a bigger one for the ceremony and photographs. Penny was so excited she didn't even notice. But when she saw the photographs later... Well, I survived, but only because I was on the coast by then and beyond her reach.

It was a church wedding. Pen wore the traditional white, and she was truly beautiful. I was in uniform, of course, complete with ribbons and that gold ring in my ear. It was at the wedding that we really met each other's family for the first time. Everything came off smoothly enough, and we became man and wife. For a 22 year old like me, it was a strange feeling. I was no longer that seventeen-year-old kid that had practically run away from home to join the Navy. But between the discipline of the military, and having experienced war, I had gone through a growing up process. I now felt ready to accept the greatest responsibility in the world: that of being a husband, and possibly a father.

After the ceremony we went to the photographer for the mandatory pictures; fortunately for me, Pen still hadn't noticed my earring, probably because so many things were happening so fast. The photag pushed us around, arranging and rearranging us until we were ready to shoot the group picture. We received the usual commands of "smile" and "everybody say cheese." He was ready to pop the shutter when we all heard the sound of running water. Kind of like a faucet out of control. The people in the group began to squirm and fidget as there on the floor at our feet a huge puddle began to form. Jean Alice, Pen's ten-year-old niece, was having a problem. Being the flower girl, and all excited about the festivities, the poor kid had lost it. That was no faucet we had heard running, it was her!

Everybody moved out of the way, out came a mop and bucket, the floor was swabbed down, and we started all over again. Eventually the pictures were taken and we all headed for the reception. Poor Jean Alice must have almost froze on the way, because remember, it was January. But kids are hardy, and she survived.

The reception came off great, and everybody seemed to have a good time. Even the strange GIs I dragged in off the street to have a drink and wish me good luck. They ended up staying all evening, and when Pen and I left around midnight, they were still there trying to make out with some of the younger girls in the place. As we walked out the door, they wished us good fortune and we wished them the same.

There was no honeymoon as such. Wartime restrictions and the short time we had made that almost impossible. Instead, we stayed at my Uncle Ernie's house for the time I was home. He was working most of the time, and my aunt was so busy with her community activities that we often had the house to ourselves. When we were at home, that is. That wasn't very often. We spent our time doing all sorts of crazy, stupid things. Between the wedding and chasing around, we spent a bundle. More money than I'd ever seen in my life. Pen and I paid for the wedding ourselves and then spent the rest of my leave going through whatever money we had left. In thirty days we ran through $2500! Kind of dumb, I suppose, but we figured that with her working and my going back to sea with no place to spend anything, we could save enough to set up housekeeping after the war. Besides, you don't get married very often in life, so we threw caution and money to the winds, and just enjoyed ourselves.

That leave, although it was thirty days plus, was all too short. The time came when I had to say good-bye to my bride and head back to the ship. So with a lot of hugs and kisses, we broke our clinch at the railroad station and I hopped aboard for the trip to the coast. I'm not embarrassed to say that despite being a very sophisticated 22 at the time, I didn't want to leave. There had been enough money left to get me a berth for the ride to San Diego, and it was a good thing. That night my eyes were more than a bit moist as I pounded my pillow and tried to get some sleep. Lying there, listening to the clickety clack of the train wheels, I knew that Pen was probably going through the same thing. It didn't help.

After that first night there was no time for me to feel sorry for myself. Getting married was the sort of thing that a million young people were doing, and our story was really no different. At almost every stop on that three-day trip to California more servicemen came aboard and there was a bit of hell raising on the way. Quite a few of the *Trever* draft had been on leave at the same time and we met on our return. With all the sailors, soldiers, and marines on the train, the MPs and shore patrol had a hard time trying to maintain some semblance of order. They were all feather merchant reservists who hadn't been in service too long, and had never left the States. Some of them were civilian cops who had been drafted, and they really threw themselves into their job. They became a real nuisance. So in a little town called Whitefish, Montana, we put about six of them off the train.

At the next stop about thirty of their brothers-in-arms stormed aboard looking for the riotous servicemen who had taken over the train. What they found were several groups of well-behaved soldiers, sailors, and marines talking very politely to little old ladies, telling sea stories to the children, and engaging in active games of checkers with the railroad porters. The storm troopers asked a lot of civilians what they knew of disorderly GIs who had put the MPs off the train back in Whitefish. Nobody knew anything about it. They couldn't imagine where they heard such reports! It was probably some inexperienced, short-timer MPs who had missed their train and were trying to cover up their own inadequacies.

Our train pulled out of the station and the party continued, but with the addition of our new-found civilian friends. I remember one nice old gal who made claim to riding troop trains during World War I. She passed around a thermos so we might all have just a touch of her hot tea. I don't know what she had in that bottle, but it would have taken all the varnish from an old rocker. When we finally arrived at our destination, those MPs that were still riding the rattler were bosom buddies—no doubt the result of the old girl's tea. We reported in to the TADCEN base and fell into our barracks. The next morning we met with base authorities and quickly found out what we would have to contend with before making our next transfer.

That Chickenshit TADCEN

After having spent several years in the Hooligan Navy, where regulations really didn't mean a great deal, we were not prepared for the restrictions and requirements of a stateside base. One of the first things we ran into was the regulation that we needed a complete allotment of clothing and other personal gear before transferring anyplace. For a lot of guys, that meant drawing a set of blues, maybe some extra skivvies, or even a blanket. But for those of us who came from the *Trever,* it meant getting almost everything. Uniforms, bedding, the works—plus a bag to carry it all. They even insisted on our having a hammock, something few of us had seen in years. But according to Navy regs it was the only way we could carry our bedding. We argued as much as we could, pointing out that no ship or station was using hammocks anymore, and besides, none of us had any money on the books to pay for all the gear we were expected to have. That made no impression on the base staff. Most of them had never been to sea and had no idea what the Real Navy was like. So we had no choice but to draw everything on the list and have our pay records show that we owed for it all. The entire thing came to about $265, and when you figure that my base pay at the time was $97 a month, with part of that being deducted for an allotment to my wife and an increase in my life insurance, it was going to take quite a while to break even. I could see myself writing and asking Pen to send me a few bucks now and then. The replacement of our missing gear was offset by the fact that they would let us file a claim with the Navy Department for our losses. Naturally, we filled out the many forms, in triplicate, to do just that. Well, that was fifty years ago, and to this day there has been no reimbursement. So much for the highly vaunted government sense of fair play we've heard so much about.

We were on the base about three days when we ran into more trouble. About five of us were walking back to the barracks after noon chow when a base jeep pulled up in front of us, stopped, and out jumped trouble in the person of one Bucky Barrett.

At first we didn't realize just how much trouble he was. You see, we all knew Bucky. He had been the chief bos'n mate on another DMS and we knew him as well as we knew anyone on our sister ships.

But the guy who came out of that jeep was not the same Bucky Barrett we remembered. He seemed to forget that we knew one another and had gone through all the same war experiences together. He began to berate us for being in improper uniform. We figured he had to be off his rocker until it suddenly became very, very clear. We were all wearing earrings!

The bos'n had been in the Navy about twenty-five years or so, and was a sailor of the old school. Strictly a by-the-book man, he had no use for what he called wartime sailors and "Pearl Harbor Avengers," guys who had come into the Navy to fight a war and expected to go home afterward. We tried to explain that we were all Regular Navy, not reserve, and had been in prior to the war breaking out. He didn't want to hear it. When he had been transferred in some time earlier, he had been sent to TADCEN for shore duty on the base police force. He was in his element, with a chance to nail people for being nonregulation or out of uniform. He had seen the sparkle of earrings, and that was enough for him. They constituted nonregulation jewelry. We argued, but to no avail. His partner called for the wagon and we found ourselves in the base police station facing a choice. We could surrender our rings until the day we transferred out, or he would put us all on report. Anything like that could hold up our leaving TADCEN, as well as mar our service record. So we handed over our treasured earrings.

But we did manage to bug him considerably when we laid those rings on his desk. We knew a bit about regulations ourselves, and insisted that he give each of us a receipt describing the item in question, and signed by him as the arresting officer along with his rank and serial number. He didn't like it, but he had no choice. We got our receipts, along with a warning. "Just watch it, sailors, like I'm gonna be watching you!"

We really didn't care all that much about the jewelry, although a few of the rings were expensive. We all had spares we could wear on liberty. But it was important that we not let him intimidate us as though we were greenhorns just out of boot camp. We also knew that the word would get around very quickly that a few of his old friends, being seasoned sailors themselves, had cut him down to size. As we walked back to the barracks, there was one thing we agreed upon. We had to get out of that chickenshit TADCEN base.

Our guys were at Camp Elliott for about six weeks, and a more miserable six weeks I don't remember all the time I was in service. There were about 50,000 men on that station for reassignment. Most of us were from sea duty, or school. All of us had several years of service and were not prepared for what we were asked to put up with. As if the order to buy new gear and the presence of Barrett were not enough, they were constantly searching for ways to keep us busy. They knew that 50,000 experienced sailors with nothing to do could only mean trouble. For them. Certainly not for us. So every day we were formed into groups of fifty or so and run off into classes of one kind or another. You can imagine how excited we were about that! There I was, a rated shipfitter with several years of experience, going through classes on first aid, signaling, fire control, and judo. Anything they might think of. Our instructors were invariably slick arms—guys who had been drafted, had no hash marks for time served, and had been given specialist ratings up to chief petty officer because of some civilian experience. Some of them had as much as three months in the Navy.

Once in a while we would have fun in class; judo, for instance. Our gang was taken to a gym where a big ex-copper was going to teach us the rudiments of hand-to-hand combat, just what we needed in the middle of the ocean on a seagoing salvage vessel. It all lasted about thirty minutes. After a very impressive lecture, he called a scrawny little pharmacist mate out to the floor to demonstrate some fancy maneuver or other. What he didn't know was that the little corpsman had been with the marines on Guadalcanal for over a year in constant combat. When the ex-cop tried to throw our little friend, something went wrong. There was a very audible snap as his elbow broke. Well, at least there was someone handy to give him first aid, along with an apology. And it did put an end to our judo classes.

There were a few other classes we enjoyed. Like the machine gun schools where we knew more about the weapons than the instructors. And the actual time on the machine gun range because we all "suddenly needed" one-on-one instruction because our instructors there were lady marines.

There were also time-consuming work parties. They would take us out to the boondocks on a truck and leave us for the day to carry rocks from one corner of a field to another. The next day another party would go out there and take them back. For our little group it worked only for about an hour or so the first day. At that point we explained to the slick arm in charge that unless he backed off and let us get some slack time, we were going to bury him under the rocks. He thought we were kidding until he found himself lying there with a lot of granite on his chest. After that we got along great. Somebody mentioned how nice it would be if Bucky Barrett was in charge of our working party.

A lot of our time was spent in figuring out ways to escape from TADCEN. Some of the guys were getting so frustrated they were ready to apply for a transfer to anything, anywhere—any kind of duty, even with a reduction in rate. But nothing worked, and we had to hang on until our orders came through. In the first week of April about ten of us were sprung. We were assigned to the naval repair base in San Diego for final transfer to the USS *Indian Island,* which we were told was a general auxiliary vessel fitted out as a seaplane tender. It wasn't the kind of duty any of us had requested, but then, we didn't expect to get what we wanted.

And a seaplane tender wasn't too bad. The ship was still being fitted out on the east coast, and by the time it came around, some of us might be off to school. In my case, school would bring an increase in rate, and would fit in with duty aboard the *Indian Island*.

Our orders called for us to be sent to the repair base, and we wasted no time getting ourselves organized as we waited for the word. The day before we were scheduled to transfer, we got together to do something we had been waiting for a long time to do. The five of us who had locked horns with Chief Bos'n Mate Barrett over our earrings trooped over to his office and demanded our property be returned. Old Bucky almost exploded. He claimed he couldn't find the rings on such short notice, and he would see that they were sent to us. No way! Some of those bits were kind of expensive and we wanted them right now! He started to get nasty until we made it clear that we didn't think he was within his authority to have taken the jewelry in the first place, and if they were not returned immediately we would have no choice but to go over to the Ad Building and file an official request for a Redress of Wrongs. That's Navy jargon meaning we thought he had broken his own regulations, that we had been wronged and wanted the matter officially dealt with, even if it meant a captain's mast. That would have been a switch. Me, going to captain's mast as a complainant! Bucky thought about it for a minute, and I guess he visualized himself going back out to sea. He screamed for one of his boys to check the property room to see if they might find a box of contraband jewelry. And what do you know? There they were! In a box of assorted items he had confiscated from guys all over the base. He dug out our pieces quickly enough and returned them, demanding that we sign the log acknowledging such a transfer of property. He also made it clear that if we were wearing them before we shoved off in the morning he would arrest us. Nothing was said about the fact that as we had walked into his office, we were all wearing our spare ring. But Barrett had to save face. We knew that before the war he had served in the Far East and the concept of face meant a lot to him. And he knew that we knew. As soon as we were out of sight of his office we all took the rings from our ears. Scheduled to leave in the morning, we didn't want to tempt fate. What we wanted was to leave that chickenshit TADCEN.

San Diego Naval Repair Base

The next morning the Navy truck rolled up in front of our barracks. Shake, rattle, and roll. I swear it was the same truck that I'd seen on every Navy base I'd ever been to, anywhere in the world, driven by the same bored, tired driver. We tossed our gear in the back and clambered aboard. In a cloud of smoke, a gnashing of gears, and a few loud clanks and bangs, we were off.

Going through the main gate, it was hard to believe that what we were seeing was the same little destroyer base I'd left back in December of 1941. But then, it really wasn't. Back in '41 it couldn't handle anything larger than a tin can, or maybe a small transport. But rolling down the street we saw dry docks that could easily accommodate a heavy cruiser, and as we watched, a fleet aircraft carrier was steaming into the harbor. Scuttlebutt had it that the San Diego base could do almost anything that might be done in the Mare Island Yard. I could believe it.

There were well over 50,000 personnel stationed there. Most of them were on temporary duty, waiting transfer to school or new construction. The remainder of them was there to work the repair base itself. Along with civilian workers on station, Navy enlisted people handled just about everything. That gives an idea of the expertise we had developed over the early years of the war. The great majority of the enlisted men lived on the far side of the base, in the very familiar two-decked wooden barracks. There was a small hospital, a mess hall, recreation building, and sports field, as well as a sizable library, a small theatre, and several buildings used for basic service schools. And, of course, the always-to-be-found Administration Building staffed by reservists. Most of them were WAVES or women marines.

In the repair yard itself there were shops of all kinds: metalworking, carpentry, foundry, blacksmith, electrical, fire control, and radar. Just about everything needed to effect necessary repairs and modifications. Along the seawall could be found gigantic cranes and derricks of all types. Along one portion of the docks were piles of lumber of every imagined kind and dimension. All carefully stacked, I found out later, in such a way so as to provide hidey holes where a tired sailor might snatch a little shuteye. Those treasured dens were usually very carefully controlled by the regular shore-based crew. Some of them were fitted out with bunks, electric lights, even pictures on the bulkheads. I saw one that was equipped with hammocks for the old-timers. The regular use of these creature comforts would cost, of course, but that was only fair because you would usually get the morning paper with your fresh coffee. From everything I could see, it would be okay with me if my new ship took a while coming around from the east coast.

Muster for roll call was about eight every morning. After roll we would all go to whatever work crew we had been assigned. When there were new guys coming in, they would hear their name called again and be told where to report for work. With so many men to deal with, it was expected that the officers would slip up now and again. I had been clued in by a buddy, that when that happened to keep my mouth shut other than to yell "here" or "yo" at muster. There was no sense being a hero and volunteering for anything. I followed his advice and joined about twenty other guys who slipped away each morning to spend the day as we chose. No work for us.

What we did after roll call was to follow a carefully developed routine we could not believe actually worked. It was too simple. Every morning we would go over to the central tool crib and check out a length of welding hose, a small sledgehammer, maybe a long extension cord—anything that the regular work crews may not have in their gearbox. Then, wherever we went during the day, we would carry that piece of equipment. When going to noon chow, we stashed it somewhere and picked it up again afterward. No matter where we might go, anybody seeing us with repair gear over our shoulders would assume we were coming from or going to some assigned job. At the end of the day we would return the gear to the crib, and repeat the process the next day. With different equipment, of course. It worked well. At least for a while.

I got away with it for about a week. Then I slipped up. Walking along the seawall, I just had to stop and watch a subchaser being warped into dry dock. I stood there too long. My reverie was broken by a loud call. "Hey, sailor, bear a hand over here." It was the lieutenant in charge of the docking crew. I couldn't very well refuse. So, dropping my coil of hose, I hurried over to give them a hand. Afterward I tried to get away as quickly as possible.

"Okay, sailor. What's your name and what crew are you

working with? I'll let your chief know where you've been."

"Oh, that's okay, Lieutenant. He's a good guy; he'll understand."

But the lieutenant insisted. So I had no choice but to show my ID and let him know I had no permanent assignment. He thanked me again and turned me loose. The next morning after roll call, before I could get away, I was attached to the target repair pens as an acetylene burner. My days as a burner didn't last very long because I ended up with my own crew to push, mainly because I had been a gang leader on the *Trever*. We worked on a lot of different jobs on different ships, and the experience I was gaining was invaluable. Quite a few of the people working there had been civilian shipyard workers that had been drafted, and they really knew their jobs. My own gang was made up of about eight men whose average age was about 35 or so. I played it smart and tried not to pull rank on anyone. As a result, we got along just fine. Still, at 22, I felt funny being the youngest man in our group. And gang leader at that! But that's the way the Navy sometimes did things. Regardless of their age or experience, they were new to the Navy. On the other hand, I had the time in, and the rank. That made me the honcho.

My time other than working hours was something else. Drawing only $25 every two weeks did not make for much San Diego liberty, so it was necessary to find other things to do on base. A lot of time was spent at the gedunk drinking copious amounts of coffee and shooting the breeze with buddies. Movies on base were only a dime, so I saw a lot of flicks. Right after payday was a good time to duck over to the Marine base and have a couple of beers at their slop chute. But time began to drag. Finally, I got smart and went back to school.

Being on temporary duty, there was no chance of my being promoted. But there was no reason not to study for the time when I might. That meant a lot of evenings went to putting in my course for shipfitter first class. It was quite a bit different from doing it casually, as I did on the *Trever*. On the base it meant going to regular classes. But I kept at it and completed the course with an average of 3.7 out of a possible 4.0, and immediately asked to take the examination. If I could get it on my records, I would have a definite advantage when going aboard the *Indian Island*. Approval to take the exam came quickly and a couple hours of questions and diagrams later, I had a grade of 3.8 for my service jacket.

Then something happened that made me reevaluate my entire future. Around the beginning of May, I received a bulky envelope from my wife. Opening it very carefully, I pulled out a big sheet of folded paper. With some apprehension, knowing her as I did, I unfolded the paper, and there in the middle in very tiny letters was one simple line: "We're going to have a baby!"

I was absolutely stunned! Pen and I had talked about a family, of course, like we had talked about a lot of things. We wanted kids. But I was still very pleasantly stunned. Me...a father? The more I thought about it, the better it seemed. I just had to tell somebody. And who better than those old guys in my work gang? They congratulated me, and a couple of the older guys took me ashore that night to initiate me into the world of fatherhood. They had kids of their own, and seemed genuinely happy for me. I guess they even looked on me as the kid they had to look after. Well, they looked after me, all right. The next day I had a hangover that cannot be described. They went along with the work of the day without their gang leader. I was sacked out in one of the lumber stack hidey-holes, trying to return to some semblance of normalcy. Those good old boys paid for the use of the facilities, including gallons of black coffee sweetened with a little hair of the dog.

When my head was reasonably clear and I was almost back to normal, these same guys gave me some good advice. Having a family would give me new responsibilities. If I could wrangle some duty stateside where my family could live nearby, then it might be good to continue with a Navy career. But if it meant being away from them for long periods of time, I should forget it. They put it this way. "Time to grow up, kid. With your training and experience, you ought to be able to get a decent job on the outside. You're going to need it to support your family."

I thought about that a lot. They were right, of course. With all rates being given on a temporary basis, I had no guarantee of promotions or pay scale in future years. And at that time I was still only second class with no clout. As much as I liked the Navy, there were other things to consider. Being back home with a family sounded awfully good to me. Why, I might even have a daughter! Wouldn't that be a blast? A cute little kid in frilly skirts! But the war was a long way from being over, and nobody knew what might happen, or where we would go. From what we were hearing about action in the Pacific, we figured on going back. So while I gloried in the idea of becoming a father, there was also a determination to get as much out of the Navy in the time remaining, before I swallowed the anchor.

The War is Over

A day or so after receiving the big news from my pregnant bride, there was another bit of news that was almost as important—news that affected us all. On May 8, 1945, Germany surrendered. The war in Europe was over. The Allies could direct their entire war-making capabilities to the Pacific and the Japanese. Those of us who had seen service in that theater, who had fought the Japs even a little bit, knew that it was going to be a long, bloody mess before the enemy called it quits, if they ever did. I couldn't help but remember those Japanese sailors in the liferaft who had refused to be rescued, preferring instead to die for what they believed. I remember the way they defiantly shook their fists as our machine guns tore them to ragged bits. Shouting their banzais as they died. We talked about it as we drank our coffee. What we had to look forward to was the invasion of the Jap home islands. There could be millions of casualties on both sides. Not a pleasant thing to contemplate. It made me think, too, of the wife and youngster I would have back home, and I wondered what this was going to mean to them. Suddenly the war took on an entirely new meaning.

There was an almost immediate change in the way things were being done on the repair base. Suddenly ships and boats were pushed forward on the schedule of repairs.

New equipment came in to be installed. And it was obvious that all of it was intended for amphibious operations. Men that were scheduled for school found their orders changed and they were sent to ships where their present skills and experiences were needed. The war in Europe might come to an end, but VE Day meant little if anything to those of us who were slated for more Pacific duty. Knowing as we did how fanatical and determined the Nips were, we knew it could still be a long war, and we resigned ourselves to it.

For the next two months work went on in the yard at a furious pace. I received work orders for jobs on a number of amphibious vessels. If it hadn't been for the expertise of the older guys in my gang, I probably would have had a lot more trouble getting the work done properly. But by listening to them, as well as watching, my own expertise grew. When the work was completed to the satisfaction of the yard officers in charge, and to the ships' captains, I knew my own records were benefiting from it. And my reputation as a shipfitter would grow.

A number of new ships came around from the east coast, and we said so long to buddies as they reported aboard. There was an opportunity to visit with them before the ships left for the Pacific, and we felt chills up our spine when we saw all the extra combat gear that had been installed. Everything from additional depth charge racks to extra 20mm and 40mm antiaircraft guns. Some of the smaller infantry landing craft had so many additional machine guns mounted it was hard to believe that the gunners would have room to move around if and when they had to use them. Still, no official word was being passed.

Then, on August 6, another big event took place that

changed the complexion of the war. Indeed, all wars forever. The American B29 Bomber, the *Enola Gay*, had dropped a single bomb on the Japanese city of Hiroshima. A single bomb that wiped out the entire city with reported casualties of 140,000. From what we could find out, it was a new weapon never before used. Something called an atom bomb, based on an entirely new principle. It exploded by rupturing the very atoms that made up the explosive material. What was war coming to? An end, obviously. But with a single bomb to a single city? The thought was frightening.

The newspapers carried stories of nothing else. Of course, no one really knew very much about it, but everyone seemed to be an expert. Some of us rushed to the base library to see what we could find out. And from what little we did find, we were very grateful that our people had developed it before the enemy did. What happened at Pearl Harbor on December 7, 1941, was a picnic compared with the potential of the new atom bomb.

On August 9, the US Air Force did it again. Another single bomb was dropped on the city of Nagasaki. Once again, it was a single bomb wiping out an entire city with casualties far in excess of 40,000. Surely the Japanese would have to surrender before their entire country ceased to exist. No nation in the world could withstand that sort of destruction and survive. Even the well-known Nipponese fanaticism and fighting ability would have to submit to this new power exhibited by America.

By August 15 it was all over. Japan capitulated, and we all breathed easier. Almost immediately, work in the shipyard slowed down as many of the scheduled conversions and weapons installations were put on hold. The word came to us unofficially that we could begin thinking of going home. Not right away, of course, but soon. We knew that we had lived through the greatest war the world had ever known. We had survived. Here and there in the midst of the celebrations you would see coffee cups raised in a silent toast to those guys we knew who did not survive, and would not be going home. In our own way, each of us thanked God there would be no invasion of the Japanese home islands. People who were planning a Navy career, those who were assigned to ships and schools that would be to their benefit in the aftermath of the war, were wondering how the sudden developments would affect them personally. The only thing we were told was to go on about our duties until told differently. In any case, it meant continuing to wait for the AG77 to come around from the east coast. The war might be over but it would take months, perhaps years, to put the world in order, and the Navy would play its part. I found myself torn between wanting very much to be part of it all, and at the same time wanting to go home to my family. I think, in my heart, the choice had already been made.

USS *Indian Island*

"Hey, Dawson, the *Indian Island* is standing in!" My gang and I were hunkered on the fore deck of an LCI,[12] contemplating the removal of some machine gun mounts we had just installed a couple weeks earlier. Ace Hawkins, the anphib's bos'n mate, had walked up to give me the news. I turned the day's work over to my senior fitter, knowing full well they could do the job without my being there, and left the ship. Heading down to the sea wall, I found several other guys who had also been assigned to the AG77, and together we went down to take a look at her.

Climbing the crew ladder of a convenient gantry crane, we could look all the way out to the channel where we could see a ship moving in. It sure didn't look like any seaplane tender we had ever known about. One of our people squinted in the sun as he said, "That ain't no seaplane tender. That sumbitch is nothing but a liberty!" Sure enough, that's what it appeared to be. One of the cargo troop carriers cobbled together by the Kaiser Shipyards.[13] Actually, it was one of the later versions. A bit bigger and more substantially built, the class was known as Victory Ships. In any case, she sure

12. Landing Craft Infantry.
13. The Kaiser Shipyards were shipbuilding yards located on the U.S. west coast during World War II. They were owned by the Kaiser Shipbuilding Company.

wasn't a seaplane tender. There just had to be a mistake.

We hung there for a while, watching as she moved in slowly, as though her skipper wasn't quite sure of what he was doing. Another sailor climbed up to where we were, carrying a pair of binoculars. Passing them around, we all had a good look at the incoming vessel. By that time she was close enough for us to read her bow numbers—AG77. That was her. AG77—the USS *Indian Island*. You never heard so much cussing as we realized what lay ahead of us. Disgustedly, we dropped down to ground level and went back to work. When the *Indian Island* tied up to the dock, we would get the gang together and go aboard and check her out. Nobody was very keen to report aboard as crew.

By that afternoon she was tied up to the fuel dock and about ten of us were there, asking permission to come aboard. At first the OOD, a baby-faced JG, was very reluctant to allow visitors to cross his quarterdeck. When we told him we had been assigned to the AG77, that it was our ship, he relented. But he still would not allow us to wander around by ourselves. "Against ship's regulations, you know." Instead, he would arrange for a tour. That gave us a pretty good idea of what kind of duty she was going to be. We were all experienced Navy men. Why in hell would we need a guided tour? We found out quickly enough.

A chief bos'n mate came to the quarterdeck, and after introducing himself, proceeded to take us around the ship. He seemed very unhappy being aboard and wasted no time advising us to apply for a transfer, as he had already done. He told us the captain was a lieutenant commander in the reserves, and the *Indian Island* was his first command. Most of the officers were ensigns and junior-grade lieutenants just out of officer candidate school. Their navigator was a chief warrant quartermaster backed by a chief petty officer. The only officer who knew anything about navigation was the skipper. Most of the crew, with the exception of a few rated men, were just out of boot camp or service school. We asked him what kind of a seaplane tender she was. He laughed.

"Seaplane tender? Where in hell did you get that idea? This bucket is exactly what her number says she is—an AG! An auxiliary! She'll be used for anything the Navy thinks she can do. And that ain't much. Cargo, troops, for all I know she may end up a seagoing USO show. It kills me to think I spent over twenty-five years in the Navy to come to this!"

With those encouraging words, we began our tour. Everywhere we went there were signs. "Go forward this way." "Go aft this way." One sign had an arrow to point the way to the mess hall. Other signs proclaimed areas to be "Officers' Country" and "Enlisted Men's Quarters." Still others identified the "Chiefs' Quarters" and the "Crew's Head." There were quite a few that simply stated "No Admittance." As we made our way through the decks, the chief was regularly saluting one officer or another. Most of them seemed younger than I was. According to our guide, "Most of the silly bastards don't even shave." He was right. One important-looking, starry-eyed ensign we passed had a piece of toilet paper stuck to his chin, obviously to seal a cut where he'd been practicing.

The *Indian Island* seemed a very rigidly controlled ship. Much more so than the Navy we had been exposed to. Experienced, rated men like me, who had come from the informal Hooligan Navy, were shocked, to say the least. The chief asked what kind of duty we were coming from. When I told him that most of us were from our four pipe, flush deckers, he almost cried, "By God! That was the Real Navy." We listened to him choke as he spoke, and wondered just what the hell we were getting into.

By the time we had completed our turn around the ship, to a man we had decided to do whatever we could to avoid going aboard that AG for duty. The few older, more-experienced crewmen we had seen all appeared to be depressed and very angry. Of course, all the young kids just out of boot camp were all wide-eyed and excited at being on a real ship of their own. So happy and thrilled, in fact, that some of them even whistled as they worked. Noticing the chief cringe at the sound, I remembered something Jack Ryan had told me a long time before. "In this man's navy, only damn fools and bos'n mates whistle."

We finally gathered at the quarterdeck, said thanks and good-bye to our escort, and requested permission to leave the ship. The baby-faced OOD gave his approval, but only after instructing us that it was required that we salute the quarterdeck and the colors as we went over the side. I wondered where he thought we had been for the previous four years. As we crossed the gangway I heard someone mutter, "Gee whiz, just like in the Real Navy." Fortunately for us, the OOD didn't hear it.

Once on the dock we talked about it for a minute or two, and then en masse we headed for the Administration Building to see about some transfer applications to go almost anywhere but the *Indian Island*. It didn't do us much good. The personnel staff had enough to do getting several thousand sailors ready for discharge and had no time to fool with what they considered a bunch of disgruntled sailors who were not satisfied with what the personnel department thought was a good ship. We should have expected that response from them. They were, after all, all feather merchants or fat-bottomed WAVES. What did they know? The closest they ever came to the Navy was their blue uniforms. And issue uniforms at that. I didn't see a single set of tailor mades in the office. I had probably squeezed more saltwater out of my socks than they had ever sailed over. But we did get some information. One of our guys was a tall, dark, good-looking devil who reminded one of Cesar Romero. He turned on the charm, and one of the WAVES broke down to talk to us; a WAVE lieutenant, no less. It all came down to this:

If we were reserves, which none of us were, we would be getting discharged right away, and certainly would not be going aboard the AG77. Those who were Regular Navy had no choice; no changes in orders were being considered. "Go aboard," she said. "Then apply for transfer to some school. Don't tell anyone you don't like the ship." If we were Regular Navy riding on an expired enlistment, like me, the best thing to do was re-enlist right away and ask for specific duty after the normal thirty-day leave that goes with the re-up. By the time we came back from the leave, the *Indian Island* would be gone and things would have quieted down to where there was a chance for some choice of duty because so many people would have left the service. She even volunteered to do what she could for us if we contacted her personally upon return from our leave.

We all went back to work, and I discussed it with my guys. To a man they were still of the opinion that the best thing for me to do would be to get out and go home to my wife and get ready for a family. I didn't get much work done the next few days, or much sleep at night thinking about it.

Every day I would see that AG77 at the dock and get the most uncomfortable feeling. Finally, my mind was made up. I had an obligation to consider, an obligation to my wife and baby. I decided to take my discharge.

By the middle of September of 1945, the discharge process was moving right along. I received my orders to report to Great Lakes Naval Station for separation from the service. A final cross-country train trip took about forty homeward-bound sailors to Great Lakes. My Navy career was rapidly drawing to a close.

Time to Swallow the Anchor

It took four days to go through the procedures to bring an end to our Navy service. Not that it was all that involved, but there were so many men to be run through the system, the personnel and medical departments were swamped. They decided to do it in stages. One day they would do physicals, on another it was filling out the endless forms the government is so fond of. Still another day was given over to signing the vouchers for our last payday. The actual mechanics of getting out only took two or three hours a day, so we had a lot of free time on our hands. Most of the guys went out on suddenly approved liberty to the nearby town of Waukegan, or even into Chicago. But I knew that once I was a civilian, every dime would be needed to carry me through that period until I found a job and a place to live. So I called my wife, told her where I was, and that in a few days she would have me home for good.

Processing out was surprisingly uncomplicated. My last Navy physical was a lot like my first. The doctors would feel us to see if we were warm, count our eyes, check to see if we were breathing; if our heart was beating, we were okay. Of course, if there were any real problems, our discharge would be held up until the matter was corrected. By that time, all we wanted was to get out, so there were very few complaints. Our pay records were brought up to date, and we were paid right to the day we walked out the gate. There was also our mustering-out pay of $300. They gave us $100 as we left, with a promise to send the balance at a rate of $100 a month. We also received our golden "Ruptured Duck" discharge emblem to be sewn on our dress blues for the trip home[14] and a small lapel button for our civvies should we choose to wear it.

There were interviews to help us decide what we would be doing after our separation, directions on how to contact the various veterans' organizations if we felt a need for help, and a lot of lectures on how to adapt to life as a civilian in the postwar world. It all began to sound very scary.

Before enlisting, I had been a teenaged kid in school. I had never really had to work for a living, or deal with responsibility. It dawned on me that I knew nothing of the world outside of the Navy gates. Certainly there was no enthusiasm for returning to the family, because I could still hear their constant admonition to get a Man's Job! A realization came to me as to why I had enlisted in the first place. It wasn't a desire for adventure, or a burning ambition to learn a trade, although I certainly wanted those things. As a seventeen year old I had actually run away from home and joined the military to get away from a life that seemed to be anything but pleasant. I think Grandma knew it back then, and it was

---

14. A cloth insignia depicting an eagle inside a wreath issued to departing service personnel, allowing them to wear their uniform for up to thirty days after they were discharged. During the war, members of the armed forces were forbidden to possess civilian clothing, in order to make desertion more difficult. The Ruptured Duck showed the military police that an individual was in transit and not AWOL. Returning servicemen thought it looked more like a duck than an eagle, hence the name.

why she, although reluctantly, gave me her blessings. But in a few days the security of the Navy would be behind me and it would be a question of making it on my own.

Finally, the big day arrived. October 1, 1945. We rolled out for reveille for the last time, took our showers, and got into our dress blues. Those satin-lined dress blues that had meant so much to me when I had them tailor made. Skintight, bell bottomed, with a custom-made white hat that was worn jauntily cocked over one eye, or hanging precariously at the back of my head. Once dressed, we headed for the mess hall for our final Navy chow. And you might have known—they served beans, stewed prunes, and hot biscuits. At least the coffee was not laced with saltpeter. There was no longer any need for the government to be concerned about our sex lives.

After breakfast, it was over to the Administration Building for a final pep talk by a four-striped captain. He congratulated us for being in the greatest navy in the world. For having taken part in winning two wars on separate fronts. In a lot of ways it sounded like the speech we had received when we enlisted. Finally, the captain wished us all a bon voyage, and our names were called to go forward and pick up our discharge papers. The US Navy, our wartime adventures, all of it would become little more than memories to be dragged out one day when we were telling stories to our grandchildren when they asked, "What did you do in the Navy, Grandpa?"

We drifted out of the Ad Building in twos and threes to walk back to the barracks to pick up our personal gear and then leave. I grabbed my bag, but for some reason couldn't bring myself to leave. Not just yet. I sat there on my bunk, looking around the dormitory, thinking of all the places I'd been, the things I'd done, and the people I'd met. Good buddies, many of whom would not be coming home as I did. My mind snapped back to the present and I noticed there was no one else in the dorm. It couldn't be put off any longer. I picked up my bag and headed for the door.

Walking to the main gate brought back still more memories of when I had first come through them in April of 1941. It seemed a lifetime ago. Passing through the big, red-brick columns, I threw a casual salute to the seaman guard, noticing how sharp he looked in his sparkling whites, bleached guard belt, and leggings. Even his pants were smooth and trim, lacking those boot camp "Maggie's Drawers." I made a promise to myself that once through that gate there would be no looking back. But I chickened out. I had to turn and take a last look at the life I was leaving behind.

There was the usual rattletrap bus rolling down the street, taking a load of recruits someplace or other. Out on the drill field I could see a company doing close-order drill, their chief calling cadence. "One—two—three—four. With your left, your left..." The old red-brick barracks didn't look any different than they did when I lived there. Over to the side was the hostess house beckoning to me to come in for one last cup of java. But a voice in my mind said, "No! Forget it! Go on home." Reluctantly, I turned and crossed the highway, and slowly mounted the stairway to the train platform. As I stood there waiting for my train, I thought of the advice given to me by the old men in my gang back at the repair base. And that is what finally brought me to my senses. I knew where my real duty lay. I had a wife, and would soon have that baby girl. And they would be depending upon me. I decided that by God, that was a real Man's Job. As my train pulled into the station, I swung aboard with no further hesitation. I was a civilian, and I was going home.

Glossary

Acey Ducey
Navy version of the popular game of Parchesi.

Anchor Pool
A lottery based on the time the anchor dropped upon arrival at the ship's destination.

Aussie
A native of Australia.

Batten Down
The closing of any watertight fixture; to secure firmly, as in preparation for a rough sea.

Battery
A group of guns installed together in a specific location, such as on the ship's bow, a deckhouse, etc.

Boatswain
Petty officer in the ship's deck force. Also known as *Bos'n*, *Bosun*, or *Boats*.

Bone in Her Teeth
A ship traveling fast enough so her passage through the water creates a bow wave, the "bone."

Boot
Navy recruit; also slang for a condom.

Brit
A person who is British; usually refers to an Englishman.

Bumboat
A small boat used to ferry supplies to ships moored away from the shore; generally refers to those rowed by island natives who come alongside a ship to sell or barter goods.

Clews
Lightweight lines or ropes at each end of a hammock to attach to hooks for hanging.

Cold-Iron Watch
Period of duty in a fire or engine room when the boilers and main machinery are shut down.

Collywobbles
A pain in the stomach or bowels; Navy slang for an unknown sexual disease.

Corpsman
An enlisted person in the U.S. Navy who has been trained to give first aid and basic medical treatment, especially in combat situations.

Coxswain
Lowest-ranking petty officer in a ship's deck force; also known as *Cox'n*. The enlisted man in charge of operating a boat, particularly its navigation and steering.

Dago
San Diego

Detention
A quarantine period in boot camp, usually the first three weeks.

Doxy
Traditional name for a prostitute, usually one who has only one customer; a mistress. Also *Doxie*.

Fart Sack
Navy enlisted man's bunk or bed. Originally referred to his hammock; can also refer to a sleeping bag or a linen a mattress is inserted into.

Feather Merchant
Navy reservist; also a sailor of slight build.

Fire Control
Central station to control firing of ship's guns.

Flush Deck
In naval architecture, refers to when the upper deck of a ship extends unbroken from stem to stern. There is no raised forecastle or lowered quarterdeck. Ships of this type may be referred to as "flush deckers," although this usually only refers to a series of United States Navy destroyers.

Four Piper
Another name for a *Four Stacker*.

Four Stacker
A destroyer of WWI vintage with four funnels (smokestacks). Between 1917 and 1922, there were 273 flush-deckers built in three classes: the prototype *Caldwell* (6 ships), the *Wickes* (111 ships), and the *Clemson* (156 ships). Four stackers played a prominent role in the early years of WWII. The USS *Trever* (DD-339/DMS-16/AG-110) was a Clemson-class destroyer named in memory of Lt. Cmdr. George A. Trever.

Frisco
San Francisco.

Galley
The compartment of a ship or submarine where food is cooked and prepared; can also refer to a land-based kitchen on a naval base.

Gedunk
Short for *Gedunk Bar* (also *Ge-dunk*, *Gee-dunk*, or *Geedunk*). Soda fountain, canteen, or snack bar on a Navy ship or naval base. The service member who works in the gedunk is usually referred to as the "gedunk guy" or the "geedunkaroo." The term was popular during World War II.

Guidon
A military standard (flag) that a company or platoon carries to signify its unit designation and corps affiliation; used to identify training companies in Navy boot camp.

Gun Battery
See *Battery*.

Hash Marks
Service stripes on uniform designating years of service or the dark stains frequently found in the seat of the underwear of an unclean sailor; also *Hashmarks*.

Hooligan Navy
Ships or stations that operate informally, without restrictions or strict regulations; also a WWII Navy pejorative for the Coast Guard.

Hot Skinny
Rumor. See *Scuttlebutt* and *Straight Poop*.

Jackstays
Heavy pipe framing used to hang hammocks in boot camp; any horizontal line or wire.

Kiwi
A native of New Zealand.

Kiyi Brush
A small scrub brush used to wash clothes.

Lackanuki
A severe "sexual disease" common among men who have been denied the company of women for an extended period of time; also *Lackanookie*.

Lash Up and Stow
Originally referred to the tying up and storing of hammocks. Now refers to packing and storing of almost anything.

Limey
English or British serviceman; the term is believed to derive from lime juice, referring to the Royal Navy practice of supplying lime juice to British sailors to prevent scurvy.

Log
Daily record of ship's activity.

Log In
To enter information in the ship's log or other book.

Maggie's Drawers
The baggy knees caused by improperly folded trousers when wearing leggings; also a red flag raised at a firing range to indicate that a shooter has missed the target.

Master-at-Arms
Navy petty officer with responsibility of maintaining order in barracks or on board ship.

Navy Strawberries
Beans—baked, broiled, boiled, or spoiled.

OOD
Officer of the deck. The officer immediately responsible for the ship's operation; the captain's direct representative. At sea, the OOD is usually stationed on the bridge and is in charge of navigation and safety of the ship, unless relieved by the captain.

Sack
See *Fartsack*.

Saltpeter
A chemical additive allegedly put into Navy coffee to reduce the biological urges of enlisted personnel. Most commonly found in boot camp.

Scuttlebutt
Rumor. See *Hot Skinny* and *Straight Poop*.

Seabag
A canvas bag designed to hold all of a sailor's possessions when traveling.

Service Number
Numerical identification of Navy enlisted men. Similar to a civilian Social Security Number.

Shit on a Shingle
A concoction of loose hamburger meat and tomatoes that is poured over dry toast and served at breakfast.

Shooting the Breeze
Bull sessions, gossiping, general discussions.

Skivvies
Underwear. A signalman is sometimes known as a "skivvy waver."

S.O.S.
See *Shit on a Shingle*.

Square Knot Admiral
Apprentice petty officer in boot camp. Identified by a rating badge showing a piece of rope with a square knot.

Steaming Watch
Period of duty in fire or engine room when ship is underway and all machinery is operating.

Storekeeper
Petty officer responsible for supplies and their distribution and records.

Straight Poop
Rumor. See *Scuttlebutt* and *Hot Skinny*.

Striker
A sailor receiving on-the-job training for a designated field (or rate); the Navy version of a civilian apprentice to a given trade.

Swallow the Anchor
To retire or take a discharge from the Navy. To leave the sea for life ashore.

Tin Can
U.S. Navy destroyer; also *Tincan*. Sailors claimed the hull plating of a destroyer was so thin, it must have been made from tin cans.

Turd Jockey
Name applied to a shipfitter who may be working on a ship's sanitary system; also *Turd Herder* or *Turd Chaser*.

Watch
A period of duty, usually of a four-hour duration.

Water Tender
Fire room petty officer responsible for controlling the water lever in a ship's boilers; also responsible for ensur-

ing that the boiler and all the equipment needed to tend it are functioning.

Weinie Wagger
Pervert who waves his genitals at others; also *Weenie Wagger.* A masturbator.

Whaleboat
Small ship's boat.

.

www.ingramcontent.com/pod-product-compliance
Lightning Source LLC
Chambersburg PA
CBHW031944070426
42451CB00007BA/125